T0358124

Wakefield Press

B Model

Miranda Darling read English and modern languages at
Oxford and modelled for seven years in London,
Paris, Milan and Tokyo.

an embellished memoir

miranda darling

Wakefield
Press

Wakefield Press
1 The Parade West
Kent Town
South Australia 5067
www.wakefieldpress.com.au

First published 2004

Designed by Liz Nicholson, designBITE
Typeset by Ryan Paine, Wakefield Press
Printed and bound by Hyde Park Press

National Library of Australia
Cataloguing-in-publication entry

Darling, Miranda, 1975–   .
B model: an embellished memoir.

ISBN 1 86254 644 4.

1. Models (Persons) – Fiction. I. Title.

A823.4

Contents

Only renown can outlive death,
And they are truly miserable
Who don't incessantly attend
To fame: life hurries to its end!

King Agramante in Boiardo's Orlando Innamorato, *ii*

Author's note

This story comes in 'fragments of vulgar writing'. It doesn't run smoothly as all things should and invariably do not. Like memory, parts of it are accurate, parts exaggerated, others invented outright. Some characters are real, others wholly fictional, still others combinations of various people.

This is not going to be the story of a supermodel – it's not even going to be the story of a very successful model. It's all about a B model – an ordinary girl, a little more pretty than most I guess but no more crazy, no more special than all the girls we know. This is the life of Justine and those countless other girls who never really made it, the ones who live between the lines of tabloid copy, whose faces are familiar but whose names no one ever knows.

Stop Talking!

Tokyo, 8.27 a.m.

Eight hands – I counted them – eight Japanese hands rummaging around in my bra and panties as if I were a disorganised sock drawer. I stood there in navy nylon underwear – lacy, they called it 'racy' – while the stylist and her four assistants adjusted straps and elastic. I'd done lingerie jobs before, and a bit of swimwear, but never in Japan and this was quite different.

The four hands working my upper body plucked at the straps once more, then slipped in, small and cold, to cup my breasts. More hands urged me to bend over, and hands coaxed my breasts upwards for fullness. Good luck to them. If they could find any fullness in my chest they were welcome to work with it.

I was never the sort of girl who should have found herself in this position. That's what makes everything stand out in my mind: things that once were completely unnatural to me became, by weird and painful degrees, the most ordinary things in the world.

I can pin down the exact day, the particular afternoon, that cracked everything wide open. My life was probably a lot like yours. I dreaded school. The absolute worst was maths, a subject that made time crawl through the halls on its knees. I was fifteen-and-a-half and I *hated* it. The numbers and symbols made no sense to me. I couldn't find patterns in my processes, I couldn't learn from my mistakes. Test papers would so paralyse me that I would stare at the blank space beside 'Name' in terror, suspecting it was a trick algebraic process that had to be square rooted or in some other way made to evolve into something it wasn't.

Every year, on the first day of school, I would resolve to Understand and Try, even in maths. I would buy sharp new pencils, sit in the very front row of the class and diligently copy from the blackboard, lettering neatly, ruling every line. But making my maths look pretty didn't help me understand it. By the end of the class my eyes would have drifted into the playground, my mind to greener pastures.

I always sat in the very last row after that first day – back row, left corner, desk against the wall. And there I would remain until the next first day of school.

The maths room was arranged in two rows of two desks with one row of three down the middle: the same configuration as economy seating on a jumbo jet flying trans-Atlantic, minus the bad movie and the plastic dinners, but just as long and uncomfortable.

My best (only) friend Gretchen sat across the other side of the room, 64A to my 64G. Miss Olyphant, the maths teacher and chief cabin steward, took great pains to ensure we were always separated.

Miss Olyphant was not a gentle woman. She wore elasticised waistbands high up on her torso and spoke through her nose, wheezing slightly. Her complexion was the colour of sweaty wax. Gretch and I hated Miss Olyphant, and we were convinced that she hated us. Of the two of us, though, Miss Olyphant disliked me more. She said I had an 'attitude problem'. Of course I did, I hated maths. I was no good at it. But it was my inability to hide my disinterest that annoyed Miss Olyphant, my quiet passivity in the face of her earnest teaching.

My maths textbook was covered in cartoon drawings of glamorous girls with big breasts and huge eyes, strange and hungry men, and nasty caricatures of Miss Olyphant. My plan was to sell the book to the girls in the year below me for more than its original price. I was sure a fellow maths-hater would love to buy a book with so many custom-designed distractions. It was to be my legacy of insubordination.

I was brimming with teen angst but the drawings in my maths book were far bolder than my actions. My cartoons shouted my discontent, my bad poems dripped blood, but at school I was known as the slightly weird, shy girl. Not Ally Sheedy in *The Breakfast Club* weird – not bizarre enough to make a movie about – just unsensationally odd.

There were no boys at my school. Maybe they thought that if they kept the boys away, the girls would concentrate on being clever. But I wailed inside. How were we supposed to have any form of social life? (A social life being the only form of life worth living at the age of fifteen-and-a-half.) If we didn't have older brothers or friends in the 'cool' group who somehow always knew boys, there was no chance.

I didn't know any boys. I knew a few faces from the bus I caught home, boys who stared and made me fidget in my seat. Gretchen was more forward. She knew some boys – mostly arty theatre types who wore black and lived in apartments with their single mothers who they called 'Julia' or 'Helen', and who ate at restaurants on school nights. Gretchen met these boys at workshops she attended during the holidays, like '101 Things To Do With Mime'.

Gretchen also knew some of the faces on our bus, sort of, and they knew her. Most importantly, she knew the name of the friend of the boy with the blond, curly hair who always stared particularly hard. His eyes burned me, burning blue. I noticed him because he didn't flinch and turn away when I returned his look. He would just keep staring, as if he had a perfect right to, not smiling, but hiding a smile, gazing as if he and I were sharing a joke.

I liked the idea of having a secret joke with a boy, especially one with giant blue eyes and a bee-stung lower lip. He always sat at the back of the bus, back row, left corner – my seat. I noticed that too.

On this particularly heavy afternoon in maths, a balled-up scrap of graph paper landed on my desk then fell to the floor, taking me away from dreams of boys on buses. A note from Gretch. I dropped a pencil and bent quickly to retrieve it. Gretchen and I always sent notes this way, all through class. Most girls did, because Miss Olyphant *would not tolerate talking in class.*

But teenage girls have a lot to say. I unfurled my note, dirty and torn. Gretch had the world's tiniest writing, perfectly neat in light-blue ink.

J – Toby's friend's name is Taber John. Not very normal.
T. might like you, Toby thinks so.
But maybe he's saying that because Toby likes me, I think.
He said we should meet them on the 365 after school.
P.S. Som–

'Justine!'

Fasten seatbelts. Oxygen masks will drop from the ceiling. I was in trouble.

'Is that a Note!'

Miss Olyphant knew it was a Note.

'Bring me the Note.'

Miss Olyphant had a policy about Notes. They were to be taken and read aloud to the class. The class would then be permitted to snigger at the contents of said Note, and at the sender and recipient. Sometimes it was funny to write an exceptionally boring note, just to see Miss Olyphant turn grey with frustration. But this note was embarrassing. I was sure neither Miss Olyphant nor the class would miss the whiff of desperation it gave off.

'Stand up.'

The dreaded command, delivered through the nose. I stood, almost

4

trembling. I was a goody-goody; I did what I was told. My bad behaviour didn't go much further than passing notes. I was a passive resister. I didn't throw chairs or get Saturday detentions and I didn't deal well with Trouble.

'Bring me the note.' I looked at Miss Olyphant, terrified now. My prideful self was being tied to the stake, and Miss Olyphant was waving a match. Her eyes blazed like burnt currants half-buried in puffy, white dough. I heard the class laughing. It would be a savage verbal rape, complete with careful inflections at just the right moment and witty asides. A crucifixion.

I put the note in my mouth, tasted paper and felt a surge of adrenaline, a moment of invincibility. I began to chew. The paper tasted like sweaty wood. The room fell silent.

I swallowed Taber John.

The sound of the ceiling fan grew louder. I was aware of a brief surge in my popularity. There would be talk of me in the playground that day.

Miss Olyphant was whiter than usual with rage. She sent me to the vice-principal's office. I took my bag and all my books with me, doubting I would be allowed to return. Catching Gretchen's eye on the way out I guessed she'd probably wait for me after school.

That afternoon I sweated on the plastic chair outside the vice principal's office. The carpet was short, brown and synthetic, like the shaved coat of a mangy dog. I rubbed my feet up and down and spent twenty minutes giving myself electric shock treatment. Shock some sense into you, girl. I wished I had been sent to see the headmistress instead, but Miss Olyphant knew better than that.

The vice principal – Miss Grillette – was a skinny, greying spinster with rigid ideas concerning the conduct of Young Ladies. She wore grey and brown tartan skirts to mid-calf, even in summer. The headmistress was also a tall, greying spinster, but she was older, gentler, benign to the point of mild senility. She would smile at you with her head cocked slightly to the side like a willow, nod a couple of times, and forget whether you were there to be praised or punished. Still unsure, she would send you away with a quotation from the Bible and another smile.

Miss Grillette frowned as I entered her office. She smelt of antiseptic sprinkled with talc, and that curious odour of musty feathers that sometimes clings to people who spend too much time alone with cats. I stepped up to her dark, heavy desk and handed her the pink slip detailing my sin: 'Disrespecting teacher, disobedience, not paying attention in class'.

Miss Grillette read the slip, looked up at me over her half glasses and asked me to explain myself.

'I ate a note.'

Disobeying a teacher was a grave infraction. The inside of my head began to spin and I almost forgot to pay attention. The window of the third-floor office was big, wide and open. I wondered what she'd say if I just up and flew away.

A week's detention, half an hour after school picking up rubbish ... Learn to respect your elders and your betters ... Rudeness and disobedience ... Your socks are too long, your dress is too short, your tie is loose, your hair is messy, where are your school badges? Miss Gillette went on, but I think she knew I wasn't a Bad Girl. She knew the extent of my petty resistance and she let me off easily – for her. Maybe she understood that I wasn't the academic kind. Maybe it was enough that I was usually no trouble, and she didn't want to risk stirring me into action.

After my detention I only had five minutes to say hi to Taber John behind the bus depot. He was on his way to the train station that day, a saxophone lesson was sending him off somewhere else. He squatted on the concrete, leaning against a wall, while I stood before him and shifted awkwardly from foot to foot. Taber John smiled and didn't say much. He had beautiful skin, like a baby's.

'Your lip is kind of crazy. It's so big.' Stupid thing to say, I know, but it just popped out.

His smile stretched wider. 'I'm a musician.'

I waited for him to say something else but he just watched me. 'Does it help your playing?'

'I can play any instrument. I'm a child prodigy. So I guess it does.' He laughed.

I was astounded by his frankness. I grew shy, but I liked him more. I hoped Taber John would become more than someone to say hello to on the bus, become a friend who wasn't a girl.

My bus pulled in and Taber John stood. 'See you round.' He flipped his hand in salute and walked off with his saxophone case over his shoulder. I made myself get on my bus but couldn't help staring after him.

I found Gretchen standing by the doors on the bus. 'Hey Gretchen?'

'Mmm?'

'What am I supposed to do now? About Taber John? He's kind of weird – but in a good way, I think. Don't you? What if he thinks I'm a dickhead? I said some dumb thing about his lip and – '.

Gretchen shrugged. 'I don't know.' She was busy staring at Toby at the back of the bus. He was busy ignoring her. Finally she caught his eye and he smiled at her. She blushed and looked away.

'I've never had a boyfriend, Gretch, or even a friend who's a boy.'

'I'm just going to say hi to Toby. I'll see you tomorrow, Justine. Bye.'

Gretch made her way to the back of the bus and I travelled the rest of the way home standing alone by the doors thinking about Taber John, my hot hand slipping as I held the shiny silver pole.

Later, at home, I thought about telling my mum about him as she concentrated on making a list of groceries. I wanted to call him a 'friend of mine', and to say the words out loud. But then I decided it might be better to keep him to myself until I had had more experience.

Milk, two pearl lightbulbs, cornflakes, cleaning fluid . . .

Secretly, standing in the kitchen, I snuck thoughts of Taber John, like taking gummi bears from my pocket, one by one, while my mother wrote her shopping list.

Sliced bread, four cans tuna, loo paper . . .

I wondered what it would be like to kiss that funny swollen lip, hold it sweetly in my mouth, like a water balloon filled with honey. My first kiss had happened a year ago, but there had been none since. A boy named Leslie had taken me into an underground parking garage by the marina near my house. He lived next door and I used to watch him through the fence. He was a year and a half older than me, one of four scary brothers who liked to bounce on their trampoline and throw knives at each other for fun. Their father was a minister – Episcopalian, tall and grey – their mother a worn-out minister's wife who had been through the baby spin-cycle three times too many and had emerged bleached and powdery. They were strict parents, enforcing their word and that of the Lord with a length of leather strap.

Leslie had put me on his shoulders and run around the half-empty garage at top speed. I squealed as my head skimmed the concrete ceiling until finally he put me down, and I stood breathless while he removed his school tie and tied my hands together in front of me. I was watching the tie, not Leslie, when he bent in for a kiss. Wet, hot, fat. At first I had tried to kiss him back, tried to pull gently at his lip like they did in the movies. But Leslie wore braces, and they scraped my lips. I became confused. I wanted to pull away, but my hands were tied and Leslie was holding the back of my head the way a starving man clings to his last coconut. He forced his large tongue into my mouth, and I had no idea how to kiss him back. I could barely breathe. Then he stopped and untied me. Late for dinner, I ran home.

Half-way through tuna and mash, my bare calves wound tightly around the wooden legs of the kitchen chair, I had to jump up, run to the bathroom and dry-heave into the toilet. My revulsion wasn't strong enough to eject the tuna and mash, but spasms shook my body as it tried to rid itself of the memory of Leslie's tongue squishing against my teeth, down my throat.

I was sure it would be different with Taber John.

This particular day after school I went grocery shopping with my mother, to the Plaza. It was a dreary urban pole where metal shopping trolleys with crazed wheels – out on every side like four broken flippers – replaced husky dogs, and the cold radiating from frozen foods kept true polar temperature. We trailed through the wasteland of iced peas and fish sticks, searching for frozen spinach. I had to tell my mother about the detentions – she had to sign the permission slip anyway – and I knew I would get a lecture.

'Well I hope this isn't going to be the start of any trouble Justine!' Reaching for the tinned tuna. 'You have enough trouble with your school work and concentrating in class – all your teachers say so in your reports. "Does not try, daydreams constantly, is distracted easily, could improve ..."'

Cornflakes and muesli into the trolley.

'Can you grab the loo paper please darling? Look at your hands! They're covered in biro!' She grabbed my wrist in exasperation. 'I just don't know what I'm going to do with you, Justine.'

'It was only a note.' I was sulking now.

'It's not just that. It's everything. I've told you a thousand times ...'

I trailed in her wake, looking for an escape. As we passed the large fridge with the products, I shivered again. I'd left my jumper in my schoolbag.

A large lady in her thirties, dressed in a black caftan, was rummaging around in the fridge like a Plaza penguin. She heard my mother's lecture and turned to look at the Bad Girl. I looked away to avoid her stare and caught sight of spinach in the freezer. I took a run-up and slid across the vinyl floor towards it. My mother was watching, but I knew she would never raise her voice in the supermarket.

I immersed my whole upper body in the open freezer, hoping to discourage my mother from coming over to finish her lecture. It was like crawling into an igloo. I wondered how long a girl could last there before she froze to death. I stayed until I could bear it no longer. Not very long, I decided.

When I emerged I saw my mother talking to the penguin. They turned and looked me up and down, seeing a skinny, scrappy teenager with her arms full of frozen spinach and nose bright red from the cold. The penguin had the same currant-bun eyes as Miss Olyphant, similar pasty white skin, and I suddenly felt alarmed.

'Come here darling.' My mother's voice had become honeyed. The penguin smiled at me, a large carton of strawberry milk in one hand. 'How old are you?' she asked me, her innocuous question seeming somehow evil.

'Fifteen-and-a-half,' I answered, cool-as-a-cucumber. Never show the devil fear.

The penguin lady turned to my mother. 'She could definitely be a model,' she said, and handed my mother a card.

Erica Webb
Model Management Pty Ltd

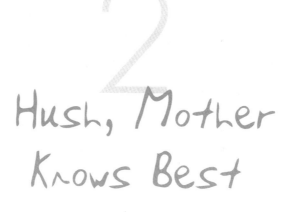

Hush, Mother Knows Best

Sydney, 4.30 p.m., Erica Webb Pty Ltd

My first meeting with Erica Webb was worse than going to the doctor.

On the way there I considered locking myself in the car and refusing to budge, or leaping out at the traffic lights. But all roads eventually led home to Mother and I realised that these tactics would only delay the inevitable. My mother was determined to make a young lady out of me and I had been given a choice: Erica Webb Model Management Pty Ltd or June Joy Patterson's School of Deportment. I had seen the victims of June Joy Patterson stepping the streets like broken show ponies, leeched of all spirit in their maroon blazers, hair pulled back painfully, nails short and clean. The Erica Webb option offered at least the hope of more freedom and it didn't end in the horrifying tradition of The Debut.

'Come on Justine – out of the car or we'll be late.'

I unlocked the car door, face like thunder, 'Bloody bum!'

'Don't swear! If Erica hears that sort ... You see? This is just what I'm talking about!' My mother scanned me with her exasperated look. 'At your age I would never have wandered around the streets so dishevelled.'

I had come straight from swimming training and my hair was a tangled mess of chlorine, talcum powder and sodden blue ribbon. My swimmers were still wet under my tunic and had left large damp patches on my chest and backside.

'You have no sense of self,' she said, turning neatly on a Parisian heel. 'I doubt Erica will want to take you on like that. The state of you!'

Exactly.

My feet were bare in my leather school shoes – I'd lost my socks in the changing room – so my toes squeaked as I followed my mother into the lift. She'd stopped speaking to me. I picked at the towel around my neck, pulling at the threads, unravelling it in small sections. My mother's manicured nail (Capri Nude) sought the up button.

Erica's office had walls of glass, and three heads – two women and a man in black-leather swivel chairs – turned to watch as we entered. My unselfconsciousness dissolved in that moment. It flowed from my cheeks, down my tired limbs, over my ankles – comically skinny without their socks on – and pooled at my feet. Fifteen-and-a-half years of living with my body and my face, and I'd never really given either any consideration. That all changed with those stares. I became in that instant vividly aware of the way I looked, and of the fact that I was being assessed on just that. It was a realisation that robbed me of myself, if that makes any sense. It made me see that I was the sum of my moving parts, and it was at precisely that moment that I began to worry about what I looked like to other people.

For the first time in my life I wanted to be my mother. She floated, cool and elegant, and didn't look out of place among the glass partitions and rows of pictures of beautiful faces that lined the back wall. I squelched along behind her, a new, dark bruise on my shin from diving practice throbbing painfully like a black heart.

Erica appeared from behind me, quick and silent on swollen feet, blocking my only exit. 'Hello Mrs Lily.'

Her words were addressed to my mother and I couldn't make myself listen. Maybe if I pretended not to be there . . .

My mother and I were herded into Erica's office, and we sat, side by side, Erica opposite us, just like at the doctor's.

Dr Webb stared at my red face. 'Have some water.'

She had one of those eerie plastic bubbles full of it. I carefully sipped at the cup she passed me.

'Have some more. It'll help get rid of those little teenage pimples.'

Her stare had concentrated on my forehead. My mother's eyes followed. Just then a woman breezed into the office looking clean, tidy and efficient.

'This is Jenny. She takes care of New Faces,' said Erica.

Jenny, my mother and Erica all pulled back their lips and smiled at me. Erica pointed me towards what looked like a storage cupboard. Jenny followed right behind me. She was very thin but even so there was hardly room to move with us both in the tiny room. Jenny closed the door and pulled out a tape measure. I could hear my mother and Erica talking outside, my mother's tinkling laugh.

'We'll . . . straighten her out . . . Oh, yes. I can guarantee an improvement . . . I see it all the . . . we get lots of young girls . . . fine career for a girl – independence, travel, money . . . Justine's got the face for it . . . grow into her bones . . . She's almost out of the gawky stage.'

Jenny circled my waist with her tape.

'So busy . . . stop-smoking clinics for pregnant women . . .'

'Oh! How altruistic . . . I do so admire . . .'

By the sounds of it my mother was telling Erica about her latest charity. Mother had a new one every month and they always consumed her. 'I'm a woman of passion,' she was fond of saying, 'one must be passionate.' This month it was antenatal nicotine patches and foetal hypnosis.

All this, however, was not enough to distract me from Jenny's wandering hands. She spoke out loud as she mapped out the new territory on a printed form.

'Height, five-nine, and you'll probably grow. Waist, twenty-three inches. Good. Hips, thirty-four. Very good.' She patted my hips happily. 'Lots of girls have trouble with their hips. Bust, thirty-three-and-a-half – we'll say thirty-four shall we, for symmetry's sake?'

Jenny was pleased with me. I must have done something right. What?

'You're spotty.' She was staring at my forehead. 'Brush a bit of egg white onto your forehead before bed and they'll disappear in no time. And water, water, water – make it a mantra. When do you stop wearing your plate?'

'Three months.'

'Well ... it'll just add to your baby-face appeal until then, won't it? Anyway you could always take it out for photos.'

Jenny pulled out a Polaroid camera and clicked, all but blinding me in the confined space. 'Two up close, one full-length – they'll love the school tunic. Genius!'

I was released from the ordeal, gasping for air. Erica and my mother turned and beamed at me.

'Good measurements – bit small on top.' Jenny read the verdict, rolling her tape measure and handing the form and the Polaroids to Erica.

'Well, she's still growing ... '

Dying actually.

'She photographs well – has something of a Nastassja Kinski – less voluptuous though ...'

Erica handed me a Polaroid. I looked like a stunned mullet.

I wrote my name on a contract under my mother's signature. She stood, I stood, we all shook hands. Picking up my damp towel, I led the way out, hoping Erica wouldn't notice the shuffling squeak my feet made with every step.

My father was characteristically vague when my excited mother gave him the news of my 'signing'. He smiled broadly and looked up from his catalogue of designer swimming pools. 'That sounds like fun!'

That's all he ever said to anything. That, and 'Sounds important' spoken in a lower voice, with less enthusiasm, if the speaker's tone was serious enough.

My mother often accused him of having left his brain at the bottom of one of the swimming pools he designed, but perhaps being quiet was his way of balancing my mother's inordinate volubility.

I rather enjoyed his lack of interest. He would never have signed me up with Erica Webb. But nor did he have the strength to save me.

3
It'll All Come Out in the Wash

Sydney, 3.45 p.m., Seafolly swimwear casting

It's like waiting for Miss Grillette, isn't it? Not that bad, maybe, but you feel the same. Sweaty plastic chair, school tunic sticking to the back of your legs. You're not in trouble, but you do look stupid.

No one else is wearing a uniform – they've all left school and you look like a stupid, ugly, messy baby. You're not the kind of girl who knows what to do with her hands. Not like your mother, with her sea-shell nails. Your nails are always scratched and covered in ink but you have too much pride to ask her to help you look good. You can't stop picking at your cuticles, can you?

Look at that girl over there – the Queensland blonde who looks like she should be on TV. She's got her hands gently folded in her lap. You'll never be like her. Face it, you're an impostor and sooner or later they'll figure it out. 'It's all about appearances – the impression you make, Justine. It's the impact.' Your impact is baby idiot with a gross, pimply forehead. Jenny's stupid egg white doesn't work.

You belong in the olden days when everyone left school at fifteen. Then you'd be finished and it wouldn't matter that you'd done badly in your exams. You're not learning anything at school. You're better off reading a book. That girl's got a big one: War and Peace. And she probably lives in Paris in her own apartment. You should just run away. But you don't have the guts.

You're too goddamn shy, the biggest goody-goody in the world. Sometimes you're just plain pathetic, you know that?

'Justine?'

That's you. You should feel embarrassed. You're an idiot. They all despise you.

'Justine? You're next.'

The head Japanese stylist stood back and examined her work on my breasts. Then she dipped into her bum-bag and pulled out a packet of what looked like Nicorette patches. She peeled off two – square and flesh-toned – and stepped up close. Her assistant pulled down my bra and the stylist stuck the first patch onto my nipple, pressing it on firmly. I stared at the square, astounded, as it clung like a limpet to the pink. 'What's it for?' I had to ask.

The stylist and her four assistants smiled, placed a patch on my other nipple, then readjusted my bra. I had a premonition that they would hurt like hell to remove. I asked again, trying to curb the wave of panic I felt at losing control of what was happening to me – waves that were breaking often here in Tokyo.

'What are the stickers for?' I demanded, turning my chest away, protecting it with my arms.

Just then, Maggie stalked into the curtained room in a yellow slip. 'Nipple guards,' she said simply.

'What?'

'They're nipple guards. Japanese catalogues and ads won't allow nipples to show, even under clothes. Nipples are porn to them, so they make you wear stickers.'

Maggie was five years older than me and considered a supermodel in Japan because she had a cover of Canadian *Elle* and some sexy editorial done in nothing but a man's shirt. She dressed lean in black and I was in awe of her.

'They'll shove one down your pants too. They feel the same way about pubes.'

Sure enough, small, icy hands were now plucking at my underpants. A look of horror must have crossed my face.

'Don't worry, they're just pads, they don't stick.' Maggie was smiling now. 'That would hurt, wouldn't it?' she laughed.

I tried to leave my body, retreat into my head. Four hands fishing around in my pants, trying to adjust my 'pubic hair pad', felt vaguely like rape. I tried to ignore it and looked over at Maggie.

She was standing by the curtain in her tiny, silk underthing, right hip out. She lit a cigarette and leant into the wall. Louche. Maggie had a beautiful face. Small, slitted blue eyes designed to keep out the Arctic sun, high, swollen cheekbones and a grown-up mouth that took well to the butt of a cigarette. She looked like she had been smoking all her life – her easy, distracted fingers, her hungry, sexy draws, the thick plumes of smoke – and she probably had. Her arms and legs were very thin, but it was her belly that mesmerized me. Maggie had just had a baby. That sounded so glamorous – a baby at twenty-one, travelling the world with her tiny son. She was somebody's Number One.

Maggie still had weird, puckered skin on her belly from her pregnancy. I had seen it when we were changing. It was rippled and uneven, and her thighs and belly were covered in silvery waves. Maggie would be modelling all the slips, so her belly wouldn't be in the photos.

I didn't want to stare but found it impossible to stop, fascinated by the sight of someone so young and fragile-looking bearing such heavy scars of living.

This was only the third time she had spoken to me that day. She was really a poor, young, single mum from Ohio, where her parents still lived, trying to make ends meet by modelling in Japan part of the year. But to me, watching her lounge against the wall, cool and ravaged, drawing manfully on her cigarette, she appeared supremely glamorous.

Japan was where they sent you when you needed cash. Sally, a red-headed Australian girl, had explained it all in a diner on my second day in Tokyo. Experienced models doing too much poorly paid but prestigious editorial work, who needed a quick cash injection, went to Tokyo. Sally was trying to suck a lump of strawberry ice-cream up her straw as she told me this. She was leaving the next day and feeling happy about it.

'If you've just started out modeling, you need to make a lump sum, enough to get you to Europe. Europe's expensive, so you need enough to get your career rolling. You're looking at airfares and then maybe a couple of weeks without work doing castings and go-sees. The Agency can advance you money, but they get shitty sometimes. Plus there are comp cards and couriers and copies of your book . . . you know how it is. Bloodsucking leeches.'

She gave a hard suck for emphasis, her pale cheeks pink with effort.

'Is Europe great? Better than here, I mean?'

'Mmm. Japan sucks, mostly. We just keep getting sent here because mother agencies are constantly doing deals with Japanese agencies who are always looking out for Good Girls.'

'What sort of deals?'

Sally looked at me with gorgeous green eyes, heavy lids at half-mast in a world-weary expression, all of eighteen years old. 'Fudge, I hate my hair,' she said. It was huge and red and curly, springing back under her hands. 'But clients here love it.' She ice-cream belched softly.

Other girls told me that Erica Webb could usually be seen driving a new set of wheels after she had sent out a new batch of what people in the industry called 'Good Girls'. Good girls worked well (often and on well-paying jobs) and had a future in the business. They were what the Japanese market wanted.

I wondered if I was helping pay for the silver BMW with the red-leather interior that Erica had driven to lunch the day before I left. She'd made a show of picking up the bill for my mineral water and Caesar salad (I felt I had to eat 'model food' around her) and kissing me goodbye on both cheeks. Just like a mother. 'Call me at home, Justine – anything you need, just call.' Looking at me fondly and fatly, she said, 'I'll miss you, Justine, you're one of my best girls.'

I wanted to tell her I already had a mother and wasn't sure I wanted to go to Tokyo at all. But Erica knows best, I told myself. 'Act professional.'

She had given me a way out of school and away from my mother and she knew it. Not an ideal way, but it was out. My mother had even been keen for me to go. She thought working abroad in the fashion industry might instill pride in my appearance. Perhaps you'll even turn out to have 'a head for business'. 'Not everyone is cut out for formal education. When I was working with Malayan botanists in Cape Tribulation . . .'

'Sounds fun!' My father had said brightly but blankly.

I was, so far, enjoying the perks of Tokyo: no school, no rules, no nagging, no Miss Olyphant, no bedtime – my own apartment even! Earning real money, travelling by myself . . .

Sally twisted and chewed her straw. 'Okay, the money *is* good,' she continued. 'That's why I bother. My friend came here last month for six weeks and went home with forty thousand cash. American!

You can get that for just one job sometimes. Loads of girls go back with wads of cash stuffed in their bras and panties. Or they roll it in toothpaste tubes or hide it from customs behind the photos in their portfolios.'

'That's a lot –'

'Yeah, but the Agency in Tokyo takes fifty per cent and, in case you haven't noticed, Tokyo is *very* expensive.'

Sally wasn't exaggerating. I had seen melons wrapped in styrofoam selling for a hundred dollars a pop, and meat cost more per ounce than gold. Not that I ate much of either. Out of sheer laziness and a mild fear of alien restaurants, I lived on rice-crackers and candy.

Everybody would stare when we (models always travel in twos or threes) walked into a Japanese eatery. The patrons weren't unfriendly, far from it, just curious. But they spoke no English, and we spoke no Japanese, and the sea of unfamiliar, searching faces was intimidating for sixteen-year-olds. So we drank milkshakes at American-style diners, and collected what we could at the European supermarket. I grew quietly thinner.

'Twenty-five cuts!' one of the production assistants screamed. 'Twenty-five cuts!'

The assistant had Maggie by the arm and was dragging her toward the set. Maggie wanted to finish her cigarette, but the assistant indicated there wasn't time.

An unseen hand in the small of my back pushed me forward while another hand cupped my breast. Fingers pulled my hair off my face while a brush swept my lips. Someone powdered my chest with great, snuffling clouds of talc to make me look pale – more Japanese, if possible.

Claustrophobia – clutchophobia – overwhelmed me. I was being grabbed, pulled and plucked until I felt like a scrap of mouldy bread in a pen of hungry hens. I wanted to scream and shake off the hands, but somehow, I was still afraid of getting a detention. I let the hands do their work, ignoring the balloon of shame gently filling my chest.

I looked over at Maggie. She too was surrounded by kneeling women, all trying to get the yellow slip to hang the way they wanted with ungentle hands.

'Twenty-five cuts!'

They were in a hurry. The production assistant's assistant reached up and snatched the half-smoked cigarette from between Maggie's lips and threw it down.

'You go now,' she said in her jagged English and gave Maggie a gentle push. Maggie's face registered shock and she turned calmly and slapped the assistant across the face.

The room stopped.

I'd never heard of anyone doing that before – apart from the rumours about Naomi Campbell in the tabloids – and I'd definitely never seen it happen. I was horrified, but inside I applauded. I felt like doing the same thing: all the hands, voices, orders in sharp, broken English.

The assistant put her hand to her cheek, more in shock than pain. Maggie bent, collected her cigarette and finished it in two quick drags. Then she handed the butt to the assistant and stepped away from the wall onto the set.

Twenty-five cuts left. In Japan, that meant twenty-five outfit changes, twenty-five shots left. A long day, but normal for Japanese catalogue work, Sally had told me.

No one had time to get emotional about Maggie's slap, not even Maggie. It was as if nothing had happened, a clean break in the air, then all back to almost normal. I looked at her, unfazed in her yellow, and thought about taking up smoking.

I stood by Maggie on the white paper backdrop, awkwardly near-naked in my blue lace underwear. I was still uncomfortable

22

revealing my body in bathers at the beach, let alone standing next to a bravely pugnacious 'supermodel', being stared at by twenty-three strangers whispering and pointing in Japanese.

It suddenly felt like porn.

It wasn't, but I was sixteen, and it felt like porn to me. My eyes floated upward, but there were no windows in the studio to dream out of. I felt short next to Maggie, who was five foot ten and a half. I wanted to reach out to her, say something witty about her slap, let her know I was on her side. I glanced up at her and her face looked weary and drawn. It was not a face I could have made laugh.

The photographer started clicking, strobes firing at every shot, a hailstorm of light. The art directors and their assistants, standing at the photographer's side, all started posing for us – exaggerated, cheesy, hands-on-hips – human tele-prompters making suggestions for how Maggie and I might position ourselves. One woman forced a huge smile and pointed at it with her index fingers. She swung her hips in what looked like a parody of an uncoordinated child learning to hula-hoop. I could barely suppress a burst of laughter.

Who were these grimacing, contorting aliens, and what was I doing here, standing under lights in my underwear, with bandaids on my nipples?

I giggled and looked over at Maggie, to see if she was sharing my joke, but she had been to Tokyo too many times. This was her life and she was tired of it all at twenty-one.

At ten that night the van came to take us home. We had been there since seven that morning. In Tokyo, you were pretty much driven everywhere, to all your castings and most of your jobs. The mini bus would come to the apartments around nine-thirty and all the girls who weren't working that day would get in. Then, for the rest of the day, the driver would take us around to various appointments. Sometimes all the girls would go in to see the client, at other times only three or four were right for the casting. The rest of us would sit in the van and wait. We spent a lot of time in the vans, smoking and talking. Each agency had one, its name usually written across the side in big letters, and you'd see them all lined up outside the casting like metal piglets waiting for their milk.

It was all about waiting – so much waiting. You longed to work, not only for the money, but to get out of the damned van.

The Agency provided the vans and the drivers because sending us out with the addresses of our appointments would have been useless. All the street signs were in Japanese, and the house numbers on every street started at number one for the first house built, then number two for the second built, and so on. Finding the right building would take forever.

Occasionally the Agency did send us out alone. We'd take the subway, which was kept immaculately clean, without a scrap of graffiti. The subway wasn't difficult or dangerous to use, except at rush hour when people would cram into the carriages with no concept – or a complete disregard for – the limitations of space. Just when you thought you could barely breathe, let alone move, another batch of office workers would plunge in. The conductors strode the platforms and shoved people in from behind. The only advantage models had is that we stood head and shoulders above everybody else. That made it easier to breathe.

The Agency would give us a photocopied map of the area and a piece of paper printed with Japanese characters. If we got lost, we were supposed to find a passerby, stop him and point to the writing on the piece of paper. Apparently it said: 'Hello. I am lost. Could you please kindly show me where this address is, please?' And then we were supposed to point to the spot on the map. Quite a sound notion in theory, but the Agency – or whoever had devised the plan – had not taken into account the national character of the people. For the average Japanese person we met on the street would consider it rude to answer 'No' to our questions, even 'No, I'm sorry, I don't know where it is'. And so, often, they smiled kindly – they were always so kind – and pointed in any random direction. And we often got lost.

This night Yoji, our driver, dropped Maggie off first. She was staying in a different apartment building – a much nicer, more expensive place, built in the shape of an octagon. I later found out that Maggie kept her baby up there with her, employing a young Japanese nanny to take care of him during the day.

Like most models, I was staying in Roppongi, district of neon and giant TV screens, the Times Square of Tokyo. I had come in for the first time at night after a flight straight from Sydney. It had been raining and the view through the wet windshield was straight out of *Bladerunner*. There were people everywhere, thousands of them, rushing past each other in great lines like duelling snakes. Neon lights reflected on the wet roads, the wet cars, wet windows. I stared at the formless black bags of rubbish and imagined they concealed body parts.

That first night I met my room-mate Michelle. Yoji knocked on an indistinct, drab apartment door in a sickly, fluorescent hallway, and Michelle answered the door in a pair of tartan boxer shorts and a grey T-shirt. She held a bowl of soup in one hand, and with her long, long dark hair and all-over freckles, she didn't look like an American model. The door closed behind me.

'Hi, I'm Michelle,' she said, standing with her weight on one leg. All models stand that way, with one hip jutting out.

I told her my name was Justine. 'You don't look very American,' I said, too tired to think about whether it was something I should say to a new roommate.

'I'm Canadian.'

'Oh.'

We soon became friends. Well, you had to, sharing a bedroom and a mini van, day in, day out. It felt like school camp minus the activity sheets.

The apartment we shared was painted light (institutional) green, with dirty, brown synthetic carpet that gave electric shocks, just like the stuff at my school. The sofa – there was only room for one – matched the carpet, dirty, brown and pilling. No matter how many of the little balls you picked off the cushions, there were always more of them. The tiny, open kitchen matched the tinier bathroom. A bedroom opened into the living room, with a telephone and two single beds. The living room had a sliding glass door that opened onto a concrete ledge that held an air conditioner and a dead plant. There was no view.

The models from the Agency and a few from others lived in this apartment block unless, like Maggie, they could afford to live elsewhere, or be bothered spending the extra money on better accommodation.

Michelle had already been in Tokyo for three weeks when I arrived, but she had only worked once. There's nothing more depressing than going to Tokyo and not working. It was expensive, boring and a long way from home. It wasn't like London or Paris or New York where – as I later discovered – you always had some kind of life outside modelling. When you came to Japan, you signed a contract that guaranteed you a certain amount of money, but also meant that, for those eight weeks or so, your agency owned you. You couldn't take the train to Mount Fuji on the weekend, or drive to see the cherry blossoms on a day when you weren't working. The Agency felt you weren't 'fulfilling your contract' if you did that. You were also in breach of your contract if you cut or coloured your hair, suddenly got bad skin or if your measurements weren't within a centimetre of what was written on your card. So you were trapped.

The contract always sounded like a fair amount of money when you signed it – usually twenty or thirty thousand dollars for two or three months. But by the end of the first week you realised that all the contract was going to do was provide for your living expenses. Rent, air ticket, visa, faxes, photocopies and the cards the Agency made for you all came out of your pocket. There would be nothing left over if you didn't work well.

This system was fine for many models who were constantly being booked. The pay on jobs was very good and, if you worked a lot, you could indeed take off with a pile of money. The contract also guaranteed that you wouldn't lose money by coming to Japan, that at least your expenses would be covered, even if you were missing jobs elsewhere.

But the market in Japan was unpredictable, and you never really knew if you were going to work well or not. Plus, as the experienced girls in the van explained during long hours waiting, the Japanese government had recently decided there were too many Caucasians in advertising, and had implemented a law saying that eighty per cent of models had to be Japanese.

Michelle wasn't working and the Agency had told her to lose weight. They said that to every girl who wasn't working, no matter how thin she was. It was their way of shedding responsibility. 'Lose weight,' they'd say, and reflect the blame back onto the girl. But it was the Agency that had read the market wrong, or simply lost interest in the girl.

Michelle was slim but she wasn't skinny. She had a shape – thighs, breasts, buttocks. She wore long flowery dresses and flat sandals that made me think of picnics by the river. She was beautiful and told me she'd worked well in Milan, that they liked 'women' there. In Japan, they seemed to only want stick-girls with big eyes, preferably blonde. But again, you couldn't predict who would work well, although everyone was constantly trying.

Michelle joined a Japanese gym, poor girl, but I never had the courage to visit it. I imagined rows of small, black-haired businessmen in shorts and white socks, cycling furiously, trying desperately to ward off the atrophy of their twenty-first-century lifestyles. I only ever saw her when she returned, perspiring and red in her grey tracksuit, always looking worried. She would only eat soup. She was only allowed soup, that's what the Agency said. Only soup or it was a breach of contract. Soup was the way to lose weight.

So Michelle ate soup every night while we watched TV. I would eat candy and crackers, and her hungry eyes were always on my snacks. We would watch Japanese game shows that involved pain, humiliation or both.

Some nights Lisa from upstairs come down with her husband, Brian. It sounds so nice and suburban, and in a way it was. Lisa was the first American model I'd met, but she was nothing like the teutonic, bitchy, Christy Brinkley clone I'd imagined them all to be. Lisa was small, five foot six, with dark hair and dark eyes. She was pretty in the way that singularly perfect features can make you pretty, but bland. She was from Kansas. In real life she was a make-up artist. She came to Japan to boost – treble – her income. She also modelled in Taiwan, Singapore and Korea. Nowhere else. When she told me this I pictured the back rooms of every Chinese restaurant I'd ever visited. It was a depressing thought, filled with the smell of frying food and pink lemonade. But Lisa wasn't able to model anywhere else – too short and not quite pretty enough – so she did the tour of Asia, making as much money as she could for the rest of the year. She always made herself up like a perfect china doll. Her skin was always clear, her nails manicured, and her hair clean and styled. She was a professional and her look was very safe. The Asian market liked that about her.

Her husband, Brian, was a model from Nebraska who worked full-time and all over the place. They were a great couple – she was motherly and perfect, he was manly and clean. They came to play

poker in our apartment. Sometimes it was just the two of them, sometimes there were others. We played with matches, coins and pretzels
stolen from the American diner, and everyone smoked up a storm.

Michelle and I had both taken up smoking. She had quit a year
ago, then started again during one of our poker games. Bored and
stressed, she thought it would help her lose weight. I took it up at a
poker game on the night of Maggie's slap. Brian and Lisa smoked
cigarettes with white filters, Asian favourites like Kent.

So we filled the air with smoke and created the atmosphere of what
I thought a real poker room would be like. I'd bought a cheap, red,
plastic visor at a department store in Shinjuku and liked to be dealer.
I don't know where I'd learnt to play poker, but I was somehow the
instigator of the games, though at sixteen I was the youngest inmate
by far.

'I could never go to Taiwan or Korea. Asia's just a mind trap,' I said
to Lisa, 'it's like white slavery.' I raised Brian two matchsticks. 'I have
enough trouble coping with this place, I can't imagine one that's Tokyo
to the power of twenty-one.' Brian folded and I reached forward and
raked in five stale pretzels. 'That's how many solar systems there are,
you know? Ours, to the power of twenty-one, all in one galaxy, also to
the power of twenty-one. It makes you feel sick doesn't it – thinking
about stuff like that.'

'My mother told me I'd get warts if I counted stars,' Michelle said.

'So did mine!' Brian laughed, and Lisa folded her cards.

'I don't mind it. I've been enough times that I have regular clients,
and I just work all day – I don't even see the city.'

'It's not sounding any better, Lisa,' I said.

'I make a lot of money,' she replied. Lisa was a very sensible girl.
'The clients pay less, but I sometimes do three jobs in one day –
I hardly sleep when I'm there. And you have to do your own hair
and make-up.'

'I've been a few times,' Brian said, 'but I don't work there. There's not really a market for male models.'

I divided a stack of cards in two and tried to shuffle them casino-style, two flip books folding into one. It didn't work, and I had to settle for a more pedestrian mix. 'Did you know that girls sometimes disappear in Japan?' I wanted to shake up the conversation. I'd heard the rumour a few times in passing while I'd been in Tokyo, and figured that Lisa would know the truth. 'Alyssa said she knew of a girl who took a job here and was never seen again.'

'I've heard stuff like that too,' said Michelle. 'About girls disappearing into, like, the sex trade.'

'See?' I added, delighted. 'White slavery again!'

Lisa collected her cards, then answered in her even voice. 'It has happened. Mostly girls who take jobs as hostesses or dancers. They answer ads in the newspapers back home. They come to Japan and their employer takes away their passport. Some of them get stuck here trying to pay off their airfares.'

Michelle and I looked at each other. 'Does it ever happen to models?' We asked together.

Lisa smiled. She had appointed herself surrogate mother, and our morbid fascinations amused her. 'It doesn't happen to models who go with real agencies – the big ones.'

'I'd never give them my passport,' I said firmly. 'No way, José.'

And I hadn't. Even when Oki had asked for my passport when I'd gone into the Agency on the first day, I had stood and waited, watching her take a photocopy then asking for it back. 'I think I must have been a spy, or some persecuted person in a previous life,' I announced. 'I have a complete paranoia of being trapped, and of customs – I never let go of my passport. I even feel trapped at birthday parties sometimes, or at jobs –'

Each day was like every other in Japan: van, casting, van, casting, van, casting. I took to sitting up front with Yoji so I'd get to see more of Tokyo. I had asked him to teach me some Japanese, hoping to learn at least something from my trip.

'Kastingu doko kana?' he would say with a smile, and I would repeat, 'Kastingu doko kana?' Translation: 'I am wondering, where is the next casting?'

One day we pulled up behind a black limo. Yoji pointed to it and said, 'Yakuza.'

My heart leapt. I'd seen all the Chuck Norris movies; I knew what the Yakuza were about. I craned my neck out the window, hoping to catch a glimpse of these famed Japanese mobsters – a partially-fingered hand, a dragon tattoo, anything at all. Yoji laughed at me. 'The Yakuza are a joke in Japan,' he said. I wasn't so sure.

At the next casting I was sitting next to Alyssa. An American, from I forget where, she was two years older than me, with long blonde hair that fell down past her breasts and never really looked clean. We were with the others, waiting to see the clients, in a room that smelt like the waiting room of a doctor's surgery. Photographs of Mount Fuji adorned the mauve walls and a stack of pamphlets sat in a neat perspex box, providing information on the advertising agency we'd come to see.

Many of our castings had waiting rooms, but they never had magazines. In some you had to sit on the floor. I guess most clients thought models were blank enough to be content staring at a wall for hours.

Most of us brought books. The reading list didn't fall in with the *New York Times* Top 100 – favourites ranged from Judy Blume to horse books. Virginia Andrews and her *Flowers* series was popular, and later *The Celestine Prophecy* popped up everywhere. Occasionally a groomed, older model would sit reading Khalil Gibran. I read comics, mainly *Archie* and *Tintin*.

Alyssa was tallish at around five-nine-and-a-half (the half is always important in a world of vital statistics), with stick arms and legs. She wore white crocheted skirts and her knees always stuck out from her thighs like small apples. Despite her Swedish hair, blue eyes, and scarecrow limbs, Alyssa was having trouble working in Tokyo because her skin was very bad, and the Japanese hated that.

Many models get spots. Bad skin was made worse by the daily routine of make-up applied in layers, removed, and applied again. Even some supermodels have bad skin but it is covered over by the expert make-up artists, or airbrushed out by vigilant art departments. In Japan, for the rest of us, it wasn't that easy. Alyssa tried to cover her spots with foundation, but the make-up only highlighted the dark, purplish patches that lurked under the powder and made her look almost ill. She was outgoing, very confident and quite unperturbed by her skin. When I occasionally got pimples, they mortified me, but I don't think Alyssa cared.

And so we waited in line in the Mount Fuji room for the casting – we never really knew what they were for, as most of us had given up asking. The answers were usually vague, or incomprehensible, or completely misleading. You would think you were going in for a toothpaste commercial and so you worked your smile like a mad woman. Later you'd find out from the girl with the crooked teeth – who had got the job – that the shoot was for pantyhose.

Alyssa went in before me. My eyes shifted to the empty water cooler in the corner, and then to the tanned girl from Florida whose bleached blonde hair, she told me later, fell out in large clumps because it was so damaged. Aussie 3 Minute Miracle shampoo had saved her life, she said. She had big blue eyes that she would cake with mascara like Twiggy, and she worked regularly. This Palm Beach Bambi's name was Danielle.

When it was my turn I was ushered in by a tiny woman in a large, beige power suit. My portfolio so far contained a test – some English

32

photographer had shot me in kiddy underwear somewhere off Bondi Beach – two ads for sunscreen and a story for *Dolly* magazine involving a garden hose. At least I had tear-sheets, photos of myself, published in magazines that I would literally tear out and put in my book.

Twelve people in suits, eleven men and the one beige woman, formed a horseshoe around the room behind formica tables. The woman nodded to me, took my portfolio and handed it around the circle. The eleven men looked on expressionless.

The woman handed me a scrap of red lycra and indicated a small door off to the side. It was a storeroom, filled with boxes and harshly lit with fluorescents. Alyssa was inside, changing back into her clothes. Skinny. I smiled. She smiled back and left me. I unravelled the lycra and groaned. I always hated swimsuit castings. It felt so stupid wearing swimmers on office carpet, so far from the sea . . .

I slipped on the suit – *Baywatch* red and too big in the boobs – and wondered how my butt looked. I tried to pull the lycra neatly over each cheek, to provide my bottom with a little dignity, but the fabric wouldn't stay put. A pair of riders. I hoped they wouldn't notice that I hadn't shaved my legs in two days.

I stepped into view, my face the colour of the bathers, and stood in the centre of the room. It's amazing how awkward your arms and hands can feel all of a sudden. One minute they're there, helping you through the day, the next they're weighty appendages that swing at your side like tree branches.

I held my tummy in and pushed my bottom upwards, hoping somehow to make my legs look instantly longer and thinner. Alyssa had been in before me. She had the lanky, easy confidence of knowing there would be no strange or fleshy bulges if she moved the wrong way. She was planks of wood, twigs, sticks. Straight edges, sharp corners. I still had the small, rounded limbs of a ten-year-old and no waist.

Under the unsmiling eyes of eleven men in suits, the woman

indicated – she spoke no English, or not to me anyway – that they wanted me to throw a few poses, to give them a preview of what they'd get for their money. There could not have been a more exquisite torture for me than this. I tried to imagine Linda Evangelista or Naomi Campbell doing it. They wouldn't have to, of course, but if they did, they would blow the room away. No one I knew was watching and I did want the job, so I pulled out my stock swimsuit poses and fired them off with a smile worthy of every Barbie babe ever fashioned. Hands on hips, left knee in front of right.

Profile. Tummy in. Butt high. Chest out.

Think Cindy C. in Miami with Patrick Demarchelier. Think fabulously sexy. Over-the-shoulder glance, hair toss, mega-watt smile.

I looked at my audience. No expression on the suit faces. Whispers in Japanese. My imagination translated for me: 'big bottom' and 'too short', 'no bosom'. The woman handed my book back. I felt a little like crying as I switched to the aerial view of myself, parading around nearly naked in a red swimsuit, smiling for these stony-faced men.

I forced these thoughts aside, shoved them into a deeper, forgotten pocket where I might look at them later. I smiled one more time, thanked them all and almost ran for the door of the box room.

Danielle walked in as I was changing, thin and brown. She smiled at me. I smiled back, and left the room as quickly as I could.

'Justiney-chan,' Oki said to me over the phone, 'prepare for swimsuit.'

I nodded then realised she couldn't see me. 'Okay – studio or location?' I asked.

'Studio.'

I breathed a sigh of relief. I didn't want to be parading around outside somewhere in a bikini. At least the studio was more contained, and there was always a bathroom.

I passed the phone to Michelle, curled up next to me on the couch, her bowl of diet soup on the table.

'Hi Oki. It's going okay.' Her voice was soft, subdued, broken. 'Still the same as yesterday . . . I know. Okay. Bye.'

Michelle slammed the phone and turned to me. 'Every day, Oki asks me if I've lost weight. How much weight can I lose overnight, for fuck's sake!' Her eyes were welling up. 'She says she's not sending me out on anything until I lose weight.' She paused. 'I'm just so fucking sick of this fucking soup!' She shoved the bowl with her foot and it flew onto the floor. Some soup splashed the television, covering the Japanese newsreader in a yellow goop.

I didn't know what to say, so I sat still.

Michelle looked over at me. 'You're lucky you're skinny,' she said, her voice calm again.

'Not as skinny as Alyssa,' I replied softly. 'Oki just needs an excuse, Michelle, you don't need to lose weight.'

'I'm fat.'

'Bullshit, bullshit, bullshit. It's the soup – it's making you upset. You can't just eat that every day. It'd drive anyone crazy.'

I got a sponge and started cleaning up. As I wiped soup off the telecaster's face Michelle giggled then stopped. 'Alyssa's pretty anna – if you know what I mean.'

'Anna?' I asked.

'Anna. Anorexia. I mean, have you ever seen her eat?'

'Only cucumbers in that little plastic tub she carries with her.'

'I can't be as thin as her, never will be. My bones alone are bigger than her thighs.'

'You wouldn't want to be that thin, Michelle.'

'They want me to – Oki and the rest of them. They spy on us, I swear.' She lowered her voice. 'The other day I was eating a Snickers – I cracked, and it was only a mini one – but that instant the phone rang and it was Oki. She wanted to talk about my contract. She said if I wasn't serious about losing weight, she'd cancel it.'

I took it all in. 'Do you really think the apartments are bugged?'

'They'd need cameras to know about the Snickers.'

'Wait.' I stood, went to the bathroom and turned the taps on full. Michelle joined me. 'They won't be able to hear over the water,' I whispered, 'Where would the cameras be?' I was horrified, but I wouldn't have put it past Oki and the Agency to spy on us. We were, after all, their investments.

I remembered a Tintin book I'd read. Tintin and Haddock in *Tintin and the Picaros*. They were in South America and their hotel had been bugged. There was a two-way mirror in the bathroom.

'The mirror,' I said to Michelle, and pointed. 'The way to tell,' I went on, delighted that my deep interest in espionage was finally paying off, 'is to touch the mirror with your finger. The tips of your real finger and your reflected finger aren't meant to touch. In a two-way mirror,' I held my finger to the glass, 'your fingertips touch.'

Michelle gasped.

I looked closely.

My fingertips were touching.

'We'll just have to be careful,' I said, then turned off the taps. 'I have to take a shower – I got that retarded Baywatch job.'

Michelle looked at me for a moment. 'That's great ... they obviously didn't think you were fat.' She said the last part in a whisper.

'Hey, Michelle. The clients eat pickled fish for breakfast and think knee socks are cool. What do they know about anything?'

She smiled. 'Fog up the mirror before you get undressed,' she called after me as I shut the door.

Swimsuit prep. I took out my pink razor and turned on the hot, waiting for the steam to cover the mirror.

My second modelling job had been a swimsuit ad – Reef Tan,

the sun oil. Erica had rung me at home on a school night and told me to prep for swimwear. I had been too shy to ask what that meant. What was I supposed to do? Moisturise my legs? Bring a towel? Eat fish?

I'd taken the day off school, and met the team of hair/make-up/stylist/photographer/assistants at Bondi Beach on a cold, sunny morning in autumn. The stylist had handed me a high-cut swimsuit, brightly patterned to suggest Happy, then pointed to the car, my changing room. I undressed awkwardly around the gear-stick, trying to hide from prying eyes on the street.

By contorting myself into several pretzel shapes I finally struggled into the suit. Then I looked down and, to my horror, discovered what 'prep for swimwear' meant.

I was a fairly undeveloped fifteen-and-a-half, and not a hairy girl by any stretch, but that gaily patterned swimsuit was so small that several stray pubic hairs were showing.

There was no way to tuck them into the suit.

I could have died of embarrassment. Outside the crew was waiting for me, surrounded by seagulls.

I panicked. I turned my attention back to my errant groin, gripped one of the more mortifying hairs with my fingers and yanked.

It didn't come out.

Someone rapped on the window. It might have been the stylist, but I was blinded by panic and all I saw was a giant head. I managed to yell, 'One second,' and the face went away.

I tried again, gripping the hair harder. This time it came out. Ouch! Frantically I attacked the other hairs, fingers pinched white, my nails digging into the tips, until I had an almost-neat bikini line.

I left the car on shaky legs, face pink, almost crying, my jungle-print bathers nicely exposed to the tourist trade. The crew smiled and hustled me over to the camera. I watched their faces carefully for signs of smirking or disgust, but there were none. I let myself float away on a massive pool of relief.

As it turned out, they only shot my face and chest.

Tonight, in Tokyo, I was taking no chances. I shaved my bikini line carefully, feeling very grown up as I did so. I was sure it was better to wax and the girls did talk about it, but I didn't know how or where to go, and I didn't have the courage to ask.

The good thing about working in Japan, aside from the money, was that most of the shoots were done in studios. There was much less chance that you'd find yourself freezing your blue bottom off in a bus station, waiting for the snow to fall as the photographer's assistant reloaded the film and some idiot assistant editor was telling you to 'Think Warm'.

Next day I found myself wearing a red swimsuit in the same style as the one I had tried on at the casting. Someone had spread sand on the floor of the studio and the halogen lights were warm. Many hands adjusted the straps on my suit, the position of my breasts, the curve of my butt. The job was only two shots – an ad for some soft-drink called 'Pocari Sweat' that tasted flat and salty and came in a blue-and-white polka-dotted can. The money was good.

A muscled, hairless male model strutted out onto the set in red board shorts. A Mitch Buchanan look-alike, he was handsome in a plastic, perfect way: American, twenty-six-ish, cleft chin like a butt, and scary in his glaring maleness.

He was supposed to be 'the boyfriend' for the shoot.

Once on the sand, he stood close to me and stared with brilliant green eyes. 'My name's Keith.'

I told him mine.

'Justin?'

'Justine.'

He kept running a hand through his sandy flop of hair. I was nervous.

Now I felt cold. Two assistants rushed in to powder my knees. The knees are always the first to go blue in the cold. They turn purplish if you have a tan.

All make-up artists have body make-up to hide the cold bits and bruises. It's thick and greasy and takes ages to wash off in the bath, but it will make your body look warm and happy even on a winter day with a south wind and the threat of rain.

Since I had started doing swimwear and lingerie, I had taken to looking very closely at all body shots I saw in magazines to see if I could spot the goose flesh on the model. I felt satisfied when I found it, as if I'd somehow glimpsed the truth behind the photo.

Keith began to rub the small of my back. 'I'll keep you warm,' he said, and pulled me in close, smiling a friendly, light smile.

I stood very still, squished against his bare chest. Should I pull away? But it was warm where our flesh touched, and I thought it might be rude to move. I mustn't seem ungrateful.

The photographer walked in. I think he said his name was Kodak. Small and elegant, dressed in black with wire-rimmed glasses, he presented an image of order and gently controlled creativity. I began to relax.

Kodak looked through the camera, mounted on a tripod in front of the sand, then up at us. 'Okay, good. Now, get closer ... turn profile, that's it ... a little left ... now be kissing for the first shot.'

Be kissing.

My body flushed hot and cold the way it had when I'd been caught shop-lifting a packet of chewing gum at the newsagent. The camera and tripod became the machine gun of a desert firing squad. The cells in my body prayed for the roof of the studio to cave in and injure the photographer enough to have to cancel the shoot.

Be kissing.

Keith grabbed me and put his dry, heavy lips to mine. Hot. My weight fell backwards. I was the cheese in a bodice ripper: *Justine, Pirate Queen, Terror of the High Seas*. I froze. Keith was pressing hard. Through my eyelids, I could see the dull red of the strobe flash firing off.

We broke and I breathed.

Kodak was pleased. His assistant reloaded. 'Same again,' he ordered.

Keith held me tighter this time, and pressed down even harder with his lips. I felt his tongue shoot out and rocket around my lips, looking for a way in. It found one, and all of a sudden his tongue was in my throat and I thought I might choke. We broke again.

I wondered if this was normal. It certainly wasn't enjoyable. He tasted of cigarette smoke, he was rough, but I had never worked with a male model before, so I had no idea what to expect. Stop being such a bloody baby, I told myself, it was only a goddamn kiss.

Thinking swear-words made me feel braver. 'Does he *like* me?' I wondered, 'or is it just part of the job?'

Down again, tongue, saliva. I didn't kiss back, but I didn't pull away.

We broke for lunch. I was starving and ready to eat anything besides boy's tongue. The lunches in Japan were always good – no damp, tuna sandwiches and bitter orange juice in Tokyo. There was usually a Bento box of sushi, chicken, rice and salad. I put on a robe and sat down far from Keith with my book. I had given up the Archie comics and bought a George Eliot novel. The girls in year eleven at home had started reading *Middlemarch* for English and I felt doing the same might Improve my Mind. I couldn't seem to get past the first chapter, but this hiccup merely confirmed that I was indeed improving my mind.

I reminded myself to eat only a little. It's hard to work swimwear when you have a belly full of rice – you need to keep it hungry and concave. I began on the sushi, but every bite of raw fish reminded me a little of Keith's tongue, and soon I pushed my lunch away.

The next shot was full length. Keith and I stood waiting. He was ignoring me. I took off my robe and we faced each other. A few shots were fired off – and then there was a ruckus.

They'd forgotten my nipple pads.

'They're standing to attention,' Keith grinned, then reached over and tweaked one. I tried to smile, stay cool, but the stylists' hands down my top distracted me.

Everything fixed, Keith and I got back into position. He held me tightly, gazing into my eyes, never once blinking. I felt like one of the white mice that people feed pet boa constrictors – confused and partially frozen, in the grip of the snake.

Kodak shot. I smiled. Keith smiled wider. The sand-rakers, the make-up girls and the stylist smiled. Keith pressed his hips into mine, and I smiled harder. I could feel a huge, hard bulge and it scared the hell out of me.

I found I couldn't smile any more.

One of his hands grabbed the top of my butt. I shifted my weight away and posed, trying to be professional. Keith shifted too, and pressed closer.

I couldn't move.

Nobody seemed to think that anything was wrong, and to get away I would have to twist free and ruin the shot. The clients would get angry. I didn't struggle.

Day over, voucher signed. I was behind a screen in the make-up room getting changed into panties and a tiny rose-printed undershirt. The make-up artist and her assistants were cleaning up and chatting in Japanese.

Keith came in behind the screen and smiled. I tried to find my jeans – cool and careless, not looking at him, like I didn't care that a guy was watching me change. Wasn't that what Maggie would do? Not give a shit?

Suddenly Keith grabbed my wrists and pinned me against the wall. He smiled, reached down and ripped my panties half off. My mother had bought me the undies – pink cotton, my name-tag from school still inside.

I wondered what they were doing at school right now.

Keith pressed me into the wall and stuck three fingers inside me.

I gasped in pain. I was in shock and we were hidden by the screen. He was wiggling his fingers around now, harder, harder, and I couldn't get away. I thought about shouting, but couldn't stand the idea of the crew seeing me like this.

'Has anyone ever fingered you to orgasm?' Keith asked in a low voice, working away furiously. It hurt. I wanted to get away but I was squashed against the wall and frozen with fear.

Suddenly he took his hand away and let go of me. He sucked his three fingers and smiled. 'Bye, pretty baby ... look me up when you're older.' And with that he left.

I found my jeans and slowly got dressed, my thoughts and legs numb. I collected my voucher – proof that I had done the job and that the clients got what they wanted – said goodbye to everyone with a cheerful fake smile, and somehow arrived back at my apartment.

Michelle was home. She asked about the job as I dumped my satchel on the table and flopped on the sofa.

'I think I might have been a little bit raped ...' I looked at her confused. Maybe Michelle would make sense out of what happened.

'What do you mean? Who by?'

'Some male model named Keith.'

'What did he do? What do you mean?'

I told her what happened, including what he'd done to me behind the screen.

'What an asshole,' she said finally. 'But he kept his clothes on, right? I mean, he just touched you with his hands, right?'

'Yeah. Whatever. It's okay.'

'I'm sorry, some of those guys are sleaze bags.' She handed me some candy and we turned to the television where a newscaster was reading in Japanese. We always watched the news in Japanese. It was funnier that way.

Michelle got a job – a Swatch Watch ad – and we took a walk around Roppongi to celebrate. It was around five o'clock, but already there were groups of businessmen, some arm in arm, swaying down the street. The last trains home to the suburbs left at seven, and so they had to get their drinking in early.

We had a milkshake at the American diner – I had strawberry, Michelle chocolate – and watched the giant TV screen in the square play the old Aerosmith clip where Alicia Silverstone gets her belly-button pierced and bungee jumps off the highway overpass in LA.

On the way back, we found men in suits lying among piles of black rubbish bags, passed out cold, being watched by a growing army of giant crows.

We stopped at a street stall and flipped through porn-ish pictures of schoolgirls in uniform. Michelle pointed at a wall of clear plastic baggies. Each bag had a photo of a young girl stapled to it. Inside the bag was underwear – *used* underwear – belonging to the girl in the photo.

'I guess it's more ... personal that way,' giggled Michelle.

'So, so seedy,' I said. 'Do the girls know where their underwear is going, or are they just the victims of crazy panty raids?'

Michelle picked up a photo. The girl was smiling coyly, her index finger in her mouth. 'I think they know.'

It reminded me of Keith. I pulled Michelle away.

September 20th or 21st, Moanday (sic)

My dear Taber,

I hope this letter finds you in good health and happiness. I have been only quite well thank you but I am better now (today). Japan is hot but nothing like the Gold Coast which incidentally is the only other holiday destination I have been to. It is so curious to see head after head of black hair when you are used to seeing other colours mixed in. Some punks in Roppongi try to bleach their hair but it seems to go orange instead of blonde (and they are very tanned and wear the most extraordinary platform shoes in colours like purple!!). I do digress but I am distracted by my rumbly tummy. Every day at lunch we go to these fast-food bakeries, like a McDonalds full of cinnamon buns. I would prefer to eat Japanese but our drivers only ever take us there. I had fifteen cinnabuns in one week and I don't even like them very much.

Do you still remember me? I am sorry to write unannounced but it is part of my resolve to educate myself. I am reading a George Eliot novel (who, I may add, is a woman!!) to improve myself. Perhaps I am hoping you will write back to me and we will have a correspondence like in the olden days. However, it is unlikely that I will get any letters as they all go into a big basket behind the door in the Agency and we have to hunt through it to find ours. Plus I might leave soon. People on the job poke you the whole time and push you around and nobody talks to you. The money is good but everything else is not really. (Except the giant screen in Roppongi that plays MTV the whole time.) Were you aware of the astonishing fact that male models only make one-third of what the girls do, and also most of them are idiots? We are all meat for hire here but at least I get a better rate. It is amusing.

Here at 2.30 p.m. I am standing in a Tokyo photo studio with some gross male model being gross, and Gretchen is having maths with Miss Olyphant. I wonder if she sits next to anyone now? Do you ever see her? Maybe you are going out with her. If you are, don't answer that question please. I never thought I could miss that class at all – and in fact I don't really. I have a friend here called Alyssa who collapsed on the job yesterday. The clients got really mad at the Agency and the Agency freaked out at Alyssa because she blacked out. So I think I might leave. Alyssa has suggested London, or maybe Paris.

My love,
Justine.
P.S. I met a girl called Maggie who has a baby and a Canadian Elle *cover. She is very cool.*

I ran away later that week.

With the taps in the bathroom on full, I told Michelle I'd get my money from the Agency and leave the next day.

'What about your contract? They can totally sue, you know.'

'I never signed one,' I told Michelle. 'I refused. I said I'd rather take the chance of making no money than be trapped.'

'I guess that was smart. I have another four weeks before I can leave.'

'Slave labour.'

'Totally.'

Oki eyed me suspiciously, but she gave me my money. I told her I wanted to go shopping. What did they care? Seventeen-thousand dollars after commission and expenses – not bad for six weeks' work when you're sixteen. I was leaving the next day.

I made Yoji drive me back to the apartment, certain that I would be robbed in the crime-free city of Tokyo. The cash padded several envelopes.

With the taps on again in the bathroom, Michelle bravely offered to tell the Agency I'd left. I hugged her. I would miss Michelle, but modelling in Japan no longer felt like a funny game – the joke seemed to be on me; it was time to leave.

Customs would only allow a certain amount of money into Australia tax free, so I had to hide it all. I stuffed a third of the cash into my underpants, which raised me up an inch when I sat down, and felt like a dirty nappy. The rest of it I tucked flat behind the pictures in my portfolio.

And then I left Japan.

40,000 feet, somewhere over the Takliman desert
Dear Taber John,

It's not that I really care either way, but can you tell me, why don't my parents ring me?

Sometimes I feel like I have stepped onto some other planet and nothing that was real before is real now. My life before seems like a dream that happened to someone else – someone very much smaller than me. Every day things happen that shouldn't be normal – but now they are. I can't really explain what I am attempting to convey to you. At least everyone around me thinks it's normal.

You know my friend Alyssa – I believe I mentioned her in my letter (did you get my letter?) – she passed out again. When they tried to bring her round they were stroking her hair and huge chunks of it came out. At the Agency they said it was the peroxide but she is majorly anorexic! I think everyone is lying to each other. And also I have left school – it is official! Because everyone will be going into year eleven except me. I thought I might have gone back after Japan but I don't think I can anymore. I can't go back to uniforms and bobby socks and detentions and geography now. THAT feels weird and uncomfortable now, like it never happened, and I have resolved the issue in my mind by determining to EDUCATE MYSELF. (I am reading Time *magazine as we speak and there is a very educational article on sharks in this week's issue which I can strongly recommend to you.)*

It is frightening how fast things move and how easily you can

46

adapt – even to food. Sometimes I eat like an American now, but I don't like it because it consists of all burgers and milkshakes and soda pop. So I mostly live on Japanese rice crackers, white rabbit lollies and a curious soft drink called Pocari Sweat that also tastes a bit like it (sweat). Maybe I am an idiot, but my mother didn't mind me not going back to school. I didn't do very well in the S.C. exams – I'm sure you would have done much better, especially if you did music! She thinks my working will lead to other opportunities and REFINE ME.

I like having my own money and also travelling alone on aeroplanes. I feel important and so adult, like I have places to go and business that attends me there. I wonder what people think when they see me. That's why I read Time *because it is interesting and because it confuses the people who watch me on the plane. Most are businessmen at this time of year because nobody is on holiday. I am on a plane now – it's my favourite bit – on my way to England. The London branch of the Agency sent a scout to Sydney and they invited me over – they are one of the top agencies and they said I could get a lot of work.*

Bye.

Sincerest Love,
Justine Lily, 16
P.S. I did go home briefly to Sydney and would have established contact with you, but I forgot I don't have your phone number.

4

Just Answer the Question, Please

Heathrow, London, 6.29 a.m.

They'd warned me not to carry anything on my person – strict instructions from Erica. 'Send your book ahead,' and she'd taken it from me and done it for me. Speed couriers were expensive, but she could afford to be generous because I was paying: it all came out of my earnings, not out of her twenty per cent.

'And your agenda.'

Her puffy hand reached for my appointment book too. Then she gave me a phone number.

I was to tell Her Majesty's Customs Officers that I was in London visiting an uncle. I should produce the phone number if pressed. The person at the other end of the line had instructions to be 'uncle' to girls coming in to work illegally.

My knees shook as I offered my passport to an officer with a handlebar moustache. I smiled broadly, trying to look him in the eye.

Liars don't do that.

I told the man I was staying a month, and visiting an uncle. He didn't ask too many questions and I was let in.

My hands were still shaking as I rode the escalator to the baggage claim. I knew I needed a whiskey, even though I'd never even tasted it before.

As I waited for my bags, I stayed cool and calm in the claim area. My espionage reading had taught me that. The mirrors on the walls weren't mirrors – I'd learnt that in Japan. Behind them sat uniformed officials licking slavering lips, watching arriving passengers for signs of guilt. Yawning, fidgeting and sweating were all possible symptoms of illegal activity, but also, coincidentally, of travelling twenty-six hours across ten time zones in a warm egg carton in the sky.

Someone was supposed to meet me at the airport. I didn't know who, but the Agency had said that someone would be there. I saw an Indian man in a grey parka holding a sign: Miss Lily.

I went over and smiled. 'I'm Miss Lily.'

'Your plane was late – I've been waiting for half an hour.'

I didn't know if the man was a taxi driver or if he worked for the Agency. I smiled again. 'I know, I'm just so glad to be off that plane.'

We drove silently through the grey streets of early morning London. My breath puffed white in the back seat of the blue Fiat, but the driver, still in his parka, didn't turn on the heater. I thought it might be broken, but I was soon to learn that nothing in England is well heated.

It was barely 6.30 a.m. but the terrace houses that lined the road were showing lights in the windows. The streets felt at once strange, yet utterly familiar. They reminded me of little parts of Sydney, parts that had taken neatly and indelibly the imprint of British colonialism.

'Swiss Cottage' was where I ended up. There didn't seem to be anything Swiss or cottagey about it. We drove along a row of crumbly townhouses, three storeys and covered with ivy, in the shadow of a giant tower of raw-concrete council flats with metal balconies that grinned like gridiron jaws.

The man dropped me off and robbed me blind. Fifty pounds for the ride. But I didn't know any better. That's when I realised he didn't work for the Agency and I shouldn't have felt bad about keeping him waiting.

I dragged my suitcase up the ivy-covered stairs. In my bedroom at home I had thought it light and comfortable, but it was growing heavier every time I lifted it.

I tried hard not to think of the morning I'd packed the suitcase, my mother standing in the doorway helping me decide what to take, warning me that Europe was cold in October and wishing me well. It seemed so far away – and it was, seventeen thousand kilometres. I was sixteen and I missed her . . .

I pressed the buzzer to the top floor. No answer. I tried again, and still no answer. I looked around. My driver had left so I was not a little stranded. I tried again.

Finally a sleepy, mumbly voice answered. Half-way through my explanation, the door buzzed open. I climbed six flights of carpeted stairs, dragging my suitcase like a pregnant crab. It smelt like somebody had been boiling hams in the hall for the past twenty years. I knocked on the small white door at the very top of the building.

'You're lucky someone was home.'

It was a girl in a grey tracksuit with long, long blonde hair. She moved away from the door, leaving it open. I walked in.

Two more girls were scattered around the living room – a high, white room with a glass skylight and an open kitchen to the left. My eyes fell first on a girl sitting sideways across an ugly brown armchair, drinking tea. She was wearing a white terry-towelling robe and looked like Betty Boop: pale skin, big green eyes, pink pout. This was TK, I later found out, from Los Angeles, California. 'Hey.' She had a high voice.

'Hi.'

'I'm Debbie,' said the blonde who had opened the door, lighting a cigarette.

'Hi.'

'I'm from Minnesota.'

I nodded, not knowing where that was.

A girl with long, dark hair and sad eyes looked up from her newspaper, then returned to it without a word.

'That's Brigitte,' Debbie told me. 'She's from Germany.'

Brigitte looked up again at the mention of her home. She was very, very thin under her thick, brown-wool sweater.

TK pointed to a door. 'You can share a room with Cristina. She's working today.'

'She's from Croatia,' added Debbie. 'Brigitte has her own room and TK and I share with Lara.'

'She's working too. She works often.'

'Catalogue mostly.'

'Money.'

'Do you work a lot?'

'Um, I do okay. Two or three jobs a week I suppose.'

'Editorial?'

'And advertising.'

'That's not bad.'

'Advertising is good money.'

'I've been to Japan,' I added.

'Me too.'

'Me too.'

Brigitte looked up and said nothing again.

I looked at Debbie. She made a face. 'Can I look at your book?'

I explained I didn't have it with me.

'Want to see mine?' she said.

Debbie photographed well. She was almost Barbie-doll-like in the pictures. She had a couple of nice Italian editorials and some sexy tests. I was relieved to see that she was at much the same stage in her career as I was, even though she was a couple of years older.

'London is a good place to get cool editorial,' TK said. 'I only want to do cool stuff.'

'Me too,' I agreed.

Debbie rolled her eyes. 'I just want to be a star.'

I was nervous as I followed Debbie into the Agency later that morning. The bookers there had never met me, all they had were the pictures Erica had sent. I reminded myself that they had asked me to come, but I still felt awkward and fidgety in my blue sweater. It itched my neck.

I had asked TK what I had to wear in London and what the Agency wanted you to do. They had strict rules about that in Tokyo.

'Whatever,' TK had replied. 'Whatever you want, it doesn't matter.'

So I'd put on my old motorcycle boots, the tight, black jeans that made my legs look really skinny and a blue jumper my mother had bought me for luck.

I was greeted with excitement at the Agency then made to wait on the leather sofa, by the watercooler.

A short, plump, animated woman came over and took my hand in hers. 'I'm Mandy. Baby, it's so good to have you here!'

I was used to gushy, but Mandy was overwhelming. She told me how fabulous I looked, then pulled out a form on a clip board. I thought she might need details like my home address, mother agency, nationality and so on.

'Hair?' she asked, and peered at mine. 'Brown–chestnut.'

'Eyes?' Her face loomed in. 'Green,' she said and wrote that down.

'Actually, they're grey.'

'What did you say, love?'

I wished Mandy's voice wasn't so loud. People were looking at me.

'My eyes, they're grey. They seem to change colour, you see, depending on . . .'

Mandy crossed out green and wrote grey. I looked at the form and noticed a series of multiple choice answers: Poor Fair Good Excellent.

'Teeth?' demanded Mandy and made me smile. She circled Good with her pen.

'Skin?' Another Good. 'You have one or two little spots – probably from flying! Hands?' I showed them: Excellent.

'Nails?'

A Fair this time. 'You really shouldn't bite them, honey!'

I grew pink from embarrassment and hid my hands under my knees.

'Legs?'

Mandy made me stand up and turn. I was relieved to see she marked Excellent.

'Body? You have a small chest, but your body looks fine.'

She circled Good.

The form finished, she filed me in a cabinet. I felt very small.

Mandy took me by the hand and introduced me to four women and a man sitting at a large round table by the window. Their names went straight out of my head as they turned to look at me, some smiling, others not. Pointy and shrill, they scared me, and I mentally dubbed them the Frights of the Round Table.

Mandy was kneeling on the floor, her head inside a cupboard. Her hipster pants had slid down to reveal the top of her butt crack, and the swell of flesh above it.

I looked away as she re-emerged with a huge stack of cards. My composites.

'We made these up when Erica told us you were coming. She sent your book over early, so we thought we'd get a head start. That way you can go on appointments right away.'

I looked at the top card. There were three black-and-white pictures on the back – body shots of me in swimwear – and my vital statistics: 34, 23, 34. The pictures they had chosen were fine, nothing I hated. I flipped the card over.

The front picture was one of the test portraits, kiddy underwear shots. I looked young and fresh and clean. The Agency name was in bold on the top. Below it was mine: JUSTIN.

I stared for a second, in case my mild dyslexia was the problem, but still it said JUSTIN.

I took a second card. Perhaps the first one had been a misprint. No.

'Um, Mandy?' I ventured. 'They've got the wrong name.' Mandy took the card.

'Why? What is it?'

'*Jus-teen* – with an "e" on the end. Not Justin like a boy.'

'Oh, I see . . .' she stared at it for a second. 'Well, you can be Justin! I like it! Justin! It's cool – people will remember it, sweetie! Don't worry!'

'But my name's *Jus-teen* . . .'

Mandy looked at me. Exasperation, my mother's look. 'We've already printed a thousand cards. They all say "Justin". It's going to cost you another five hundred pounds to have them done over!'

I had been in the Agency thirty-five minutes and already was half a grand – *sterling* – in debt. I couldn't afford another five hundred, nor could I risk inviting Mandy's displeasure so early in the game.

'Don't worry,' Mandy said, 'Justin's great – I like it much better than Justine!' She took her place at the round table and took a gulp of tea from a mug smeared with red lipstick. 'You're much more than plain old Justine! Justin Lily! Cool baby, cool!'

And that was the end of that.

I was Justin.

'Look what they've done!' I held out a stack of cards to TK and Debbie. We were eating baked potatoes at a café near the Agency. It was four-thirty in the afternoon and we'd not yet had lunch. I had spent the day walking – lost most of the time – through the West End, visiting advertising agencies. I was hungry and my feet were sore. It had been dark in the streets since half past three.

Debbie took a card. 'I think you look really good in this photo. It's a good head shot.'

TK glanced over. 'It's pretty cool.'

'Look what they've done to my *name*.'

Debbie and TK stared at it. Just then we realised that no one had thought to ask my name yet.

'My name is *Jus-teen*. With an "e" on the end.'

'I knew it was something with a J.' TK blew on a forkful of potato. 'You have a "J" vibe.'

'What should I do?'

'I like Justin.'

'What did Mandy say?' Debbie flipped the card over.

'She liked Justin.'

'She was only saying that because she can't be bothered making you new cards. Mandy doesn't really understand cool.'

'She told me I would have to spend another five hundred pounds to get them remade.'

'Just leave it. Justin is cool – and anyway, that way you can feel, you know, that it's not really you that people are rejecting, but some chick called Justin.'

TK had a good point.

'Plus,' said Debbie, 'you never know what picture they'll put on your card if you let them do it again. They always pick my worst photo for the front of mine.' I saw a thought skip across her face. 'Have you got your book yet?'

'Yes.'

'Can't you at least wait until we're in the Agency or something?' TK said to Debbie.

'Why?'

'At least look at it under the table.' TK had lowered her voice.

'I never get why you're so embarrassed about being a model, TK.'

I did. I handed the book to Debbie as discreetly as possible. 'It's the whole "look at me I'm beautiful" thing. It's embarrassing,' I said.

'See? Justin feels the same way,' TK said to Debbie.

'Well, I don't care. I like being a model. Who cares?' Debbie spent the next ten minutes engrossed in my pictures. TK looked over her shoulder; I sat in my head.

I spent the next week dragging myself across London, going to go-sees to meet the photographers, ad agencies and clients. They took a card, called me Justin and for the most part didn't pay me much attention at all. I answered the same questions hundreds of times, in the same way: 'Where are you from?', 'How old are you?', 'What work have you done?', 'Isn't that a boy's name?' I didn't bother explaining the mistake with my name after the first casting, where my story was met with a blank stare. From then on I just shrugged.

I never knew where the hell in London I was, rarely saw daylight as I spent those pale hours underground on the tube or waiting to see photographers in their white-painted studios. But I didn't mind all that terribly because I was only too glad to get out of the weather. I hadn't had time to buy a winter coat, in fact had no idea where to get one I could afford, and my hands were often so cold they could scarcely unclasp my satchel and show my book. My nose would go bright red and run furiously every time I stepped indoors, which didn't help the aesthetics at all. London was full of models and they were all so much cooler, so much more beautiful, so much more stylish than me in their big winter coats. I wanted to be anyone but Justin the whole time.

At nine in the morning I would leave the flat, after tea and toast with vegemite (brought in my suitcase) in the semi darkness with TK, and I wouldn't get back until well after eight on most nights, sometimes later. Days full of Polaroids, forms, smiles, questions, names, addresses, streets, faces ... And it was always wet. I smelt wet wool everywhere, even in my sleep, and I was so tired, so hungry. I could never seem to find anything I wanted to eat. I had been photographed so many times that I felt faded, as if each copy of me had taken a layer off, as if I was becoming a paler version of myself with every Polaroid snapped.

This is another form to fill in. Please do so in BLOCK CAPITALS.

1. Your new name: JUSTIN

2. Are you a supermodel: NO

3. Do you want to be a supermodel: YES

4. Is there any chance of you becoming a supermodel: NO

5. Are you beautiful and sexy: NO

6. Do you have a famous boyfriend: NO
   (Name, if applicable: _____)

7. Do you have a boyfriend: NO
   (Name, if applicable: _____)

8. Do you have a wardrobe full of cool clothes: NO

9. Have you had any embarrassing experiences this week: YES
   (Please give details: LAUGHED AT COOL PHOTOGRAPHER'S JOKE. RUNNING NOSE RELEASED LONG, CLEAR COLUMN OF SNOT ON TO PORTFOLIO. WANTED TO DIE.)

10. Do you have spots: YES
   (Where, if applicable: FOREHEAD; ONE ON CHIN)
   If you have answered NO to questions 2, 4, 5, 6, 7 and 8 you have failed the Real Model Questionnaire. You will have to leave our most exclusive club now. You do not quite fit in.

5

Don't Make Such a Fuss!

Mulberry casting, London, 2.05 p.m.

Dear T J,

I hate being who I am and if you were me you would too. Also if I see another sandwich I will die.

So far, I have not gotten a job. But today Mandy (booker) told me I was working Wednesday – Just 17 mag. Not great at all but at least I have a booking. I was getting worried that they would realise they had made a mistake and send me back to Sydney if I didn't work. And as I will be 17 this year I suppose it is an appropriate job. But I bet you anything they put me in pink mohair doing something really uncool.

It never stops raining here. It is always dark and everybody looks so cool. I want to get some cool jobs – The Face or ID or something, not stupid teenage fashion. But maybe that will happen later.

Why am I writing to you? You probably don't even get my letters, or care. Is it almost Christmas? I don't want to go home. I can't remember what my bedroom looks like. My mother sent me a postcard from Western Australia where she is trying to bring pearl farming back to the local mangrove community. Also I smoke now and she wouldn't like that. My dad is fine.

I would really like a pair of white, leather ankle-boots and a winter coat. I will have to ask Mandy where to go shopping. She calls herself my London mum – weird mum! She wears mini-skirts all the time and pats all the girls on the bum as they go past, and wears loads of make-up, especially lipstick. Still, they say you can't choose your parents. I think she really wants a boyfriend – I heard her complain to Serena Blonde, the head booker (who is very scary) that 'there aren't enough men who can love in this galaxy'. Maybe there just aren't enough men who think her make-up looks good.

How is your music going? I haven't drawn anything since I left Sydney. I've probably forgotten how. None of the other girls draw. Lots of them don't even read books. I have given up on George Eliot and Time *magazine. I am concentrating on other magazines at the moment like* Vogue, The Face *and such like, and sometimes I read a book about Hollywood but I can't remember the title. I also have four blisters on my feet as my motorcycle boots are killing me. I have to go because the TV is on.*

LUV
Justin
P.S. I feel ugly.

I was on a beach somewhere warm, alone but not alone, in the way you can only be in dreams. I was unearthing silver cutlery, neatly tied in blue ribbons, and a bunch of supermodels were looking down from heaven and saying: 'What a beautiful noise that silverware makes.'

Only it wasn't a beautiful noise anymore – it was loud thumping. I woke in the dark. Cristina, my roommate, was swearing under her breath in Croatian and rubbing her shin with one hand.

I groaned. 'For god's sake – just turn on the light Cristina.' It wasn't dawn yet, and the pale yellow of the streetlight outside wasn't helping her see.

I shielded my eyes from the brightness. Cristina was standing above me in a tight black dress and spike heels, just home from some party. Four in the morning, according to her red digital clock. Her short, black hair stood out at all angles, her lips were chapped and red, but she still looked awesome. In one hand she cupped a pair of lace panties.

'I need you to help, Justin.'

Her voice was always dark and husky, like a man's, and her accent was thick. She also always got right to the point, perhaps because she didn't have the luxury of her own language.

'Are you in trouble?' I asked, still fuzzy. Cristina could usually take care of herself. 'What happened? Are you okay?'

She tutted in annoyance: 'I am fine – it's not like that. I need you to help me to do something.'

Oh, oh. I didn't really want to be involved in one of Cristina's hare-brained schemes at four in the morning, but I doubted she would go away if I didn't. 'Why are you holding your panties?' I asked her after a bit.

She looked down at them proudly.

'I have Mick Jagger's sperm.'

'What?' It was easy to misunderstand Cristina because of her accent. I hoped I had.

'I have his come in my pants.' She beamed at me with her amazingly white, pointed teeth.

'Um, that's ... great.' I had to ask. 'Um, why?'

She pursed her lips at me in frustration – she thought me slow tonight. 'We made sex, I took his sperm and now I want to have his baby.'

That stopped me in my tracks. I knew she was a fan of the Rolling

Stones, but I had obviously underestimated her fervour. 'You want to have his baby? How?' I didn't really want to know what she had in mind.

'It has to be inside me – I have to put it inside, now! Quickly or it dies.'

I was getting a little scared here. 'Okay,' I said slowly, buying time, wondering if the girls upstairs could hear me if I screamed. I decided they couldn't. 'Why do you need *me*?'

She grabbed my hand and dragged me toward the bathroom.

'I make handstand,' she said.

'And…?'

'And sperm all goes inside to make baby Mick.'

'No way, Cristina.' I backed off. 'There's no way I'm touching his – '

She wouldn't let go of my hand. She looked at me with her fierce Croatian eyes. 'Please?' she said quietly.

We made a deal.

I stood outside the bathroom door for minutes, my toes freezing.

When I heard Cristina say, 'Okay, ready,' I took a deep breath and went in.

She was kneeling on the edge of the bath, face down, her hands in the tub. A plastic turkey baster lay discarded on the floor next to her spike heels. I stepped carefully over it and went over to where she was kneeling. After two attempts, I finally got her into a handstand, leaning her feet on the bathroom wall for support.

She had read in *Cosmo* that doing this for three minutes would greatly increase her chances of conceiving. I had recently done a job for *Cosmo* and heard the women there brainstorming their stories over a drunken lunch, laughing at their ideas, but I didn't say anything to Cristina, upended over a tub at four-thirty on an English morning. She had lost her elder brother to a rogue mine only the year before and didn't need to hear any more bad news.

We were sitting on the floor and the line in front of us appeared interminable. There were at least fifty models, boys and girls, in the crooked stairwell, perching on railings and squatting on the cold concrete. The casting was for a Diesel campaign and the money was good, not to mention the street cred and exposure – a delectable morsel of a job if ever there was one. TK and I were sitting on our portfolios to keep our bums from freezing.

'It's amazing how many models there are. I mean, look at all these people – all here for one job,' I mused.

'But if you think about it, these would be almost all the cool models in London – don't you think? All the ones who have to go on castings, that is.'

I nodded, scanning the pool of leather, beanies and lace shawls. 'Everyone does look very cool – well, almost everyone.'

'Okay,' she said, 'bored now. What's the most embarrassing thing you can think of to do in this situation? Think of something really bad – but not obvious, like flashing your tits or singing. It's got to be *subtle*.'

'What's yours?'

'How about, if you walked in here and saw the line then tossed your hair, and said in a really loud voice, "Excuse me, can I get through?! I'm a *working model*."'

I smiled. 'That's pretty bad.' I cringed at TK's scene, but loved the danger of imagining such utter humiliation.

'Your turn. But be subtle or it doesn't work.'

I had to think about this, but the game was right up my alley. Self-mortification had become my artform; I had been playing this game all my life. 'Okay. How about sitting at the top of the stairs, right where everyone walks past, with a huge, brand-new, hardback copy of *War and Peace*. You're only on page two, but you keep sighing really loudly and saying, "This is mind-blowing – the most important novel of the century, surely." And shaking your head in wonderment.'

'Embarrassing for you definitely, but check her out.' TK pointed. A girl sitting on the stairs held a copy of James Joyce's *Ulysses*. She looked up every few seconds to add to the conversation with bored, blank eyes.

TK looked around the room. 'That guy over there is cute.'

I looked over.

'The one in the studded denim vest with crooked teeth. He has a funny face.'

TK had managed to single out the most unattractive guy there. He looked like he needed a thorough scrubbing and a good feed. Weedy was okay by me, but dirty was another matter.

'So ...' The Muse of Mortification landed lightly on my shoulder. 'Go up to him, smile shyly, then ask if you can show him your book.'

TK gasped, horrified. 'Beautiful – the simplicity.'

'I think I win ... He's so –' I couldn't quite think how to describe him.

'He reminds me of my ex-boyfriend.'

I was glad I hadn't voiced my disparaging thoughts.

'He was an actor – in LA,' she went on, 'but he was pretty cool. He's actually really famous now. He was, like, a teen idol when I was dating him. I was only seventeen.'

I wanted to ask his name, but thought it would be uncool and so I simply encouraged TK to tell the story she wanted me to hear. 'What happened?'

'He was making a movie near my school. That's how I met him. I did ballet and was always wearing these pink tights, with my hair tied back in a bun. I was cute, in a crooked-skinny way. He used to come to watch me when I had a dance class.'

We shifted a little as the line edged forward. I saw TK give Dirty Boy the eye. 'Did he really look like that guy?' I was trying to imagine which teen idol on earth resembled the model in any way.

'Yeah. It's like, the teeth, the look. I don't know. Something.'

'Anyway . . .?' I prompted her.

'Anyway, we partied. It was cool. Then he moved to New York to do plays and I started modelling in LA. I went to New York for a bit but, it just didn't work out. You know – the movie-star thing. He tried to hit on my young cousin once when she came to visit.

'That's bad.'

'And he swears he wasn't unfaithful to me, but you know what? I was so young at seventeen that he could have been doing anything. When I look back on it, I'm sure he was cheating on me. Some girl named Rose, I'm pretty sure. She's an actress too, though not a famous one. She's done a few cool things I guess.'

'So did you dump him?'

'Yes. Well, sort of yes. I don't know.'

'Were you upset?'

'I cried for months. He's the kind of guy who is so much fun that everyone seems dull in comparison. He gets you hooked, and then he works it so that he forces the girl to dump him, not the other way around.'

'Did he break your heart?'

TK didn't say anything. She was looking at Dirty Boy. 'I wonder what his name is?'

'Mandy says she's suffering from a broken heart. She was in love with a photographer named Simon, and they were together for about four years – and then he dumped her for a blonde model from Weehawken, I think it was.'

'That's so lame.'

'Yeah. She's always crying about it. I see her sniffing in the bathroom.'

TK gave me a funny look. 'You're such a ditz. She's doing coke in the bathroom – that's why she sniffs. She's not crying.'

'Oh.' I felt très stupide.

'Brigitte's the one who's always crying because she misses her boyfriend. She's got some guy in Paris – he's a photographer too. Older, though. I think he's about forty.'

'Brigitte's only nineteen! That's a scandal.'

'He's the one who got her into modeling. Discovered her with her parents at some dire seaside resort in Germany and whisked her off to Paris. They live together.'

'That's weird. Her parents would just let her go off with some sleazy guy?'

'I bet he charmed them with promises first, or set her up with an agency then found her again. Anyway, my bet is that he thought he would jump-start his career by finding a girl who would be a supermodel.'

'Like Mario Sorrenti.'

'Yeah. If you do all these stories with a young girl who then gets to be a supermodel – you're set. And he controls her absolutely.'

'She's so anorexic.'

'I think she's just trapped. Probably believes everything this guy tells her.'

'He might be a nice guy.'

'Right.'

'Well, it seems there are a lot of broken hearts around.'

The line shifted forward again. I lit a cigarette for myself and one for TK. At least we could smoke. Everyone was. The stairwell was dense with fog of carbon exhalation.

I saw Dirty Boy look over at TK.

She was wearing a ratty leopard-print jumper under a navy coat, tights and wooden sandals. Her curls were pinned off her face with two red clips. She looked cute in a funny way, like her clothes had fallen on her from a high shelf. She felt him looking and blushed, nibbling on her cigarette. When she smoked, TK took quick, shallow puffs, as if she had never learnt to smoke properly.

'Justin,' she said, 'I'm twenty-two and it's too late for me to be Darcey Bussell, but I could still be good. I think I'm going to take up ballet again.'

Mandy sent me to L'Oreal to have my highlights retouched.

'They do all our girls for free, lovey, and they'll do a beautiful job – just tell them what you want!'

A girl with cropped, burgundy hair and multiple ear-piercings led me through undecorated corridors to the interior courtyard of the L'Oreal offices, somewhere off Kensington Church Street. From there, another girl with cropped, burgundy hair and multiple ear-piercings took over. We headed for a large, steel door that, by the looks of it, could have led to a radiation shelter.

The girl typed in a code, then held her finger up for scanning. The steel door swung open after some beeping sounds and we entered.

The smell of chemicals was overpowering. There were no windows, only the hum of interior ventilation. I felt like Justin Bond as I followed her through the hallways. 'What's with all the door codes and secrecy?' I asked my guide. 'Do you build bombs as well as hair products?'

She smiled.

'No, but industrial espionage is rife in the hair care business. L'Oreal spends millions of dollars on research. We can't risk someone from a rival company slipping in and nabbing the fruits of our research.'

I was impressed. 'How do you know *I'm* not an industrial spy?'

The girl smiled again. 'Oh, we can tell. We keep files of faces, and we're trained to look out for certain things.'

We turned a last corner and I found myself in what a lettered door proclaimed to be the 'Testing Centre'.

About ten women – all but one elderly – looked up from their chairs as I was ushered in. Each was in a different stage of some unusual hair treatment. One had foil twists in her hair that seemed to be attached to mini jumper cables. Another lady sat underneath a clear, plastic dome with green goop in her hair. Yet another was having the largest mass of curls I'd ever seen blow-dried by an assistant in a white coat.

My guide left me and I grew nervous. I told the young man who dressed me in a black plastic sheet that I was here for highlights.

He smiled and said, 'Greet, we'll get ye all sorted oot then. Mair name's Gareth.'

'Okay, Gareth, hi. I just wanted to get my highlights touched up where they've grown out. Mandy said you guys would take care of it.'

'Mandy's a greet girl, no problem.'

He didn't appear to find my request strange, and I relaxed.

Someone brought me a cup of tea and I pulled out a copy of *ID*. Gareth came back with a lady in a burgundy bob. I made a note to self: be sure to ask for *blonde* streaks.

'This is the girl, Linda. We're going to give her highlights, to lighten the face.'

I faked a smile but Linda didn't notice. Just get on with it, I thought, and turned to Gareth. 'I just want my *blonde* streaks touched up.'

'We'll git ye sorted oot then.' Linda was from Scotland too. 'Now, oor processes may be a little different to what she's used to, Gareth, so tell her we're very good at what we doo, and to just relax.'

Whatever. Just no burgundy. Or I'll kill you.

Gareth began mixing purple goop in two clear glass bowls behind me. I could see him in the mirror.

'Why is it purple?' I asked in my most innocent voice.

'That's the colour bleach goos when you mix it with the activator.'

I nodded. He said bleach, not burgundy. Good.

'Well, it certainly smells strong.'

Gareth laughed.

I looked up and noticed that all the ladies in the room had their beady eyes on me, curious as hens. I imagined that these were the eyes that usually stared out from behind lacy kitchen curtains in the terrace houses encircling Greater London. I buried myself in my magazine and let Gareth git oon.

My bum was feeling flat and sore, like the sit-bones were too near the skin for comfort after four hours of sitting still in a plastic chair. People had come in and out, examined the texture of my hair, the colour, its length. A class of white-coated students – Advanced Tech – had come in with clipboards and watched Gareth intently. He had 'prepped the hair', and done various other things which I had endeavoured to ignore.

'We're going to strip the follicle of extraneous pigmentation. The head will have to sit here . . .'

I tuned out again.

Now my hair was covered in the strong-smelling purpley stuff, and I was getting grumpy and bored. Suddenly my scalp started to tingle – like when you get a fright and your hairs stand on end. The tingling grew stronger until it was an itch, a burn, until it felt like my head was on fire.

'Gareth!' I screamed, not caring an ounce about old hens now. 'My head's burning!'

Gareth wandered over far too casually for my liking. 'That's the natooral process,' he said and handed me a knitting needle. 'Scratch it wi this an' it'll feel better.'

I snatched the needle from him and started attacking my scalp. It relieved the burning for about – half a second in the place I scratched but did nothing to help the rest of my head. My eyes were filling with tears. I scratched furiously then threw the needle on the floor. I looked up at Gareth, tears streaming from my eyes. 'Get it off me, Gareth.'

'Just a few more minutes . . .'

'Now!' I stood up, ready to run my head through the wall if necessary. Two assistants came rushing through the doors. At first I was afraid they might try to hold me down, like night nurses in an insane asylum, but they led me slowly towards the sink, past the staring women, and put me in a chair.

'Ookay then – time, people,' cried Gareth, 'it's time.' The assistants tilted my head back and aimed the hose.

I felt cool and watery relief spreading over my scalp.

There was still burning, but it wasn't as bad. A small group had gathered by my head, umming and ahhing.

'Is that enough?' the head washer asked Gareth.

'Ask her if it still burns – that's how you'll tell.'

'Does it still burn?'

'A little, yeah.'

'Shampoo her one more time then,' ordered Gareth.

I nodded gratefully, docile as a lamb now. Anything to take the pain away.

They towel-dried my hair, then ummed and ahhed some more. I was feeling very kindly towards them all now.

'Does it look good?' I asked brightly.

I settled back, happier now that the end of my ordeal was in sight. I had been locked in the windowless basement full of burning and fumes for five-and-a-half hours.

They dried my hair with the blow drier where I sat. It blew too hot and hurt my now-tender scalp, but I didn't complain because I just wanted to get out of there.

Gareth and his disciples clustered around my head once more and coo-ed. '*Lovely* colour. Gorgeous.'

'Show her your genius, Gareth,' whined one of the assistants.

They wheeled my chair to the mirror and spun me around to face my reflection.

'Perfect.'

I felt the hot/cold touch of horror on my shoulder.

I blinked and looked again, to be sure.

I had the all-too-familiar feeling of prickly nausea that comes with a grossly unwelcome surprise. Miss Olyphant and the note, the bikini line . . .

I had been transformed beyond recognition. I no longer knew my name, and that certainly wasn't me in the mirror.

It was worse than burgundy: I had become a blonde. A no-doubt-about-it, hands-down, cor-blimey, platinum blonde. A Debbie Harry, rock-and-roll groupie, reach-for-my-tits-and-feel-me blonde.

'What have you done?' I croaked. 'What have you done?'

Gareth smiled widely. 'Looks greet doesn't it – suits you to a tee.'

'I wanted streaks,' was all I could say, 'highlights,' I went on dumbly, 'a little more around the front, a little less around the back – a natural, sun-kissed look that would bring out my eyes . . .'

'It *is* streaky – you have beaootiful highlights in there.'

Two of Gareth's Advanced Tech students examined me in the mirror.

'See here,' said Gareth, 'a natural, streaking effect – highlights if you will.'

'Oh yeah, yeah,' they purred to their guru of hair. 'Great streaks, Gareth – so natural. They bring out the girl's features.'

'But it's all one colour! There are no streaks!' No one listened to me. They all continued smiling: the head was talking but it was of no importance.

Linda came in.

'How did the highlights come oot, Gareth?'

'Superr,' smiled Gareth.

'Lovely, lovely,' echoed Linda. 'You did a greet job on her.'

'But it's *not* streaky – it's all one colour, all *blonde*!' I could feel my eyes welling up in frustration. *'I'm a blonde!'*

'Get Susie to show the head oot – our work is done.' Gareth clapped his hands twice, then he and his assistants disappeared through the doors and left me alone with the stares of the old women.

None of them appeared to have moved at all since I had first come in – and all of them seemed just as curious as before.

Susie, the burgundy girl with the secret codes, led me out through the maze and I told her what had happened.

'Gareth is a genius with colour,' she said, smiling over her shoulder.

'But all I wanted were gentle highlights. He totally bleached me.'

She shrugged and opened the outside door. 'You're better as a blonde. Blonde is better.' Then walked away.

It was almost dark outside. The sky had begun to drizzle icy rain. I kept glancing in the shop windows as I passed and not recognising myself. I noticed people on the street staring at me too. I wanted to buy a hat but decided that I had better get used to my new head, try to embrace the brand-new me.

I passed a fish and chip shop with an open doorway. The boiling oil in the frying vats gave the room a dirty, yellow glow. A teenage boy slouched in the doorway reading a folded newspaper and wearing a slinky, purple shellsuit. He looked up as I crossed in front of him. He had spots on his forehead and smelt of hot wax.

'Hey!' He leant out into the street. 'There she goes. My dream girl.'

As I walked on into the night, towards my bus stop, my mouth grew itchy then broke into a small smile.

The girls at the flat were matter-of-fact, offering their professional opinions.

'Photographers like blonde hair because it catches the light.' Lara O'Hara was sitting at the kitchen table sewing name tags on the toes of her socks, her ankles neatly crossed.

'What are you doing that for, Lara?' TK was sitting on the floor, her legs split out on either side like a pair of tweezers. Her hair was slicked back into a tight bun and she wore pale pink tights and ballet shoes.

'Our socks are always getting mixed up in the wash. People take my clean socks. This way, everyone will know who they belong to. Besides, did you know that you burn eighty-four calories an hour when you sew or knit? Although ironing is better at a hundred-and-twenty.'

TK bent her upper body toward her left knee, so her response was muffled. 'Whatever.'

The television was on and Cristina was curled up on the floor feeding 20p pieces into the fat, old payphone. She was shouting into the receiver in Croatian. The line was bad and she was apparently fighting with her boyfriend. The only words I recognised were the English swear words.

'Fuck you fucker. Shit. Cunt.'

For someone whose grasp of English was still quite rudimentary, Cristina seemed to be fluent in Swearing.

I watched the news on TV – an IRA bomb going off somewhere in London and a baking contest in Devon. I drew a caricature of the runner-up in the cake competition on the back of an envelope (old-fashioned fruitcake made with pork fat and candied rind – Mrs Barton). I thought I had captured the absence of chin and cheekbones rather well, and the flowered apron needed no further embellishment.

'Do you think I look more like Amber Valetta or Eva Herzigova?'

I looked up. Debbie was reading *Vogue*. She was always reading magazines.

'In that picture, Amber – except you hair is different.'

'Police stepped up their efforts to stop the bombings and to secure the area –'

'You fucking cunt shit!'

'What about in this one? Kate Moss or Jamie Rishar?'

'Jamie without question.'

Debbie looked at the photo again.

'Yeah. I agree. Do you think I should get a tattoo like that?'

'I've always baked my scones this way – my mother always did, and her mother, so I suppose you could say it's quite a tradition in Devonshire.'

Brigitte yelped. We all turned around. It was rare that she ever made a noise. Her bottle-opener had slipped and crashed to the floor. She stared at us with eyes like a frightened animal's. She was trying to open a bottle of wine.

Lara sighed loudly and got up. 'Let me do it, Brigitte.'

And the capable Lara uncorked the white wine in a flash. She beamed her megawatt star smile at the sullen Brigitte, who merely snatched the bottle back and crept into her room, locking the door. Lara went back to her sewing with a shrug.

'She's getting far too thin.' In out, in out, perfect little stitches. 'Someone should tell the Agency.'

'Mandy knows. She's seen her. But Brigitte still works – no one cares until the clients stop booking you. Fact.'

We all nodded. Fact.

'Why is she always in her room? What does she do in there? I only ever see her when she comes out in the morning for her weird oat breakfast.' The mystery had preoccupied me for some time. 'I think that's all she eats all day, that breakfast.'

'She sits in her room and drinks wine. I went in once and saw all these bottles.'

'Wine is so fattening,' Lara said, not looking up from her sewing. 'It's full of calories – it can have more than beer, which has twenty-nine per hundred mils.'

Lifting her head, TK asked, 'Lara, how many calories in half a cup of Kraft peanut butter?'

Lara was horrified at the mention of peanut butter, as if the name alone might pile on pounds. 'Never touch the stuff, but it –'

'No, wait. Something obscure – potted shrimp!'

'Potted shrimp has three-hundred-and-fifty-eight calories.'

'What about a bread roll?'

'Brown? Crusty? Two-hundred-and-fifty-five.'

'Ketchup?'

'Heinz? One-hundred-and-seven. A hidden source of calories, people don't realise.'

'What about Debbie's Garlic Bites?' The packet lay open and half-finished beside her.

'Five-hundred-and-twenty-eight – no, sorry, twenty-nine.'

I checked the packet and started laughing.

There was another loud crash and a torrent of swearing. Cristina had kicked the payphone over and was spitting on it.

TK giggled.

'What happened, Cristina?' I couldn't help smiling at her perfect rage.

'Fucking cunt is full of shit.'

'Your boyfriend?'

She turned her fierce eyes on me.

'No!' She really was very loud. 'Phone! Phone is full!' It was full of money and we could no longer make calls out. Cristina stormed out into our bedroom.

'How very glamorous this modelling world is – wouldn't you agree girls?'

The other girls ignored TK's comment. I smiled at her, lit another cigarette and turned back to the television.

You feel pretty cool don't you? Like you could kick some Tokyo butt. You might have been in awe, back then, of what you see now in the mirror. Admit it. The hair changed you into something – a real model? A fashion doll? Somehow you became a product and a character all at once and you don't think it's all bad, do you? You will never like yourself, but has this brought you closer? Peace through artifice?

You only feel cool because Cristina is swearing into the phone and because you know what TK's thinking about Lara right now and because you can lie here with the girls in your sweatshirt and smoke and feel like you belong to it all. These girls don't mind sitting next to you – not like at school. And you are enjoying the reflection of yourself in the window aren't you? Admit it. You are such a vain idiot – look at the way you glance slyly from the TV to the window and back, and how you feel glad that there are people in the room with you who can bear witness to your new coolness with eyes trained to spot and admire exactly that.

Don't you understand that it is precisely this detachment from the moment that makes it impossible for you actually to be a part of any world? The constant calculation and appreciation and desperation that runs the engine of your mind will never go away and will make sure that you will never be able to live wholly engaged in a single moment. Unless you count extreme pain. But even then you seem to move outside yourself – even just for a second. Can't you see that the girl in the reflection is doomed? You do feel lost, don't you?

This is not a world of mothers and daughters. You know that. You are all orphaned from your families and your homes. You just bob in circles near the surface, disoriented, drawn to the first bright light on the horizon.

6

Sit Still, Please!

It had seemed like a good idea at the time but now ...

I was the only girl in our house who had not gone home, or at least somewhere, for the holidays. I had accepted Mandy's exuberant invitation to Christmas lunch when well-lubricated with Seabreezes at the Agency Christmas party.

'Darling! Do come! It'll be so much fun – just you, me and some of the girls, lots of food and drink. Like one big happy family. Sweetie! I can't wait! Go on, say yes!'

I didn't even know if she could cook, but she did live within walking distance, somewhere in Finchley. I was, so it transpired, the only girl in the Agency to accept her offer.

Mandy seemed a little surprised to see me on her doorstep at one o'clock on Christmas Day but she covered it nicely with a squeal of excitement and a big hug. As I was standing a step lower than her on the stoop and as she was wearing her 'special occasion' boots with the fifteen-inch heels, I found my face pressed into her chest, cheek to cheek with one of Santa's knitted elves.

'I like the jumper, Mandy.'

'Do you?! My mother knits, darling! Isn't it the most gorgeous thing you've ever seen? Come in! Come in and meet her – don't you love it?! And *red* is just so *me*!'

I was relieved to smell turkey as I walked in. Mandy's mother, stout in floral print and a plastic apron greeted me with a jolly, hearty 'Merry Christmas' then began a conversation made up of disjointed, Christmas-related statements that she could never seem to finish. '– but this turkey! … Birds, you know … and I put it in at ten this morning!! … cold outside you see, but with the pudding it should all come up roses!' she ended with a satisfied flourish.

I nodded. 'Yes. Dreadful. I mean, wonderful.'

She beamed at me, happy that I felt the same way.

I handed Mandy her Christmas present – a fluffy, white, mohair hat (Russian style, with earflaps) and the world's largest Smartie box (she always kept a jar of them by her desk, 'for energy!')

'So you can refill your jar … I don't have … anything for your mother …'

Mandy's thanks were a little flustered. 'So *sweet*! Love it love it love it! Yours is … upstairs. I'll nip up in a minute.'

She put the hat on and examined her reflection in the window (it was already almost dark out).

The kitchen table was set for two, the thick plastic tablecloth (tropical fruit print) shining clean, two Christmas crackers by the side of each clear Perspex plate. Two table settings became three.

Mandy embarrassed, whispered, 'She's a bit dotty the old mum. I told her a million times you were coming, but what can you do? Age!'

'Do you live here too, Mrs …?' I realised I didn't know Mandy's last name.

'Oh call her Betty, Justin! You crazy thing! She's Betty!'

'Isn't Justin a boy's name?'

'I know, Mum, but she's from Australia! Anyway I think it's so cute. A cute little girl with a boy's name – clients love it!'

'Charlotte is nice…'

'Charlotte is so Victorian, Mum! You can't call her Charlotte! Anyway – she already has a name, don't you Justin?'

'It's actually Justine,' I told Betty.

'I love Justin! It rocks!'

I really wished I had gone home for Christmas. The brown walls and the avocado carpet were closing in, the tumble of words burying me until I couldn't understand anything at all. Betty was Mandy's mother, no doubt about the genetic link there, but less manic.

Betty carved the turkey and I thought about my own mother and father. I had wanted to show them – Mum in particular – that I had grown up and grown-up people didn't always go home for Christmas. But also, I admitted to myself, I had expected her to try and persuade me otherwise. I felt hurt that she hadn't begged me, and wanted to hurt her back a little. So I stubbornly decided to stay in London.

My mother seemed to understand perfectly. 'We'll miss you Justine – but London will be beautiful at Christmas!' she said, before asking me if I knew anything about the illicit trade in Persian cats that went on in the bowels of the fur industry.

My father had asked about my plans and replied, 'That sounds like fun!'

It was not fun.

Mandy's mother pulled out a huge bottle of whiskey and set it on the table. It had always seemed like such a man's drink that I had never drunk it before – but there would never be, it occurred to me, a better time to begin.

'Down the hatch, love. Good for you! Have it neat, will you? Some like soda … defeating the point isn't it? The bubbles …' Betty trailed off.

'Thank you so much for having me.' I cautiously sniffed the glass of whisky.

'Go on! It'll warm the cockles of your heart, dear.'

My heart was feeling particularly cold, damp and empty so I downed the tumbler. The coughing fit that followed made my eyes water – thank god – so Betty and Mandy didn't see the tears in them, or notice my trembling lip.

If you start fucking crying now I'll disown you, you sad-ugly brat.

I downed another glass. It made me feel braver and I smiled at my hostesses. They were onto their fourths already.

Mandy's cracker was the only one that went off and mine was missing the paper crown. 'Take mine Justinbaby! It's red! That way I can keep your lovely furry hat on!' And she did, all through lunch.

I drank another glass of whiskey and felt myself sink down into the chair, having had two bites of turkey and a sliver of roast potato. 'That was delicious . . .'

Mandy interrupted. 'Question: What did the tomato say to the squashed tomato?'

'What *did* the tomato say to the squashed tomato?' Betty responded.

'Ketchup!'

The crackers were providing us with conversation. That was a funny one.

'Why didn't the skeleton cross the road?'

'Why did the chicken cross the road?'

'*No*, Mum! Why *didn't* the skeleton cross the road?' Mandy paused. 'Because he didn't have any guts!'

I actually fell off the chair laughing, but now it was my turn.

'Two peanuts were walking down a dark alley – and one of them was a salted!'

I cracked up. Mandy and Betty stared at me, which only made me laugh harder. Betty's purple paper crown had titled to an absurd angle. Mandy's head was still encased in the white fur and her large left breast had shifted a little, giving the smiling elf on her jumper a lascivious leer.

'I don't get it.'

'Where's the question? That's not a real joke!'

'These crackers are crap!'

'Come on, don't you see?' My body was shaking with laughter. I felt sick. Their confusion was only making me laugh harder.

'It's about peanuts – salted nuts – '

'I have salted nuts down at the pub with Robert – well, that's his name but we all call him – '

'Shut up Mum! Who cares about – '

'Mandy! Don't swear!'

'I didn't – '

'You just swore at me, young lady and – '

'Shut up isn't swearing! Fuck is swearing! Fuck! Shit! Hell! Cunt! That's swearing!!'

I couldn't stop laughing. This was dreadful. Mandy and her mother began screaming at each other, Mandy a white teddybear with a red, human face, her mother an orgiastic Roman emperor, jowls now purple as her crown.

I jumped up, knocked over my chair, ran to the lavatory and threw up my two bites of turkey and sliver of roast potato. I heard a plate smash in the kitchen. Slipping cautiously into the hallway, I grabbed my jacket and made a run for the door.

It was five minutes to five and the rain had started. My paper crown – I had forgotten to remove it in my haste – deflated under the raindrops and became wet pulp. My throat was burning, head revolving. A car went past and caught me in the headlights. I jumped back and stumbled on the gutter, falling backwards onto the hard pavement. Looking up, I lay for a minute and noticed there were no stars in the sky at all.

It was late afternoon and beginning to snow madly. I walked out of the Old Street tube bent almost double into the wind. It was already dark. This had better be good, I thought.

I was on my way to a job for *Dazed & Confused*. Everyone wanted to copy their pictures of skinny, Vaseline-covered boys and awkward girls in supermarket underwear.

'*Dazed & Confused* is so so *hot*!! They love you baby! They've got such a buzz going!' Mandy told me when I called into the Agency.

I had thanked her for Christmas and given her a potted plant to pass on to Betty. Mandy had been upset that I had aborted my supper. 'I had a whole evening planned, baby! Old movies on the sofa! How did you get home?! Your hand looks funny!'

It was swollen from the fall off my chair. I started to tell her about my walk home from her place, about the gutter, but halfway through my story she turned to talk to a stunning African model from Uganda (tall, shining black).

The *Dazed & Confused* offices were in a huge converted garage, painted white, the roller-door still in place as the front door. Katie, who worked there, poked her head through a trapdoor in the floor – her office was below ground.

'Go down the back, sweetie.' Her head was level with my ankles. 'How are you? Dave's shooting in the studio.' Then her head popped back down as I stepped over the hole.

The studio was in the far corner of the garage where the walls had been painted white and the corners smoothed into curves to eliminate shadows. Dave, the photographer, was prowling around the lights with his assistant.

Dave was tall and skinny, with scruffy orange hair a little longer in the back than the front. He wore skin-tight navy jeans – dirty – that hung low enough to reveal the tops of yellow Y-fronts, and a thick, woollen reindeer sweater. His eyes were pink-rimmed and heavy-lidded, mildly reptilian in a face covered with freckles, or scales, depending on which way the light hit it. I'd met him before and had instantly developed a mild crush.

His assistant was cool and Asian, wearing all navy, with a pierced lower lip and those weird plugs that look like champagne corks in his ears. They were firing off the strobes and calling numbers to each other, both in Cockney accents.

Emma was doing make-up – I'd worked with her before. I liked her because she babied me. I liked her soothing voice, her soft curves, her crooked front tooth.

'Dave! Let's shoot Justin first. All right?'

Dave nodded his head from across the room and shouted a vague yeah in reply.

'It's going to go late tonight, babe, you don't want to be last,' Emma told me.

It was freezing in the studio, and I fought the urge to wriggle some blood into my freezing veins – it was better for Emma if I stayed still. 'So, what are we shooting?' I asked.

Emma's reply came, muffled by a paintbrush between her teeth. 'An orgasm story. Dave wants to shoot six faces having orgasms.'

'Oh.' I guessed that might be cool. I hoped I'd get at least one full face shot out of this, something I could use in my book anyway.

'I'm going to do your make-up real sexy,' said Emma. 'So you won't have to work as hard to do your orgasm expression.'

She painted my lips a perfect, hyper-glossy red, so shiny I really did look like one of those blow-up sex dolls.

Dave's assistant came over carrying four six-packs of lager and two bottles of vodka which he dumped on the make-up counter. 'Here Em – they were out of lime.'

'Did you get me straws, lovey?'

'I forgot.'

'I'll need straws, Kevin, especially for the girls. I'm not doing their lips over.'

Kevin shambled off in his oldest of old-school trainers.

Emma added a beauty mole in black with her paint brush, right by my mouth, just like a Victorian prostitute.

'Nice touch.' It came out 'Naas souch' because I couldn't move my mouth.

Emma smiled. 'It's all about sex, baby.'

Then she smeared Vaseline from one of those giant, wholesale jars onto my eyes, to give me sleepy, snakey lids, and flushed my cheeks with blush for sex blood. 'You look insane, darling.'

'I think I might be insane, letting you do this to me. But I love it,' I added in a hurry. You should always compliment the make-up artist on her work, it's only polite. And Emma had done a great job to make me look like a sex-flushed hottie. My lips looked enormous, and even to me I looked like a girl who'd blow anyone in a high-class nightclub for a bottle of champagne and a line of coke.

There was a rumble as Katie and her assistant Fenella emerged from the trapdoor to greet a Japanese film crew who had wandered in through the gap in the roller-door. Katie looked great in jeans, chain-mail and a tiara – a long-haired Joan of Arc-gone-glam. Fenella wore a pair of boy's superman pajamas, with cape, that would have looked better on Kevin.

The film crew seemed to be expected, although you could never tell with Katie because she took anything in her stride. Their two cameras were already rolling. I could hear Katie: 'Are you MTV Tokyo? Who are you guys? Kobayashi? Are any of you Kobayashi?'

Their English appeared to be non-existent. Katie and Fenella strode down to the studio, the film crew following them devotedly.

'Anyone here speak Japanese?' Katie looked around the room, hands on her skinny little hips. 'Kevin, you do. You're from there. Come over –'

'I'm from Manchester – I've never even been there.'

'But it must be in your blood somewhere . . .'

'I'm Korean.'

Katie shrugged and clapped her hands.

'Okay then.' She turned to the man with the microphone who appeared to be the spokesman. 'Knock yourselves out then.'

Emma handed me a can of beer and a straw. 'Drink up, but mind your lips.'

I took a careful sip. 'It's really warm.'

'You should just drink it – you'll need something. I could give you the vodka if you want.'

I shook my head. 'This'll be dandy.' It fizzed up a lot more than beer should as I sucked it up the straw, but I liked the picture I created in the mirror – a plumped-up dolly bird in an old black sweater, cheeks and lips flushed, drinking an enormous can of cheap lager through a straw. I looked twenty-five, but I was still only sixteen.

The Japanese film crew spotted me and hurried over. I pretended not to notice them crouched at my side with cameras and booms and an ongoing Japanese commentary by the man Katie called Kobayashi. I sucked at my beer, pouting softly and widening my eyes. They loved it. Of course they did. I had learnt enough about modelling in the last few months to know how to strike the perfect naïve pose.

Fenella and a guy called Roger – skinny, pierced, probably the designer and definitely gay – dressed me in a white-leather, fringed-collar thing. It fastened around my neck, the tassels hanging down to my belly button, covering my chest in an on/off fashion. Still, there wasn't much to cover, and I was onto my second beer, through a straw and on an empty stomach, and it was all just fine. Dave came over and poured a little vodka into my lager can, spilling half of it. I stared at his freckles close up and pouted, but he didn't really notice.

Four boy models arrived – only this was London and you'd never have known they were models, unless you were one yourself. Three were skinny, pale and dark-haired, with beautiful purple bags under their eyes. The other one was reddish – his skin and hair were almost the same colour, and his eyes were very pink. He might have been the boy from the latest Katherine Hamnet campaign plastered all over the tube, or he could have been Dave's younger brother. They had a bottle of Jack Daniels with them and they kissed everyone in the room. They were all named John.

Roger fitted my white-leather knickerbockers while Emma clipped red hairpieces to my head. Fenella was doing something with my shoes – strappy alligator heels with lace socks.

The film crew didn't know what to film first. One camera went with the John boys and their whiskey to a corner of the studio, the other followed Katie around like a potty lamb. She had seniority and got the sound mikes.

Dave had a vaulting horse from some old gym positioned in the middle of the set. I was to be riding it like some half-witted rodeo queen.

'What I want,' explained Dave in his beautiful voice, 'is for you to pretend you're coming. Pretend you're on the edge of an orgasm, build up, and then let it come. I want to see it in your face, your lips, your eyes – everything. Got it?'

I nodded. I had no idea what I was doing – I'd never had a goddamn orgasm – but I'd seen enough actors come all over the screen to know how to imitate one well enough.

One of the dark Johns had put on Prince's 'Little Red Corvette' and I was boozed. The strobes were firing, I had my head back, my lips open a little, my eyes closed. I rocked back and forth, my back arching, trying to think of Sharon Stone in *Basic Instinct*.

'Yeah, baby, that's fan-fucking-tastic.'

That was Dave. It spurred me on. I could hear Roger saying, 'Pure sex! You're amazing! Think *sex*!'

What would your mother say to all this?

Dave stopped for Kevin to reload. He came over to me. 'You're gorgeous,' he said in a low voice, 'you're doing great.'

I looked around. Everyone was watching me simulate an orgasm on a wooden horse – the film crew from Japan, the four Johns, Fenella, Katie, Roger and a few other people I hadn't seen before.

Emma stepped in to powder my face and gloss my lips again. 'Do you want me to get rid of them?' she whispered, gesturing to the audience.

I nodded and Emma and Katie told everyone to get themselves some booze and move away.

I imagined my face up on the giant TV in Roppongi square and wondered if anyone I knew would recognise me. I doubted it. I was not the same girl I had been in Japan.

Three more people came out of the trapdoor in the floor and joined what was now pretty much a party. Roger and some guy with an orange mohawk had their shirts off. Fenella was canoodling with one of the Johns on a poo-brown beanbag. The other two Johns were doing forward rolls on the studio floor. 'We're experimenting with another mode of transport,' cried one of them, 'an alternative to walking.'

The film crew was going around, trying to interview people in Japanese and getting a lot of football songs from the boys and giggles from the girls. I noticed that red John had a ferret under his shirt. It was probably around eight or nine at night, but there were no clocks and I had no idea of the time. I was glad Emma had told Dave to shoot me first.

More pictures, more sweet-talk from Dave – either the booze or me was starting to fall in love with him. Or his voice, at least.

'Fucking amazing,' he was saying. I could hear Roger next to him. 'You're a star baby, you're going to be a bloody star.'

I guess that would have been enough to make some models come for real. But I stuck to my mental pictures of Sharon and rode the bucking bronco, head lolling like a dandelion.

Roll change.

Red John came over with Emma. She glossed my lips again, powdered my nose, asked me if I was okay.

Red John held up his ferret. 'You can pat him if you like,' he said, 'his name's Fashion Boy.'

I reached out a hand. I didn't really want to pat Fashion Boy. His body scared me. He looked more like a snake than a cuddly mammal, but I thought it would be uncool to be grossed out. I gave the ferret two quick pats. He felt soft and bony, unnatural. I was glad when Dave was ready to start shooting again.

He shot me closer this time – eyes, tongue, mouth, mole.

'You have a face men would go to war for.'

Last shot! I heard a scream. My eyes flew open in shock, Dave snapped, we all turned to see what had happened. The shirtless man with the mohawk was hopping around screaming 'Fuck! Fuck!' and gripping his hand, surrounded by the camera crew.

'What happened?' shouted Katie, not bothering to go over.

'Fucking Fashion Boy bit me.'

Red John was holding the ferret close to his chest. 'Sorry, guv, he doesn't like fags – no offence man, but that's just the way he is. Live and let live.'

Mohawk was on the floor now, Roger at his side. 'Get a rabies shot – you'll be fine,' said Roger as he helped him to his feet.

Mohawk was bundled off, his hand wrapped in his T-shirt. Red John lit a cigarette and called out a farewell. 'Peace.'

The party resumed.

I could see Kobayashi with his microphone, standing in front of the two cameras, the retreating mohawk in the background. Kobayashi smiled out at his invisible audience: 'Dazed and Confused!' He bowed. 'Cool Britannia!'

It sounded like he said 'Cruel Britannia', maybe he did.

Vivienne Westwood threw a Whores and Pimps party. It was somewhere fancy, a grand ballroom with a giant centre staircase made of marble that ran up three floors. There were chandeliers hanging high up from an almost invisible ceiling and liveried footmen dressed in purple.

The horde of paparazzi at the front entrance took no notice of TK and me as we followed the red carpet in from the street. I think a few flashes may have popped, but they were almost certainly accidental.

I decided that it might be even harder to ignore paparazzi who are ignoring you than hungry ones out to suck your blood. Walking along the red carpet that night, under the spotlights, was like stepping on to a stage to no applause.

'Most embarrassing thing you could do right now?' whispered TK.

I rose delightedly to the challenge – the moment was dripping with potential for horrible self-humiliation. 'Stop in the middle of the red carpet, throw a dramatic Oscars pose then shout: "Take my picture – I'm a fashion model."'

That brought an earsplitting grin to TK's pale face. I took her hand for moral support and climbed the stairs.

Most people at the party had interpreted the theme to be Regency pimps and prostitutes. There were ringlets, powdered faces, beauty marks, rouge and gravity-defying boobs. The make-up reminded me of my orgasm shoot. Many of the girls hadn't bothered with dresses at all and pranced around in bloomer-type shorts and tiny bustiers – old-fashioned hooker lingerie.

Some of the boy Regents had gone mildly Mardi Gras, with giant, foam hairdos in yellow and orange pyramids, steel corsets trimmed with wire lace, and fishnet tights held up with leather buckles.

There were, of course, the requisite number of seventies-style, super-fly pimps – most guys are dying to dress in those wide-collared shirts and mirrored sunglasses, dangling a cheroot. Had the theme been 'Jane Austen's Morning Room' or 'The Probe to Mars', I could still have guaranteed you at least a handful of white boys playing at pimp.

Cream pies were being passed around as hors d'oeuvres and people were picking the cherries off the tops and using them as nipples.

Someone licked my shoulder as I walked past and whispered 'Great dress.'

I turned to TK. 'What is this party for and *who* invited us?'

'Mandy. It's some underwear thing, I think. Who knows, maybe there'll be goody bags.'

TK wore a tight, white dress with black, patent vinyl stilettos, blue eyeshadow and too much hair. We hadn't decided yet on whether she looked like a prostitute or some pretty mid-western insurance clerk out for a night on the town. I envied the dress – I'd always wanted a white dress.

I had found a black number for five pounds on the Kings Road. It was a satin Cheongsam-style dress that fell to the floor. A gold zipper spiralled the length of the dress so I could be unpeeled, like an apple, in three seconds flat. You could adjust the zippers to reveal as little or as much as you wanted. I took a look around the party and thought it better to unzip the bottom to crotch-skimming level, and the top to threaten my bosoms with exposure. I felt more equipped to handle the crowd then, and grabbed two glasses of champagne from a she-male harlot.

'I'd say there was never a better time to go bottoms up.'

TK took another glass with a smile. 'You bet.'

After the champagne the room felt warmer, and the cream-pie people no longer seemed as odd.

We found two gold chairs along the wall and sat down, glad to give the heels a rest.

'I told Mandy today that I was leaving the Agency,' TK told me, rubbing the arch of her foot. 'She did her full speech on how my career would go down the tubes if I left the Agency, and how I was going to be such a star – everyone in the Agency had such plans for me ... blah blah. I told her I'd think about it. When I walked out, Sophie smiled and waved, and called me Helen. Go figure.'

'Is she here tonight? Mandy?'

'Probably. Since when has she missed a chance to soak up free booze and hunt for a guy?'

'She's not bad, TK, and she's suffering from a broken heart.'

'I know, but she's my booker – *our* booker – and she's always boozed, or hung over, or completely hyper and I just can't deal with her madness when I'm, like, calling from Milan to check my chart, or trying to get any sense out of her.'

'I know what you mean,' I nodded, lighting a cigarette and exhaling towards the chandeliers. 'She means well, but she's not a good booker. And she'll never tell it to you straight – it's always "Baby! Honey! You look amazing!!" Bullshit, bullshit, more bullshit until you forget what you were mad about. I mean, look at my hair.'

'It looks good, and that's not the point,' replied TK. 'We had this discussion last week. You have to have a serious talk with her, Justin, and then not listen to her crap. If she's here you should do it tonight. That way it's neutral territory – and you don't have to walk through a whole room of bookers who have probably guessed the truth or seem to be seeing you for the first time. Just tell her she has to start taking care of you and sending you on good castings or you'll change agencies.'

My reply was interrupted by people streaming towards a makeshift stage at one end of the room. There appeared to be a judging table in the centre of the stage, covered in a white tablecloth and lilies. TK and I looked over, reluctant to leave our seats.

The lights went down, music started, and a girl appeared on stage in two very small pieces of fur. She started dancing to Prince's 'Cream', taking the lyrics to their literal extreme. The crowd cheered and clapped, and a few shouted 'Pamela!'

Suddenly, Mandy appeared at my side.

'Hi lovey!'

She gave me a big hug and two kisses. Her lipstick had already smeared itself over the outline of her lips, a Ferrari red that always meant GO in her case. I noticed her eyes were glassy.

'Hi hon,' she said to TK with a smile, to show she was above it all.

I decided to jump in here and save us all. 'Hey Mandy, what's happening on stage?'

She turned back to me. 'It's a stripper-dancing competition thing. Whoever wins gets to be Vivienne Westwood's lingerie girl in the ads.'

Mandy looked up at a gyrating girl with cropped, white hair and no chest. 'I don't see why Vivienne couldn't have used models in her competition though – I'm sure one of *our* girls would have been perfect.' She looked at TK. 'I could have got any of you up on that stage.'

I dove in again. 'There's no way, Mandy, that you would have asked anyone in our agency to do that sort of thing. I don't even know what you call it! Get real.'

I laughed and stopped a man with more champagne. The three of us toasted. Mandy had her arm around my waist and was squeezing tightly. 'Look at that tiny little tummy of yours – it's so cute!' she was saying, squeezing it again and looking at TK as if to say, Look at all the love and attention you're missing out on.

TK wasn't biting. 'Did the Agency drop Federika today, Mandy? Is that true?'

'She was too big!' Mandy did not mean famous. 'We gave her a few weeks but she just wouldn't lose the weight! What can you do?! I gave her all my diet tips – nothing seemed to work!'

Mandy was no rake herself so I wasn't surprised her diet tips had failed.

'Big girls just don't work!' She hugged me tighter. 'Not like you Justin-baby!'

I hated her for that.

TK turned away as a Spanish girl named Tia grabbed her elbow – perfect timing as I was getting tired of Mandy's rubbish.

'Doesn't Naomi look great?' Mandy pointed to the glorious super-model on the arm of either Robert De Niro or his twin. 'She's amazing! We made her whole career, you know. And she's such a darling!'

'Mandy –' I summoned my courage. This chaotic woman should not be helping me make my business decisions. 'I need to talk to you.'

I felt like some troubled teen in an American family sitcom, but there was no other way.

'What is it, sweetie?'

'Not here, Mandy. I have to go to the bathroom. Come with me.'

She took my arm and we set off in search of the ladies.

Mercifully, it was unoccupied. Most of the guests were watching the show, and there were bathrooms on every floor, thank god.

This was one of the good ones. Nice lighting, linen hand-towels, and a make-up bench with soaps and hair products.

I sat on the bench.

Mandy was calmer now. She'd got the vibe that my news might not be something she really wanted to hear. Then she seemed to put two and two together, remembering that TK and I were friends, and her face drooped.

'Mandy,' I said, looking at my feet, 'I'm not happy with the way my work is going. I think that maybe you're not really pushing me hard enough for good editorial ...'

I was such a wuss that I couldn't even say it in absolutes. I didn't think, I knew.

'What?!' Her eyes were horrified.

'You're my booker – the only booker out of six I can talk to at the Agency, and you're usually out-of-your-head busy. You send me on any old casting and half the time it's all wrong – the address, or the time, or it's something I won't do.'

Mandy was starting to panic. 'I sent you to Diesel the other week – '

'Me and every other model in London.'

'You did *Dazed & Confused*!'

'That was the first really cool job you got me. I'm always doing teen mags or ads. I just want a bit more from you. And if you can't do it, I shall have to leave.'

Mandy's concern had nothing to do with my threatening to leave. Not directly. It was just that if two girls defected – two of *her* girls – it wouldn't look good to her boss.

'Look, you're going to be a star, the whole agency has plans for you.

This was exactly what Mandy had told TK. I wondered if there was a Booker Handbook she had consulted somewhere.

Mandy reached into her pocket and dumped a pile of coke on the make-up bench. She cut two fat lines, rolled up a ten-pound note and handed it to me. 'Go on, sweetie – my treat.'

I took the bill from her. I had never done cocaine, or any other drug, but this was not the time to appear vulnerable. And besides, I reasoned, the fact Mandy was offering me coke proved that I was perfectly right. Why should I accept a booker whose answer to job dissatisfaction was drugs?

I smiled and snorted my line, surprised how easily the powder disappeared. Mandy took the note and did hers, and then leaned into the mirror. 'We have great plans for you!' she exclaimed to my reflection. 'It'd be a huge mistake to leave us!'

'I need more work, Mandy,' I said soberly, although the coke was making me want to jump around, smile and agree to anything. 'It's purely business, nothing personal.'

I felt very sensible, very grown up, very in control – glad I had watched all those mobster films. The responsible, pulled-together model. 'I'm sure we can work it out.'

'Listen sweetie, you don't really want to leave, we'll do it together!' She was almost pleading now. 'I'll push you hard, I'll send you out on all the primo stuff, I swear! You're more than just my girl, you're a friend.' She moved in until I could see the lipstick on her tooth. 'We'll do it together, sweetie, together.'

Then she grabbed me and kissed me passionately on the mouth.

Her tongue was wet, her lips soft and so wide that they covered my entire mouth. I was so surprised that I found I couldn't pull away. I suppose I should have expected something like this, but I hadn't.

Just then the bathroom door swung open. 'Justin?' Tia yelled. I broke away from Mandy's mouth as TK walked in.

Mandy took her handbag and whispered, 'See you tomorrow, honey.' She made air-kissing noises at Tia and TK, then swept – with a wobble – out of the ladies. She had never looked so utterly mad.

Tia and TK were staring at me.

'What?' I said.

'Are you okay?' asked Tia.

'Why?' I looked in the mirror.

The area around my mouth was bright red from Mandy's fire engine lipstick. I grabbed a tissue and started wiping.

'That woman,' I said, beginning to laugh now that the shock had worn off – or perhaps was setting in – 'is so mental, it's terrifying.'

The red wouldn't come off. It was designed to stay on lips, and I guessed faces too. 'I think she thought she could French-kiss me into staying with the Agency.'

Tia pulled out a silver vial from a chain around her neck, unscrewed the top, snorted two neat hits of powder off a so-cute-you-could-die matching spoon then offered it to me.

I shook my head. 'Mandy was, um, kind enough, thank you.'

TK took the vial. 'This is the cutest thing I've ever seen!' She handed it back to Tia then looked over at me. 'She's gross – Mandy, I mean.'

'Actually, it wasn't a bad kiss as far as they go,' I replied seriously.

TK threw a box of tissues at me.

'I'm serious.' I was laughing. 'I may have discovered the answer to my man troubles – or lack thereof. Lesbianism.'

'You'd make a really bad lesbian, Justin.'

'Why?'

'Because you're boy-crazy, you idiot,' said TK, picking up another box of tissues.

I threw a toilet roll at her before she could launch the tissues. She grabbed one from a stall. Soon, there were rolls flying through the air in every direction, leaving paper trails behind.

Tia grabbed both cans of complimentary hairspray. She attacked my head until my hair stood on end and the room was so full of fumes we could hardly breathe. We collapsed out the door, choking and laughing, and almost killed one of the foam-head boys in platform boots – who was talking to Robbie Williams – as he keeled backwards on the stairs, overpowered by the smell.

Rock and roll baby doll. Is that what you want to be? Is that who you think you are now? Nothing can touch you. You sit there blowing smoke rings, a demented china doll, porcelain features crinkling, puckering, gasping. You'll always be a fish out of water.

'Tia's beautiful, isn't she?'

TK nodded. 'She has a beautiful body.'

We were in a cab on our way home. It was raining outside and I was smoking my last cigarette. The cocaine had made me smoke far too much.

'That was heroin in the vial.'

'What?' I stared at TK's outline.

'Mandy told me Tia snorts heroin. It wasn't coke. She snorts so she doesn't get needle marks.'

'Bullshit.'

'I've heard her talking about it. She says coke makes her too edgy and the heroin keeps her thin.'

'She doesn't look like a heroin addict – I mean, she's very thin, but ...'

'... she's not drooling and covered in sores? The community service announcements make you think that all heroin addicts are basket cases – that they live like rats, crouched in dark sewers, murdering for money. Some are like that, sure. Heroin is shit. But others snort or shoot pretty high-grade heroin so they don't need a fix every day. They hold down jobs so they can support their habit without crime and keep their families – but they are completely addicted. Tia is one of those and there are loads more like her. We just don't notice them.'

'Shouldn't Mandy do something?'

TK looked at me and I felt her arch her eyebrows in the dark, as she always did when she thought someone was being obtuse.

Debbie sipped her tea and stared at me. 'It's obvious.'

'What is?'

'That you're a virgin.'

'What are you talking about? Why ... what ... how can you say that? You – '

96

'See? You're blushing. You're all shy and twisting pieces off the couch.'

She was right – I had a ball of mouldy, green wool in each hand.

Debbie smiled. 'It's okay, you know, but it's not really something you can pretend about, is it?'

I stared into my mug and wondered how many cups of tea had been made in it to give it so many brown rings. Maybe tea mugs were like tree trunks, you could tell their age by counting the tannin rings ...

'I lost my virginity at thirteen.'

'Okay, Debbie, you know what – that's not helping me feel better.'

'Don't be ashamed!' She was almost laughing, whether it was at me or my embarrassment didn't matter. 'It was with my neighbour in his coal cellar one lunch-time. We snuck away from school. It was cold and all I could think of was that it felt like having to pee, only painful. Everyone knew when we came out because we were both covered in black dust. But no one really cared – everyone was doing it.'

Brigitte walked in and Debbie stopped talking.

'Hi Brigitte,' I called out. But she only said hello and went straight to her plastic bin full of muesli. (She used apple juice instead of milk, and I hated seeing her oat-crusted bowl in the sink in the morning – it made me want to gag.) She filled her bowl and disappeared into her room. I thought I heard the door lock.

'She always seems so depressed,' I said to Debbie. 'What's wrong with her?'

Debbie lit her ninth cigarette and blew smoke out of her perfect nostrils. She smoked Newports – mentholated cigarettes – and the green smell clung to her. 'She's not sure she wants to be here, or even modelling. She has some boyfriend in Paris, an older guy. She needs to have a plan.'

'A plan?'

'Yeah. The only way to survive this modelling circus is to have clear objectives – you have to know what you want, and what you have to do to get it. Otherwise you get lost and sad and eaten alive.'

I nodded gravely at what I saw as deep wisdom. 'Well, what are your goals?' I leant forward so I wouldn't miss anything. Debbie had the right idea about life.

'I plan to sleep with every guy on *People*'s fifty-most-beautiful-people list, and a couple of the girls as well.' She sat back and smiled. 'I've done five already – well, four-and-a-half. Blow jobs only count as halves.'

'And that would make you happy?'

'Yeah. I'll probably get famous somewhere along the way. I'll get photographed with some star, and voilà!, I'll be a household name. I might even get married, have little star babies. It'll be great.'

'It's not that simple, Debbie, you have to do something to be famous.'

'Right,' she said sarcastically, 'that's untrue, girl, so untrue. Just watch me. I'm going to make it happen.'

Only that afternoon, Debbie had sat on the top of a double-decker bus thinking about how her favourite movie was *Pretty Woman*. She'd watched it at least thirty-five times – the Minnesota winters were long – and she knew every line of dialogue. When she found her prince, Debbie would know exactly what to say, to the letter.

She realised, with the heat from the bus radiator melting the soles of her cheap boots, that she only wanted to be *Pretty Woman* if she also got to be Julia Roberts. The idea of Vivian going home to play housewife and take a part-time job at a nail salon didn't do it for her. She needed to go to her prince and step into Julia Roberts' life. That was the charm of the movie. There were no questions left unanswered and all the answers were happy ones.

We all knew what happened to the heroine after she climbed

down that fire escape – we read about her every day – she became Julia Roberts. And to Debbie the two were synonymous: find thy prince and thou shalt be Julia Roberts (or at least Reese Witherspoon).

Debbie had been married before, at sixteen, to a boy from her home town. The boy was going to open a garage one day, his own garage where he could be the boss. The marriage had lasted five months. In those months, Debbie had discovered modelling and the glimpses of glamour were enough to turn her already loose head. One turn down the makeshift catwalk of the Minnesota Mall (biggest under-cover mall in the world) and all of a sudden Rick and his dreams were never going to be enough. She lauded herself for being smart enough to see that early on in their relationship and escape before it was too late. (Too late for Debbie meant too old – about twenty-five.)

She left Minnesota and persuaded herself that the marriage had all been Rick's idea. The further she moved from her home town, the clearer this became. By Los Angeles, she was convinced that Rick had manipulated (by London it was 'threatened') her until she, sweet ingenue of sixteen, had had to say 'yes'.

Debbie thought of herself as Nastassja Kinski in *Paris, Texas* and even began remembering cow bells tied around her ankles. She knew she had what it took and nothing was going to stop her going as far as she wanted.

The bus conductor loomed. 'World's End, please.' Debbie flashed her travel card.

The passport picture was good, she thought, examining it for the hundredth time. Her eyes were huge in it, green flecked with gold, and curtained with dark, heavy lashes. Her narrow face didn't look too long and her light freckles had disappeared under the bright flash. Her straight, blonde hair and heavy, straight fringe gave her a wide-eyed look that she could exaggerate to good effect when it came to matters of men.

Her child-like frame hid steely determination and resilience beyond her years. She was fuelled by ambition, cigarettes and adrenaline.

And instant mashed potatoes with lots of butter. Eating was a bore to Debbie. She missed the comfort cookies, marshmallows and burgers of American diners. Already her grey, wool miniskirt hung loose on her hips and her grey, wool stockings encased twig-like legs, ever so slightly bowed. Debbie had no love of fashion, she was not 'cool' and didn't try to dress that way. She was Minnesota through and through, but she knew she never wanted to go back there. And she was prepared to do anything not to.

The windows of the bus were steaming up and the floor radiator scarcely warmed her toes. One day she would move through these streets in a limousine. Everyone had to start somewhere. And that's just where she was now, somewhere.

A week after our conversation, Debbie made the front page of the *Evening Standard* and the *Sun*. She was pictured – wearing a Dalmatian-print coat and huge black shades – climbing over the wall of the home of the charmingly middle-aged movie star R., three days after his much-publicised split with his model girlfriend.

The media coverage was frenzied. Debbie did interviews for *Hello* magazine, *OK*, *Heat*, *Woman's Day* and a host of others. Video images of her running up to the Agency doors, her hand raised against the cameras, wearing tight, tight black, appeared on the evening news. It was all about Debbie.

She didn't come home for three nights after that. We all assumed she was holed up with R. somewhere. Then Mandy told us Debbie had landed a huge job for the lingerie label Victoria's Secret and was on her way to Barbados. Some execs had seen her face in the news and decided they couldn't miss linking their new campaign to such a 'bankable star', and snatched her up.

The payphone in our apartment rang. It was Debbie on her way home from the airport. 'Just calling from the limo, darl,' she said. She wanted us to go out with her – me, TK and 'whosoever else wants to come.'

'We're going to dinner with Ali,' said Debbie. 'You know Ali, you met him at Brown's the night I got into that fight with Björk.'

Debbie had got really high at a record launch – she'd been dating Nellee Hooper (the famous music producer) at the time – and become convinced that the teddy Björk was carrying around on her back was her long lost Sukey from childhood. She'd left it somewhere on the I94 during a family road trip in Mississippi and had missed it ever since. She had confronted Björk, and, when the singer didn't appear too willing to return Sukey to her rightful owner, Debbie had lunged for it, and the three of them had hit the ground rolling.

Björk won the fight, and Debbie had sulked in the champagne lounge for the rest of the evening, trying to convince Nellee, and anyone else who would listen, that Björk was really a man, and therefore didn't deserve her 'Best Female Artist' Grammy.

All I could remember about Ali was that he was Middle Eastern – Lebanese perhaps – and that he had huge hands covered with scars that might have come from non-accidental cigarette burns.

So that night we ended up in Ali Baba's Cave, a glitzy joint that reminded me of what I thought Las Vegas must be like. The entrance hall was all black mirrors, floor, ceiling and walls. Further in, oil fountains sparkled pink in the low light, and gold-plated palms lined the way. The floor became black marble veined with gold, and the ceiling sported huge gold stars.

The restaurant itself was huge, with murals of the desert on all four walls and leather booths, trimmed with real tiger skins. Barry White was piped in from some invisible source, and his voice was making the room vibrate ever so slightly.

Can't get enough of your love, baaby.

Debbie sat at the centre of a booth looking fabulous and tanned. Beside her sat the much-read-about and seen R. TK sat on his other side. Ali sat between Debbie and me. Three beautiful female attendants hovered around the table in gauzy veils at any one time, henna-ed hands refilling and replacing as we consumed.

Curious as it was to meet such a famous actor up close, to have his eyes bore into mine, it was Debbie who fascinated me that night. Her head was thrown lightly back, her delicate throat exposed, and she tinkled with laughter. I'd never known Debbie's laughter to tinkle before – it had always been a rather endearing mid-western 'haw haw haw'. But in the space of two weeks, it had become a tinkle. How I hated my laugh.

Debbie was wearing a divine gossamer gown, sewn (by hand) to look like a series of delicate black cobwebs. I knew the dress was designer, and I knew how much it cost – I had worn it the other day at a shoot for German *Elle* and the assistant stylist had kept telling me to be very careful when dressing, undressing, eating or walking. The gown had to be returned.

Debbie glanced over and met my gaze. She smiled, her teeth white against her Barbados tan. She'd acquired one of those film-star smiles that float around the room, beaming, but never alighting on any one person. She glowed, she was elegant, she was famous, just like she'd said she would be.

R. leant over, lit her cigarette and whispered in her ear. That tinkle again.

Ali was asking me how much I made on jobs. Money, its causes and effects, was his favourite topic.

'It all depends,' I said, taking a deep drink of my vodka tonic. 'I get almost nothing for editorial, and up to twenty thousand for a big ad campaign, or a long-running catalogue job.'

He twinkled at me in an avuncular way. 'Are you investing the money, or are you spending it all?'

'I save some in the bank.'

'You know,' leaning in conspiratorially. 'You could buy one of my fighter planes for twenty thousand.'

Ali dealt in old war machines – second, third and fourth-hand tanks, ships and planes. He bought them in places like the Balkan States, Afghanistan and China, did them up, then sold them to rich collectors in the west. I had a suspicion he probably dealt in not-so-vintage arms too.

'For twenty thousand,' he went on, 'you could put a down payment on a Russian bomber – with guns and maybe a few bombs.'

Suspicions justified.

'I could have it for you in a month.'

'I couldn't buy a Russian plane!' I cried, lighting my tenth cigarette, liking the idea tremendously. 'Why would I want a fighter plane? I'm a model, not the Mujaheddin. I'm just trying to get on the cover of *Vogue*.'

Ali smiled. 'You limit yourself. Expand your thinking, Justin. Think big. Twenty thousand – you buy my plane, maybe the guns, maybe not. You live in Australia, am I right?'

I nodded and exhaled my smoke towards the ceiling in a steady white stream. I supposed I did.

'Think how easily you could fly home with an aircraft of your own. You could renovate the inside – lots of room for sofas, a movie theatre, beds. You could bring your whole family over. And go to the Bahamas for the weekend, anything you wanted. You get yourself a good pilot – and voilà! You'd be crazy not to.'

I was beginning to think he might be right.

'What about the guns?' I asked Ali. 'What would I do with those?'

'Hold the magazines hostage. Threaten war if you don't get the jobs you want.' He laughed. 'You can do anything you want.'

'The guns scare me, Ali. I don't think I would want to buy the guns.'

'Just the plane then, no problem. You give me twenty thousand – you pay for all renovations yourself, but I will throw in a free hot-tub with Jacuzzi jets, because you are my friend. What do you think?'

Thankfully, one of the veiled women sashayed over and whispered in Ali's ear, causing him to frown and saving me from ending up with some radiation-saturated pile of scrap metal somewhere on the Afghan border.

'We'll have to go out the back way,' Ali announced. 'Myrta says there is a crowd of photographers outside, waiting for R. and Debbie.'

Debbie held up a hand. 'It's okay, really. I don't want to trouble you. Why should those pesky paparazzi make us change our plans?' She smiled at the table. 'I'll be okay. I'm just going to the ladies – back in a second.'

R. and Ali stood for her as she got up.

'Come with me, Justin.'

I found myself following her without thinking. I heard R. say to Ali, 'She's handling fame amazingly well.'

Debbie gazed at her reflection in the mirror, then pulled out a pot of lipstick and started touching up her mouth.

'I guess you did it, Debbie,' I said, smiling. 'You look great, by the way.'

'I'm going to be on the cover of German *Elle*,' she said, perfecting her cupid's bow lips.

'I did a shoot for them too. In that dress. We might be in the same issue.'

Debbie pressed her lips together. 'I made Cassie do my face before I got off the plane at Heathrow. I knew the press would be waiting, goddamn hounds.'

'Right,' I laughed.

Debbie straightened up.

'What's so funny?' she demanded. 'They've been dogging my every footstep – I can't get a moment's privacy without some crazy paparazzo snapping his flash.'

'That's great – and there I was preaching that you had to do something real to get famous. I guess you were right to laugh at me.' I leaned against the wall – a paper mural of *The Thousand and One Nights.*

'What are you saying, Justin? That I'm just famous because of R.?'

She looked at me angrily in the mirror, her lips set in a hard little line.

I was taken aback. 'But you *are* famous because of R.! Those pictures of you climbing the wall – '

'Initially, that's true – but now I'm famous in my own right. I've earned my fame, I've paid my dues, and it's my face you'll see on bill-boards. Not R's.' She spoke slowly, as if to a moron. 'And those pictures were just a cheap attempt to get people to buy the tabloids – do you think that I asked for this circus wherever I go?'

'Well, yes, Debbie, I do. I remember what you – '

'You're just like everyone else, Justin. I thought you would be cooler than that. Envy doesn't suit you.' She turned back to the mirror.

'But Debbie, remember how you explained that you had to have a goal in modelling, and that yours was to sleep your way through the fifty most beautiful people until you became famous too? Now you are. So doesn't that mean that this *is* what you wanted? What you set out to achieve?' I still thought she might be joking.

Debbie sighed with practised exasperation. 'All R. and I want is to be left alone. We're just two normal people in love. I don't see why the world is so interested.'

She snapped her beaded purse shut in contempt and pulled the bathroom door open. 'I expected more from you, Justin,' she said over her shoulder. 'It's very disappointing.' Then let the door swing back in my face.

7

Say Thank You to the Nice Man

It might have been Halloween – I know it was sometime in October. We were in an under-heated studio in Camden, the Lemonade Factory they called it. We were shooting an ad campaign for some body lotion that sounded like 'Nivea' but wasn't. I was in a bathrobe and Mr Pearl was applying foundation to my left thigh.

Mr Pearl was small and thin, with a shiny bowl of dark-brown hair that swung in time with his hips. He was very good at what he did, and his specialty was flawlessness. He could make everyone look perfect, so he got a lot of advertising jobs. I'd worked with him before, mainly on beauty jobs, but it had always been with other models who knew him well, and we hadn't had the time or the attention span, Mr Pearl and I, to get acquainted.

His assistant, Maia, a hefty, pierced girl, was painting the toes of my right foot sea-shell pink. I watched Mr Pearl applying flesh tone with a sponge, his touch deft, his clean, shiny hair hiding his face.

'Oh, baby, you're cold,' he said, rubbing the goose bumps on my leg. 'Annie,' he called across the room to the studio assistant, 'can you bring us a cup of tea? Make that three, one for me and Maia, too. Thanks, lovey.'

He went back to work and I tried to think who or what he reminded me of. 'Mr Pearl,' I asked, 'what's that you're wearing around your waist?'

As a young, blonde model you can get away with asking indiscreet questions (and no one asks why you're late if you tell them you got lost).

Mr Pearl looked up and smiled. He had a nice smile. 'It's a corset, sweetie. It makes me look slim, trim and fantastic.'

He had a kind, lilting, lisping voice. I took a good look. The corset looked like an extra-wide leather belt that fastened at the front with eye-hooks, and at the back with straps. Mr Pearl seemed in danger of being completely bisected by it. His lower ribcage and hips stood out like an exaggerated hourglass, his waist so narrow I could have put my hands around it.

'But you don't need a corset – you're tiny,' I reminded him.

'You can never be too tiny, Justin.'

'Is it bad for you? I mean, does it hurt? – squash your insides?' I wondered if it would do anything for me, a tiny waist like that.

'Oh, we suffer for our beauty, don't we? Do we ever make the sensible choice?'

Growing shy, I picked up a pair of his scissors that were lying on the bench. He almost snatched them away. 'Oh, no, lovey, don't play with those. They cost two grand a pop.' He took them quickly from my fingers. 'And they're very, very sharp. My magic foundation could never cover a river of your blood, play with this instead.'

He tossed me a Velcro hair curler and looked at me in the mirror. 'I like your hair like that. None of that punk grunge teasing, just clean and beautiful.'

Suddenly I knew why Mr Pearl felt so familiar – he reminded me of my mother.

I lit a cigarette and reached for the *Daily Mail* lying under the mirror. Mr Pearl was now working on my right thigh, Maia on my right calf. She had finished my toes.

I pointed at a cigarette. 'Do you mind?' They didn't – of course they didn't.

I took a gulp of too-hot tea and almost choked on it, and the front page. There was a picture of Debbie and R. leaving Ali Baba's Cave. Half of Ali was visible behind R., along with the top of TK's head and my legs. Debbie had her dark glasses on, one hand outstretched, as if to stop the photographers. She had made sure her hand didn't cover her face, and to grip R.'s arm for support. She looked good, I had to give her that. She knew how to play the role.

Mr Pearl looked up. 'Are you okay, doll?'

I coughed, pointing to the front page. 'Did you know that you have the honour of painting the very legs that appear on the cover of today's *Mail*?'

'They're your legs? They look fabulous.'

I smiled at him. 'Let's not go nuts.'

'Well they do – you have beautiful legs.'

'They're your legs?' asked Maia. I nodded. The crew gathered round to see my legs on the front page of the *Mail*.

'Nice pins,' whistled the young photographer's assistant.

'You've been photographing them all morning.'

'I know. But nothing's ever as real as when you see it in print.'

'You're almost famous.'

The crew dispersed, taking the *Mail* with them.

'Don't you think it's sad that I'm pointing out my legs in the newspaper? I mean, it's a picture of Debbie, a story about her, and I'm pointing out my legs.'

'I think it's great.'

'No you don't. Neither do I. But it is funny.'

Mr Pearl agreed it was funny. I wanted to tell him about Debbie, but I knew I couldn't do that. 'I guess,' I said, throwing down the newspaper, 'I guess that's what I get for being a B model.'

You'd think it was ridiculous if you knew. It is. I am.

I pulled out my drawing book for the millionth time that evening. It had a red-leather cover, and I had bought it a month after arriving in London, when I had suddenly remembered that I liked to draw. But all its pages were still blank, save the first, where I had stuck in the old envelope with the cake lady's caricature.

I had tried to draw many times since then, but could never get anything onto the page. Tonight I tried again but nothing would come. Instead I found myself writing down Mr Pearl's compliment: 'You have beautiful legs'. I stared at the sentence and it felt good to see the words on paper, as if they were suddenly more true. I continued, transcribing the assistant's whistle: 'Nice pins'. Underneath I carefully copied something a photographer had asked me the other day: 'Do you have your mother's lips?' I had replied in the affirmative and he said: 'I can see why your father wanted to kiss them'. So corny – yet I felt better with each compliment that I remembered and wrote down.

'You have a face men would go to war for' – good one, from the *Dazed & Confused* shoot. And I remembered the compliment from the oily boy the night I became a blonde: 'My dream girl'. That was my favourite flower and I wrote it in large letters. The title page I drew in pencil, heading it *Book of Compliments* and adding a rose in pencil that turned out better than I feared. I was embarrassed, yet that didn't stop me. I needed the affirmation. I planned to carry the red book secretly in my satchel and look at it whenever I felt crap about myself (which was often).

TK got the Diesel job so we went to the pub to celebrate, even coaxing along Lara, who didn't drink or smoke or indulge in any loutish behaviour so pubs were irrelevant to her 'lifestyle'. I told her she should be a good friend to TK and show her she wished her well. An appeal to decent human nature always worked with Lara.

Cristina followed us without complaint. She had just rowed with her boyfriend Milos over the payphone again and was glad to get out of the suffocating air of the apartment.

Debbie had called and we told her to meet us at The Landsdowne in Primrose Hill. 'Nice choice, girls,' she purred, 'love to – but I'm in Hawaii. Swimwear for Gottex – very sexy, very European. R. is with me. Big kiss darlings.' She had even 'mwaahed' into the phone.

And then there was Brigitte.

She wouldn't open her bedroom door or answer our entreaties. Finally TK tried the handle. Brigitte had forgotten to turn the lock.

She was curled up at the foot of the bed, lost in her sea of itchy, brown wool. She looked like a starving woodland creature, all big eyes and fur. I was scared to touch her in case I hurt her tiny bones with my big hands. We all just stared at her.

'Brigitte.' Cristina stepped forward, her voice soft. I had never heard her speak like this. 'Come wid us now.'

She reached out her hand, and I half expected Brigitte to whirl around and sink pointy teeth into it. But she just looked up at Cristina with her little monkey face.

She must have seen something in Cristina's eyes that made her trust the wild Croatian girl. Maybe it was the bruises on her black pupils from seeing so much too soon, the anguish of a dead brother and a homeland torn apart – things Cristina never spoke about aloud spoke silently to the wasted Brigitte. She took Cristina's hand without a word.

Cristina found Brigitte's coat and put it over her shoulders as gently as a mother, and we went down the road to celebrate. Even Lara was impressed.

The pub mercifully, was less full than usual. We took a table near the back and ordered pints of beer. Even Lara made an exception to her firm rule of abstinence. I think we all felt that coaxing Brigitte out of her room was another reason to make merry. She still hadn't said a word. I had ordered her a Guinness for nourishment but she hadn't touched it.

'You have to look after yourself, Brigitte, you're too thin.' Lara the mother hen was pecking gently. 'You'll damage yourself. You should see a counsellor.'

'Lara.' TK could feel Brigitte's terror mounting at the attention – we all could.

'I'm serious. She should see a psychiatrist. She probably has all sorts of unresolved issues that she should face. I'm going to speak to Mandy about her tomorrow and –'

'Don't talk as if she's not here.' I wanted to stop Lara's self-help train from crushing the fragile Brigitte.

'She needs help. Someone has to say something.'

'Lara, stop it.'

'I don't care what you say – I'm going to Mandy tomorrow. And someone's going to have a talk with you.' She looked right at Brigitte.

Brigitte fought back tears. Cristina kissed the tiny girl's hand with its papery skin, and drank from the untouched Guinness. Her Balkan features crinkled in disgust and she pushed the glass away from both of them.

'So, when's the Diesel campaign coming out, TK?' Lara sipped her beer as one would hot tea.

'I don't know – a month or so, I guess.'

'Who was the photographer?'

'Rhett Someone.'

'Tall, lanky, rock-star type?' That was me.

'Yes. That's him.'

'Were there any nice clothes?' asked Lara.

'Pretty cool, in an urban edge sort of way. I had, like, big jeans and this little tank top and I had to sit on this guy's lap.' TK turned to me. 'You'll never guess who the guy was, J.'

'Dirty Boy!'

'Who?' TK was puzzled.

'The guy in the studded denim who you said reminded you of your ex-boyfriend!'

'You call him Dirty Boy?' Her eyes lit up.

'It slipped out.'

'Doesn't he shower?' Lara's smooth brow furrowed in concern. 'That's disgusting.'

TK ignored her. 'I like that. I was bummed out when he told me his name was Lonnie. It's pretty hard to be cool if your name is Lonnie.'

'Or Cyril.'

'Or Leslie.'

'Or Guy. You'd have to have a pretty strong personality to carry off Guy.'

'I like Dirty Boy,' TK insisted.

'People can't really help their names.' Lara seemed genuinely concerned.

'So, was he nice?' I needed details.

'He was so sexy – he has these crooked teeth and a bit of a lisp. I love lisps.'

'You mean, like a speech impediment?'

'I have a huge crush on him.'

'So, what happened?'

'I had to sit on his lap all day. There were eight other models in the photo – one of those Calvin Klein group set-ups – and I had to pretend we were hot for each other.'

'Did you make it wid him – the boy wid the dirt?' Cristina always cut to the chase. She'd grown up in a place where time was short.

'Cristina! I don't believe in sex before marriage ... but we had to kiss.' TK rummaged in her bag and pulled out a Polaroid.

It was a close-up of TK and Dirty Boy kissing. Well, they had just finished kissing and were pulling apart, their mouths hungry and open.

'I love how there's a string of saliva between our mouths – it's so dirty-sexy.'

'So you really kissed him full on.'

'He's a good kisser. Tongue and all.'

'TK! When are you going to see him again?'

'He's going to call me.'

'You are not vagina.' Cristina announced.

TK and I giggled and Lara looked horrified.

'What do you mean?' I asked.

'Vagina! Vagina!'

A group of hip men in square glasses and an old lady at the bar turned to look at Cristina. We giggled more. She was oblivious.

'When there is no sex – when you are a child – you are vagina.'

'Virgin,' whispered a mortified Lara, 'I think she means virgin.'

Brigitte hadn't spoken or changed her expression yet. It was unnerving – if anything could have provoked a reaction, Cristina's comment should have. It was as if Brigitte had departed London weeks ago and left her body propped up in the corner, emptied of soul.

TK spoke up. 'I'm not a virgin. But that doesn't mean I believe in sex before marriage. I think people should wait.'

'I'm waiting,' said Lara.

Her comment made me feel better. I didn't want to be the only virgin at the table. Although Debbie had guessed my secret, the others didn't know.

'Really?' I wanted to know more.

'Really. I've never had sex. I'm waiting until I find the right man, and then we'll get married and I'll sleep with him then.'

'Have you never been tempted?'

I could sense jealousy in TK's question. She had hoped to shock us with her unorthodox views on sex, but Lara had pipped her fair and square.

'Never. I have very well-developed will-power.'

Lara sat back, calculated on her fingers all the kilojoules she had consumed that day and converted them to calories. '1 pear, 40 calories; broccoli, boiled, 24; lemon and herb cod steaks, 195; lager, 29 per 100 mls'. She allowed herself another sip of beer. Lara was nineteen-and-a-half kilos below the desirable Weight Watchers weight, a fact of which she was proud.

Cristina shrugged matter-of-factly. 'I'm making sex with Milos since two years. My first boyfriend. I like it. It's not bad. Maybe you die tomorrow and you never know sex.'

'Well, I'm going to wait until I get married too.' TK was trying to reclaim the conversation as her own. 'That's what the Bible says. And anyway, guys lose interest if you give in too soon. Virginity is a state of mind.'

That didn't make any sense to me. It seemed to me that virginity was indeed a very physical state. But I did not want to involve myself in a debate that might require me to answer personal questions about my experiences. Anyway, I thought to myself, if virginity is a state of mind, losing it could be too. I decided, then and there, that I was no longer a virgin. From now on, I was going to be sexy, as if I knew what it meant. I lifted my pint and silently toasted the popping of my cherry.

I had to get up at five the next morning and the air in the apartment was freezing. The oil radiators wouldn't start up again until seven, so I wrapped myself in the itchy grey blanket from my bed. I had to be at a shoot for *Cosmopolitan* by seven and the beers the night before meant I could barely remember my name. Cristina was snoring lightly as I crept towards the kettle in the kitchen. All was dark.

As I groped along the wall for the light switch (they always seem to migrate south in the dark) I heard a noise. Brigitte's door opened slowly and I heard a muffled thud. Her outline emerged, dragging a suitcase, and headed for the front door. She didn't notice me, and I was too unnerved to disturb this odd scene.

She opened the front door and was about to step forward when I managed to force her name out into the dark. 'Brigitte?'

She looked up, startled, and saw me. Not a word – she simply stared a moment. Then she turned back to her suitcase, stepped toward the open door and slipped through the crack. I knew Brigitte was running away, far from us all, back to her parents. It made me want to call mine – they seemed somehow closer in the dark. I found the phone by moonlight and dialled, afraid to turn on the lights in case the memory of them, suddenly so palpable, should slip away.

My father answered the phone sounding vague. 'Your mother is with those ... the ones that run ...'

'What are you talking about Dad? What runs?'

'Races.'

'She's at the horse races?'

'No, dogs. Sounds like fun. It's a charity because they aren't loved.'

'The dogs?'

'They are dreadfully neglected once they can no longer run ...'

He was reciting my mother's propaganda.

'I see ...'

'It sounds serious.'

'Okay Dad. Will you tell her I called . . .?'

I clicked the receiver, lonelier than ever.

The Honourable Jeb Hoochy was a model handbag. He dangled from the perfectly formed arms of beauties of all nationalities. He was especially partial to blondes from the Eastern Bloc with a limited command of English, but any cutie under eighteen would do. Jeb was short for Jebbery, and he was directly descended from Lord Jebbery Hoochy, Purveyor of Wives to the Crown. There was however little that was honourable about him.

It was rumoured that the original Lord Jebbery had received his title for services rendered in helping to procure three of Henry VIII's wives. When marital disharmony in the King's household threatened to disrupt Lord Jebbery's appointment, he discreetly excused himself to Scotland, where he farmed sheep for the rest of his life and retained his title.

Jebbery the descendent was a horror film director, specialising in sequels, prequels and scantily-clad lasses. He was president of Hoochy Coochy Productions and had offices in Soho furnished with leather sofas and bloodied props from *Hedge-Clipper Maniac VI: Up the Body Count*, his greatest success to date.

Auditions were held almost every day in the HC offices and passers-by would hear scream after blood-curdling scream through the closed second-floor windows. Jeb's audition technique never varied: he would ask the girl remove her shirt and bra and scream at the top of her lungs for as long as she could. Jeb, presiding in a leather swivel chair by Olivetti, would compliment each and every candidate sincerely for her time and talent. Every girl who entered the offices of Hoochy Coochy Productions came away feeling special. That was Jebbery's gift. He could make any girl in the world feel like a queen.

Jeb was an enthusiastic lover who showered his adored girl with gifts, but his attention never lasted long. Those who didn't know Jeb scornfully called him a playboy; those who did know him agreed, but with a smile. He wasn't an overly attractive man, but neither was he so gross that his charm could be overlooked. He had dentist's teeth and bleached, blond hair and his modest looks made him more friends among men than perfect jaw bones would have.

All in all, he was the best Jebbery Hoochy that money could buy.

His taste in suits was flashy. He favoured shirts of shiny, midnight-blue unbuttoned to his navel, but wore them with aplomb.

Jeb was a friend of Mandy. They had met backstage at the London fashion shows and seen each other every season after that, Mandy with a different hair colour each time, Jeb with a different girl. Mandy found him glamorous and Jeb found Mandy's job as a booker in the biggest model agency in London very useful. He was invited to all the large Agency dinners and his status as Mandy's friend made the girls relax around him.

Jeb had been married before, about two years ago, when he was a fresh thirty. He had been window-shopping for lovelies at a fashion show – autumn/winter Alexander McQueen – when his future wife appeared on the runway in a tartan bustle and little else. She was pouty and sixteen, with blonde hair to her hips. Jeb had been struck dumb. After that, he followed her from show to show, sitting in the front row as she tossed her hair, and slowly befriended her backstage. Her name was Raimie and she came from Small-Town Nowhere, America. Raimie liked to party hard.

After her last show of the season – a wispy affair for Ghost – Jeb and Raimie hit the champagne, the town and the drugs and soon they were flying. In the back of a rented white limo (Jeb always travelled in limos) he decided they shared a love bigger than the two of them and the only conceivable thing to do was become man and wife. He had the car stop in Bond Street and bought two beautiful gold wedding bands.

Raimie thought that marriage was a great idea and wondered where they could get more ecstasy.

They were married in four hours and went missing for four days. At some point – when she was coherent enough to drool down the receiver – Raimie phoned her mother with the good news and her mother raced over from America. By then the drugs had worn off and Jeb had fallen to earth. He realised he wasn't ready for a wife, especially one bought duty-free at take-off, and wanted a refund. Raimie suffered a bout of dementia from the prolonged mood-enhancer binge and had to be temporarily institutionalised. The marriage was declared null and void, Jeb narrowly escaping prosecution because sixteen is the legal age of consent in Britain, and because witnesses at the show attested that Raimie had indeed gone willingly. The beautiful gold rings from Asprey held up well in court and spoke for Jebbery's good intentions, as did his aristocratic ancestry.

Since the incident, Jeb had worn his wedding ring on a chain around his neck. He claimed he liked to look at it while he made love to a girl, watching it dangle between her breasts. He said it reminded him to keep one foot on the ground at all times and not make the same mistake again. Not all divorces are as smooth as his first had been.

This was all information he freely admitted to me at our first meeting. It was at an Agency dinner somewhere in Chelsea – *Riccardo's* I think. Both Mandy and Jebbery had been benefiting from the political unrest in the Balkans. The fighting and air raids were driving more Eastern beauties than ever westward into their hands, and many of them were natural blondes. These girls had to be entertained and introduced to the right people – there were dinners almost every night. Mandy invited me and I came for the food. I was seated on Jebbery's left and his attention never left me. He ordered for me without my noticing – something fishy – and I heard him tell Mandy not to order the pasta. 'You'll balloon, Mandy. Straight to the hips, baby.' Mandy blushed. 'Order the Dover sole.' She did and I wondered whether Jeb thought I was fat, ordering the fish like that for me.

TK was at the table too, but Mandy had been careful to sit us apart. We were often criticised for whispering to each other. Someone had invited Dirty Boy Lonnie. I saw him get up and change seats so he could be next to TK. When he sat down at her side, I saw her femininity shift into high gear. Her skin flushed and her eyes warmed up. Her lips filled with blood and she twisted her hands together in half-affected shyness. She looked beautiful and I think Dirty Boy was bewitched. But I could not observe them long – I had my hands full with my newest acquaintance.

Jebbery would not allow my attention to wander. I thought him arrogant, but also strangely charming. No man had ever worked so hard to keep me happy, even if it was just over dinner. Jeb filled my wine glass often and was ready to light my cigarettes before I even had them out of the pack. He complimented me endlessly: the baby whiteness of my hair and the baby-curl of my upper-lip. He liked the fact that I was not quite seventeen. I was deeply suspicious, yet his attentions were so exaggerated that I felt he could not be real. If he were not real, I had nothing to fear. And Jeb was providing some great material for my secret *Book of Compliments*.

'May I?' He reached forward lightly, straightening a rogue fold on the sleeve of my T-shirt. 'You're just a wrinkle away from perfection.'

It was difficult to maintain a cynical wall under the barrage of gallantries. His story about his wedding helped keep me wary. I teased him about it, and about his shirt, his name and everything else. Jeb fought back with flattery. It became a war of attrition.

His finger traced the iron-on number on the back of my T-shirt.

'Eight. It's my lucky number. There's something beautiful about the way it curves and swoops around like that. Endless. It has no beginning and no end.'

'That better not be just an excuse to wipe your fingers. If you've lost your napkin, take mine.'

He smiled at me gently, like a piranha, and kissed my back through the cloth.

I spun.

'What liberties!'

This was starting to feel absurd, like a Victorian flirtation. I felt I should reach for my non-existent fan. I took a cigarette instead.

'I bet you are wonderful to kiss. That lip –' he groaned softly and his face quivered.

'I bite.'

His face cracked open like an egg and he started laughing, a wonderful laugh.

'You don't mind me going on like this?' he said. 'I adore flirting with you. It's the only way I know how to talk to a woman.'

'I don't mind. But only if it's in fun.'

'We could do that, you and I – be flirting friends. What do you think?'

I rather liked the idea.

The notion of befriending a man like Jeb appealed to my need for small rebellions. I knew people would be shocked, but I wanted to try on the Bad Girl's clothes for a little while. I wanted to party with the big kids.

So when Jebbery smiled his conspiratorial smile, lowered his voice and eyes and brought out some small, red pills, I took one. He told me they were MDMA, but he could have said ASAP, PMT, or ABCD and it would have meant as much to me. They were bright and pretty and Jeb was daring me with his eyes. 'Take it with a sip of wine – that'll kick it along.'

I watched him take his then did likewise.

He smiled at me. 'Pretty little things, aren't they? They liven up the party.'

I sat back, pressed my lips neatly with my napkin and waited for the compulsion to stick needles in my arm to hit me. In school they told us that all drugs led to heroin, and that the slightest deviation from the road of absolute abstinence would land you directly into a straitjacket or prison-issue jumpsuit. But right now, the need to feel cool outweighed the danger – I thought I'd probably look quite good in a tight, belted, white jacket. Very Helmut Lang meets Joan of Arc.

It's all about that, isn't it? About being the hero in your own story. Is that why you're tempted by Jebbery's drugs? Is that what the heroine in your story does? Heroine/heroin – a small matter of an 'e' to keep one from the other – take an 'e' and become a heroine. You just want to be Joan of Arc and you think the little red pill will make it happen.

There were six of us in the cab: TK and Dirty Boy, Mandy and her newest squeeze – Raoul, who she liked to refer to as 'the Lenny Kravitz of Spain, darling!' – Jeb and me. I took the snap-up seat, the only other option being Jeb's lap which, at this stage, I preferred to avoid. The roads were slick and the streetlights glowed in horizontal lines as we sped past. I let their fire and colour play on my pupils, not focusing, and listened to the wet road hissing under the tyres. The windows steamed up and the glass felt cold and hard against my cheek.

Raoul and Mandy were smoking. I looked at their faces, sliced into slabs by the flying icy light, searching for signs of depravity. I knew that they too had chosen to party with the red pills and was waiting for the devil to emerge.

Within myself, I felt only a soft warmth, a caramel custard feeling lapping up against my tonsils. I was relaxed, lightly heavy and my senses burned. I smelt and felt everything, heard almost nothing and saw in muddled flashes.

I loved Mandy for the care she had shown towards me, and Jeb looked so cute holding Mandy's purse like that. TK was kissable by the window. My dear, dear friend. Raoul had star potential, and even Dirty Boy sat like a wicked rock god, his greasy hair merely unkempt in the dark.

The world made sense to me, and at the same time it didn't matter. Nothing did. Only the flying, and the lights and the smell of smoke and wet wool. Someone was repeating my name over and over and over.

We went to a club. The strobe felt hot on my face and the DJ turned the volume up from some aerie above. The beat got heavier and louder and the dance floor started to shake. I felt like I was being rattled around in a giant ribcage – hot, sweaty, dark and damp – with an unseen heart beating loudly close by. Bodies brushed past me, faces flashed in time to the strobe. I could feel the molecules in the air around me. I fought my way to the bar, not bothering to excuse myself to the people whose feet I trod on – most were too hypnotised to notice – and found fresher air at last. My pupils adjusted to the dim light away from the dance floor and I rested my arms against the cool, grey marble bar as I leant in and ordered a cranberry juice. Clear red was such a beautiful colour. Beautiful. I felt my soft arms, soft legs, soft heart. I was relaxed as cream pie.

Turning back, I watched a shape detach itself from the crush of dancers and drift towards me.

A body leaned in. It was a muscled guy with a goatee, not tall, but very wide. He smiled. The cream-pie grin vanished from my face.

'Would you like a drink?'

His eyes were earnest. I stared at his nose. It had a ring in the left nostril, silver and pronounced, like a calf's tag.

'No, thank you,' I said, holding up my juice.

'Sure?' He signalled the bar-tender with a hammy hand, and ordered himself a Corona with lime. He wanted to know my name and I had to repeat it for him three times. No one ever got it the first time.

He offered 'Corey', as his, unsolicited, obviously proud of its sturdy connotations.

He took a manly swallow of his unmanly beer and, leaning in even further and pausing a beat, said, 'Parlez-vous français?'

So many thoughts rushed my crowded head they caused a traffic jam. Nothing came out.

He tried again, his voice lower, huskier this time. 'Parlez-vous français?'

Unperturbed by my look of horror, he went on: 'C'est le language d'amour ... it's the language of love.'

Did I imagine that wiggle in his eyebrows?

I was desperate for Jeb to come and save me. A sleaze to save me from a sleaze – although 'sleaze' was probably unfair to Jeb. My body felt too soft and I lacked the strength to tear myself from the bar.

Corey was still talking with a fake shy smile. 'I'm sorry, you looked like someone who might understand. You see, my grandfather was French – at least half-French – and I find the cultural gap between England and France very tough. I'm torn.'

All of a sudden I knew beyond any doubt that Corey listened to acid jazz and usually wore a beret.

He went on. 'I have to get out of here. I can't stay in London – this place is too small. No one here understands my potential.'

I guess he thought an almost seventeen-year-old platinum blonde model might. I searched for a way out.

'New York. That's where it's at. New York, the city that never sleeps –'

An arm whipped around my waist like the tail of a snake and spun me into the crowd. For a second my world was confused. I was lost in a tropical jungle of limbs, darkness and animal sounds.

Jeb whirled me onto the dance floor, holding me, tightly. 'God I get jealous when you talk to other men.'

'Jeb.'

'You looked like you needed saving.'

I nodded and relaxed into his arms, so strong on my back. I wanted to cry for a second. So safe and strong. The tears poked hot.

'Baby, baby, baby. I'll always be your prince.'

Noticing my welling tears, he held my face between his hands.

'Kiss me.'

The feeling broke. The tears froze.

'No.' I pulled away. He didn't try again, just smiled and stroked my hair.

'No one's ever got to me like you. Those eyes,' he whispered, 'stop making those eyes at me.'

I closed them and smiled.

Jebbery Hoochey was a cliché, but he was a great, bad man.

In a dark corner far from me and oblivious to all but each other sat TK and Dirty Boy. TK was drunk, but not terribly – just enough to let her fantasies muscle out reality and her face to become soft and willing. Dirty Boy was perfect. He spoke in perfect non-sequiturs and his thoughts on films, clothes, books, babies and ice cream were perfect. He had even lived in LA for a while and liked ballet – watching it, that is. TK became the fourteen-year-old ballet student from Los Angeles again, shy, sweet, gorgeous and pliable. Dirty Boy instinctively became the actor who had broken her heart.

TK had finally met someone who could become whoever the situation required, just as she could – a djinn like herself. So when Dirty Boy kissed her – hard and messy – and took her hand, dragging her off growling, 'Come on doll face, we're out of here,' doll face followed, giggling.

Faces at eight on a Sunday morning are delicate affairs. Especially when they've had only three hours' sleep and a bad cup of tea. Mine felt particularly tender that cold morning as I fumbled in my coat pocket for a cigarette.

'Do you mind?' I gestured with my lighter, but I wasn't really asking. Zander the make-up artist lit a cigarette himself and smiled under his perfect cropped head. He was as gay as Christmas with a streak of mean steel under his tight sweater. I knew him from other jobs.

'You can do it at your age. It's when you get to mine that you really feel it.'

'I didn't drink.'

'It's the lack of sleep that kills you.'

I glanced at my face in the mirror. It was pale, but otherwise unscarred by my outing the night before. I thought I looked rather dramatic, wrapped in black wool, cigarette smoke rising to soften the bobbing of my loose white head.

'It's only Vaseline. You don't need anything else.'

That was Zander again, as he dipped and smeared the paraffin wax on my face. The cold of the studio was making it harder than usual and it pulled at my skin. My face underneath it felt hot and clammy.

I raised a hand and watched it shake gently like an Aspen leaf. My heart felt unsure and my head light as Zander pulled it this way and that on its delicate stem. I resolved to get more sleep next time.

'Who's coming today, Zander?'

Rhett, the photographer, slid in at that moment, wearing rock-star pants.

'Mornin' Justin,' he said.

Rhett was cool in the way that people who never give you – or the world in general – more than cursory attention are cool. He appeared entirely self-contained and never wore shoes over his socks, hence the sliding. He was a fan of the Rolling Stones and bore a fierce likeness to Ronnie Woods.

I knew how to play his game.

'Mornin' Brett.'

'It's Rhett, baby. Not Brett. Rhett.'

He didn't like that. Score: Justin 1, Rhett 0. I inhaled deeply and stubbed out my cigarette.

The other model, Rebecca, was five-feet-ten-and-a-half and pale as vanilla. Miko the stylist had dressed her in leather and heels – Teutonic über-babe – and she could barely walk the stilettos were so sharp. I smiled at her in the mirror, but she wasn't looking.

'Is that too tight?' Miko was crouching by her left ankle.

Rebecca shook her head. 'I can bear it,' I heard her reply, softly as a mouse.

Rhett saw her as she walked onto the set and whistled softly. Rebecca smiled and lifted her chin a little higher.

She was twelve years old.

Her mother watched from the sofa, hand-bag in her lap. She wouldn't take her coat off and sat like a woman waiting for answers in a doctor's surgery.

Either way, I thought, the prognosis wasn't going to be good.

I didn't want to talk about Rebecca – her age or lack of it – while she was there. I wanted to wait until I got home to TK, but Zander felt differently.

'It's the mother – pushing her into this, isn't it?' he said quietly, his mean streak flashing. 'I mean, fucking hell, she's twelve. Look at her. She's too terrified to move.'

I watched Rhett trying to coax some life into his model, moving her parts like Lego, and shook my head. 'It's too easy to blame the mum. Rebecca's probably wanted this ever since she was strong enough to hold a magazine.'

My emotions were mixed. I felt pity for Rebecca; I understood shy awkwardness so well, although I was better at hiding it now. I felt jealous of her height and her extreme youth – I wished I was younger, just by a year or two. I resolved to be very kind to Rebecca if I got a chance.

Zander wasn't finished. 'Who gives a flying fuck how old she is, if she's a good model. But she's stiff as a board.'

The polaroids were not coming out well and I could sense Rhett's frustration. He made Rebecca turn to face the backdrop and the strobe fired off at the back of her head. I felt the girl's shame all the way to the make-up mirror, but tossed it off as quickly as I could. People were pack dogs and they could smell weakness in others. Zander especially.

Rebecca came over to have her vaseline re-applied. Miko held out a scrap of studded leather for me. I dressed there and then, having long ago abandoned my modesty in front of strange gay men. Miko pulled the buckles of my dress in tight and told me, as I sacrificed an inch of lung, that we all have to suffer for our art.

'Don't you agree, Zander?' Miko slid his arm around Zander's waist.

'Agree with what?'

'That we have to suffer for our art. You have to look good, or you're nothing.'

Zander dipped his fingers in Vaseline and wiped them on Rebecca's sweet face. He had an opinion on that, and most things. 'It's what's on the outside that counts – that's all anybody sees. Nobody's beautiful on the inside – we're full of blood and guts and snot and pus. I'd rather be gorgeous on the outside and a perfect bitch on the inside.'

I saw Rebecca open her eyes and look up into Zander's. He smiled. 'Beautiful people get away with murder.'

In the fashion world, Zander made perfect sense. That's how people survived and that was what Rebecca was learning today. I pictured them all filled with oozing black pus and sores, honey-glazed venom spewing from their mouths like fountains of poisonous sweet and sour pork.

'Honey? Justin, baby? We're ready for you.' Rhett was changing the roll of film and didn't look up as I walked on set.

Rhett 1, Justin 1. Even stevens, I conceded.

We were shooting an ad for German Gillette. The slogan was unintelligible but it had something to do with smooth steel and sharp edges being desirable.

Rhett wanted to add ambient smoke to the pictures. 'Can we get a cigarette, please?'

Zander offered one of his and Rhett brought it to me in his stockinged feet. I parted my lips slightly and kept my hands on my hips. Rhett hesitated an instant, then placed the butt carefully between my lips. He wouldn't meet my eyes but I stared into his as he brought out a box of matches and struck one. This time he met my gaze, fumbled with the match and dropped it.

Justin 2, Rhett 1.

By the end of the day, Rebecca had been advised to get some more experience and sent home with her mother, Miko was crying because Zander was being mean to him, Rhett had a splinter in his foot and the score was Justin 31, Rhett 25.

I was proud of my victory over such a worthy opponent. The fact that it was Rhett's studio gave him an advantage but I awarded him an extra five points for the aplomb with which he handled Rebecca, her mother, Zander, Miko and the German art director who popped in at intervals to remind us we were running over-budget and out of time. That made us almost even.

Grow Up!

TK reacted with a satisfying degree of outrage when I told her about Rebecca. This wasn't playing fair at all.

'I felt so old next to her,' I complained.

'And you're not seventeen yet. That's ridiculous.'

'Still.'

'And her mum was there? That's something I suppose.'

'Bit embarrassing though.'

'Do you think it's the money? Maybe they need the money … maybe that's why she's starting so young.'

'Partly – but I think she's chasing the glamour. Aren't we all?'

TK scratched her skinny wrist and slouched further into her seat. Her torn black T-shirt had a Budweiser logo on it. It didn't go with her pink floral skirt, but that was the whole idea.

'Sure, we all want to be stars I guess, if it comes to that, but hey, I'm just doing it to get away from LA. Modelling is the easiest way to live in a foreign country and make money. The Agency finds you a place to stay, they get you a visa, they hook you up – it's better than backpacking and there's always the chance you'll make a lot of money.'

'I do okay.'

'Yeah. But you get a lot of advertising jobs. I get editorial that doesn't pay. I'm so broke. The Agency have to keep forwarding me money. But I only want to do cool stuff anyway – I'd hate to be like Lara and just do catalogue every day.'

'I bet she's making loads of money,' I said.

'But it's got to be so depressing! Doing shit clothes and shit make-up and the same shit poses every single day. There's no creativity there. So boring.'

'It's pretty boring anyway. At least you'd know why you were doing it, if there was a big cheque at the end of every day. Lots of stability – like a proper job.'

TK nodded. 'That's the way Lara sees modelling. Some girls look at it like a serious job that you do like any other. They are always perfectly groomed, on time and smile a lot. They go to all their castings, do all the catalogue jobs and get paid lots of money. They are never cool and they will probably never be superstars – but they will have a long, steady career earning very good money.'

'I don't think I would want a long career doing this. I would rather be a star for a short time – make a bunch of money doing cool jobs then retire.'

'That's what everyone wants. I wish I was Kate Moss.'

'She's cool.'

'I'm going to start doing make-up, or styling. I'd like to be a stylist. I mean, I have to lie about my age already.'

'How old do you say you are?'

'The Agency told me to say nineteen, but I say twenty. Two years isn't such a big jump.'

I felt strangely cheated. Here was TK claiming youth she no longer possessed. And in a world where extreme youth is a precious commodity, I almost felt like she was stealing some of mine.

We agreed that we should probably start trying to think about a future outside modelling. My notebook had lain bereft of compliments lately. Soon we really would be too old.

'Hobbies. And maybe an education.' TK herded peas on her plate with a spoon. 'That's what we need.'

Although she ate almost everything except meat, TK liked to play with her food. The slower you ate, the less appetite you had. The less you put in your mouth, the skinnier you remained. Something like that.

'What would your hobby be?' TK asked me.

A hobby was something people in learn-to-speak-French books were always going on about. My peas slipped off my plate and rolled off the table. 'I like drawing.'

TK nodded sharply.

'And painting,' I added, hoping to provoke another nod. Her approval somehow helped me hope that I could one day be good for something other than hanging on the periphery of the fashion world, that I could move out of modelling suburbia.

'So do I. And I have my make-up thing.'

'What happened to ballet?'

'He's getting back with his girlfriend.'

'Who?'

'Dirty Boy.'

'Since when?'

'He was kind enough to tell me the morning after that dinner. Remember? When we went to the club.'

'I know. I remember. You were in the corner.'

'I never slept with him. But he was so perfect. We lay together all night, snuggling. He wanted to, but I told him I was waiting till I got married, and he was cool with that.'

'So?'

'We had ice cream for breakfast, just like I used to with my boyfriend in LA. Then he said he probably wouldn't call me for a few days because he was trying to get back with his childhood sweetheart. So I barred him.'

'Good you didn't sleep with him, then.' I didn't look at her because her voice had gone funny and I knew TK's pride would suffer if I caught a glimpse of tears or anger.

'I know.' TK lit a cigarette. 'We should start taking classes and going to museums.'

'Okay.'

I wanted to help TK change the subject but it sounded suspiciously like school to me, those excursions that invariably fell on rainy days. You'd pile into the bus with wet raincoats and a packed lunch. The museum floors would be slippery from the wet shoes and your sandwich would get squished under heavy text-books, sadly unrecognisable as the lovingly prepared cheese-and-ham-on-brown-bread-with-the-crusts-cut-off it had started out as. Things smelt bad and your feet got tired.

I wasn't anxious to relive those days. But then again, if it would give my life meaning, distinguish me from the twelve-year-old models snapping at my heels, then that is what I would do.

9

Play Nice, There's a Good Girl

It was my seventeenth birthday and TK made a plan to take us to the National Gallery. The exhibition 'Botticelli: Images of Love and Spring' had been hung the week before and it sounded girlie enough to visit without feeling like we were taking this art interest too seriously.

Sure enough, it was a wet day and our shoes squeaked on the marble floors. There were raincoats and umbrellas dripping on stands in corners and uniformed guards checking bags for bombs. TK made cheese and lettuce sandwiches and brought a pink cup cake with a candle that we were not allowed to light inside the gallery. We sat in front of *La Primavera* because it was huge and beautiful and the figures in it almost life-size. TK had her sketch book out and was beginning on Beauty, the middle Grace.

'So, which one's Chastity?'

'I think the one on the left – I like Beauty's hair. It's good to draw.'

'Jeb's going to call his daughter Chastity – if he ever has one.'

'I think he's joking, Justin.'

'If they stepped out of the painting, they'd be weird-looking, wouldn't they?'

'The Graces? Yeah, I suppose.'

'I mean, they're beautiful in a waxy way, and in context, but the Agency would never take them on.'

'I know. Isn't that awful? They'd tell Chastity to lose weight first of all.'

'Lovely hands, great hair, but her upper arms are the size of your thighs.'

'And they'd probably send her to the sun bed a few times.'

'Beauty would be put on a diet and told to smile more – and they'd send her to the hairdresser for a more "modern" style.' I was still slightly bitter about my forced image change.

'What about Love?' TK asked.

'She looks too old . . .'

TK read from the exhibition catalogue: '"Womanly beauty was not understood as a self-justifying quality that merely existed of physical charms; on the contrary, it was seen as the direct consequence of virtue, a connection between external beauty and important inner values." There you go – that's what this Dr Zollner says.'

'Their world does look kinder than ours, doesn't it? It must have been quite nice to live in a time when innocence was prized, not despised.' I said this quietly in case it provoked TK to probe into exactly what sort of innocence I had in mind. I still squirmed whenever anyone talked about sex. TK still didn't know (hadn't asked, thank goodness) that I'd never had a boyfriend. 'Sometimes I think it would be quite nice to have an arranged marriage – don't you?'

'It would take a lot of the hassles away, but you'd have to trust your parents to pick well.'

'I'm not sure mine would. My mum would choose an uptight Frenchman who believed in his 'n' hers manicures and lemon-yellow skivvies. Dad would forget who he'd chosen.'

'I *know* mine wouldn't pick a good one. I'd be married off to some weird guy who knits and studies black holes and has a log cabin in Maine.'

'Can you imagine if we suddenly landed in the Renaissance world?' I was captivated by this idea.

'They'd find us hideous,' TK declared, quite delighted at the thought.

I had another idea: 'Can we count all the stuff we do for those "arty" creative magazines as "art"?'

'It depends whether you think art imitates life or the other way around.'

'We models are in big trouble if life copies art. Any real world created around the magazine shoots I do will be pornographic – and hard and cold and dirty and grey and just pretty crap. It's not a world I want to live in. Maybe we should go on strike, for the good of human kind.'

'And who said models couldn't change the world!' TK the sarcastic revolutionary.

'I don't think anybody's ever bothered to think that we could –'

'I don't want to try and talk about art anymore.'

'Right. What could be worse than two models trying to discuss a painting they know nothing about with words they don't understand. I kind of love the cringe-factor.'

'At least no one can hear us. We just have to pretend this never happened.'

'The model's dirty, shameful desire for knowledge. Okay.'

'Anyway, I bet guys were the same back then. Born hunters who love the chase, the women all playing at Mysterious Flower.'

'Sounds like an erotic card game.'

'Playing hard-to-get drives men mad. I bet the women in that painting were masters at it.'

'What do you mean?' I asked.

'You probably do it instinctively, it's female nature. We know men need to feel that we are a prize they have won, or they won't treasure us. And so it's up to us to make them feel that way.'

'Don't men just think you're being weird, or mean?'

'Maybe, but they love it. Most of the time they don't notice, they only notice their growing desire. You just have to be clever about it – you're never mean, just unavailable. Or very busy, or intensely interested in everything but them.'

'I've never done that. I don't play games.'

'Yes, but how many relationships have you had?'

I blushed and shifted my eyes to another painting. They lit on a nude Mars. I shifted back to Chastity in the spring.

'Look,' TK went on, 'I've seen so much heartache around me – so many girls desperate because they've been abandoned by men who obsessed over them. And they always lose their man because they cling and cry. I've never lost a man.'

'What about that actor?'

'I could have had him back, you know. After he had made me miserable, I went away and he started calling me again. But I couldn't go back, or wouldn't. I don't know which.'

'I think you have to always be witty and charming and make an effort to look nice, but I don't think pretending not to like them will work – or should work.'

'The heart lies,' TK concluded dramatically.

'No.' I didn't want to believe that. 'It can't lie – it can't even talk. The heart is like a cat.'

A school group passed between TK, me and the painting, distracting us. The kids were about my age – uniformed, noisy – and I watched them as TK buried her head in her sketch book.

'I'll leave you to draw, TK. I'm going for a wander.'

I followed the school group at a distance, then hid behind a pillar to watch more closely. Taber John popped into my head as I watched one of the boys chewing his pencil. I felt a strange smile creep up inside me, followed by that same weird longing I used to feel in the playground – the longing to belong.

My eyes scanned the group and stopped on a couple slightly to the side, obviously the king and queen of the year. He had dark, curling hair, left a little longer in the back. The collar of his blazer was turned up in a rakish way that no one else could have pulled off and he grinned broadly. Yet he was so attentive of his queen. That's why I was mesmerised. He kissed her hand, and kept his arm around her waist.

His queen was blonde – natural blonde – her skin pale, deep blue eyes lined with heavy black lashes. Her profile seemed cut in white marble, so smooth and sure. She had a school scarf bundled around her neck, blue, black and yellow. It forced her long hair up around her face, enhancing her fragile youth and beauty, contrasting with the severe grey and blue of her school jumper and skirt. I knew that seeing her in plain clothes – ill-fitting jeans and a large red T-shirt, say – would ruin the effect.

The girl was well shaped – not skinny – the perfect, ordinary shape of a slim teen. I wondered if I had looked like this girl when I had been at school. Our uniforms were similar, but I had never had a boy to adore me as she did.

I longed to be them so hard my heart almost broke itself.

The girl pushed her king off playfully, then ignored him, then acted coy, snuggling up to his neck as if for protection. The boy was smitten. Their friends – none as handsome or pretty – stood around watching, acting disinterested, but I could tell they were rapt. Beauty and confidence are magnetic. Coupled with a mild contempt for the world, they are riveting. I realised the queen was subconsciously playing the mysterious flower game TK had just described. Maybe she was right . . .

Had I become some crazy teen pervert, shadowing school kids

through public spaces? I could feel the girl's joy. I smiled when she did, and gazed adoringly at the boy through her eyes. I half-listened to the teacher's lecture, took her reprimands to include me and stood up straight, not talking, not touching the paintings.

When the group moved off to other paintings, I began following them down the hall. The queen suddenly spun and caught sight of me. I suppose I half-expected her to recognise me, send me a warm smile perhaps ... Was I not one of them too? I had talked out of turn and giggled as well ... Yet the girl's eyes, when they meet mine, were a stone wall. The blue was no longer warm; it was icy cold, hard and blank. My stare bounced right off hers and I turned away, stung.

I stood by the basins in the ladies room, looking at myself in the floor-to-ceiling mirror the gallery had kindly provided, trying to figure out how other people saw me. I did not look the way I felt. I looked skinny-scrawny in my dark blue jeans, my trainers almost comically big, wet and scuffed on the end of my legs. My white blonde hair was a tangled mess, matted with old hairspray in a crazy rock-bitch style, and my punk-bands poked their studded faces out in childish rebellion. My heavy sweatshirt dwarfed my already small features.

Punky Barbie – she's such a hit!
All she does is smoke and spit!
Get into Barbie – Punky Barbie!!

I heard the Mattel toy jingle loud and clear in my head. I'd seen Barbie at a supermarket the other day. I had picked up the box and read about her:

Dream Girl.
Rooted hair, vinyl head, arms and legs, twisting waist, poseable and bendable legs. Bonus fashion outfit. Eleven inches tall.

My eyes were as hard as those of the queen. Even I didn't want myself.

'Hello.'

A plump woman in a raincoat was smiling at me, standing too close, staring hard.

'Have you ever thought about becoming a model?'

I stared at her in disbelief.

'I'm a booker at Faces.' She handed me a card. 'I think you have lots of –'

'Leave me *alone!*' I was suddenly very angry at Erica Webb.

The woman's smile ran from her face like sand. I dropped her card and it fell on to the floor, where I carefully stepped on it on my way past her.

'What happened?' TK looked up from her sketching, 'You look funny.'

'I know. I didn't realise I look the way I do. I'm not normal anymore.'

'You're okay.'

'No. I was watching school kids over there and I saw what I am supposed to be like. I realised that's supposed to be me with them, over there, but I can never be that way. They won't take me back. I'm like a newborn puppy touched by human hands. The mother dog rejects it.'

'Now you're not being normal. Let's go get a cup of tea'.

Dear Taber,

I can't think if 'John' is your last name or not. I don't think I ever asked you at the bus stop. I thought of you the other day because I saw these teenagers on a school excursion. If we had gone out together maybe we would be like them now. Do you think we would have gone out if I hadn't left? Or maybe we might have kissed? It's just a speculation. But now there is no going back, I am not trying to go out with you. (I know you know that and anyway I am so far away and you probably wouldn't want to anyway.)

Even though I have just turned seventeen I am not a teenager. Are you, do you think? Do you know what I mean by this? Sometimes I miss wearing my uniform, which is probably crazy because I hated it then but now I almost want it back. You will be finished school quite soon, I think. Will you play music when you leave? Could it be your career? I have been wondering about my career but modelling is fine for now. Anyway, once you are in it it's not like you can just leave. It's not like waitressing or other ways to make money when you are a teenager because it is a Life. It changes everything and it feels irreversible. I feel removed from everybody who is not in fashion.

What I need to do is just model and not think about other stuff – just be like a model and work and party because it is too late to change anyway. And you shouldn't have regrets. Plus it is all very fun. I am going to Paris for the shows which I have never done so wish me luck because it'll be scary. Also did I ever tell you I ate a note about you once?

Big kiss
J. (Justin) X

Respect Your Elders

Le Carrousel du Louvre, Gaultier show, Paris, 7 a.m.

Although it was only seven in the morning we were already drinking champagne out of quarter bottles with straws so we wouldn't ruin our lipstick. I was so jumpy I had run to the bathroom three times since six. The make-up artist, Eugene, kept looking up from painting Kirsty Hume's lips and giving me knowing glances, intimating he'd like to share in my bounty. I let him believe that. I'd rather he thought I was a fellow druggy than let him know it was my first-ever show.

Le Carrousel buzzed like an aviary full of beautiful birds. But instead of birds there were girls in different stages of make-up, some completely naked, some glamorously dressed, others still in their day jeans (with stiletto boots). They stood or squatted cross-legged on the floor – smoking, drinking, chatting in French, English and Spanish into phones, to each other, to hair and make-up artists, and to little dogs they had brought along.

I quailed. They were sure to smell me, see me, stop me. Tell me there had been a grotesque mistake, laugh, turn away.

Eugene ran up to me. 'Justin!' Quick. I'm ready for you now.'

They all knew my name, were acting like I was meant to be there, handed me champagne. The bubbles made me feel better and I decided to drink some more.

I was plastered when I went out on the catwalk, thank goodness. My nipples were hanging out of my flesh-coloured, see-thru slip. I wore a tiny black G-string underneath. My heels were gold and I had rhinestones glued to my face.

The music pounded like surf, so loud I could feel it. I let myself be carried on it – out from backstage, onto the stage, into the flashbulb assault, along the runway. I floated helplessly in the foaming waves down, twirl, twice, and back.

Backstage I was stripped bare by two women dressers.

Put that on. Take that off. Hurry, hurry, hurry. Don't touch that. Get it off. Put it on.

All clawing at me. I was laughing in a high-pitched way – I could hear it outside my head. No one had time to calm me down. Eugene powdered my face from a compact and held a line of cocaine up to my nose on the mirror. I inhaled and ran to find my place in the line-up. My heels were so high I staggered up the stairs.

The dresser grabbed me: 'For Christ's sake get a grip.'

I could barely hear her over the music. Her hand accidentally tore my halter top right off as I turned away. She screamed in horror but I was gone, hustled out by the man with the ear piece. Suddenly I was on the catwalk again. The flash bulbs went and this time they were for me, for my totally bare breasts.

Keep it together you fool. Do not fall: step, step, do not trip, step, step, do not fall, step, watch out for the girl in front, she's that scary German model, step, stop, beat, turn. 'You're falling from grace . . .'

The words of the soundtrack made me laugh.

'. . . *falling* . . .'

Place one foot carefully after the other, allow hips to swing in a delayed, exaggerated sway. Stare straight ahead, grin like a jack-o-lantern.

I was scarcely aware I was missing my top and so was the crowd. They found the leather shorts, leather braces, bare chest and big smile fabulous – 'just divinity' one fashion journalist was later heard to gush.

Stop. Hustled straight off, then straight back on for the finale. Jean Paul Gaultier came out waving, his close-cropped hair newly whitened, his big blue eyes smiling. I happened to be closest to him, so he took my hand and we bowed to applause and flashbulbs.

'*Can't you see, you're falling from grace.*' The words echoed in my empty head.

Backstage there were television cameras trying to capture the Glamorous World of Fashion through a blue haze of cigarette smoke. The place was even more crowded – now with boyfriends, well-wishers, leeches, reporters and fabulous nobodies ogling famous bodies. I felt I might drown.

Hands grabbed and stripped me of my last scraps of Gaultier. Naked, I found my bag and shook out my crumpled jeans, my red boots, my off-the-shoulder jumper in white. My hand was trembling as I lit a cigarette and took another quarter bottle of champagne. The other girls were changing into street clothes as well. My eye caught a jagged honey blonde leaning against a wall, talking to an androgynous girl in army fatigues embroidered with dragons. I recognised that lean body, that casually-flicked cigarette, the way the hip-bone jutted out over the waistband of her faded jeans. It was Maggie, the model mum who had delivered the resounding slap and made me want to take up smoking at the lingerie job in Japan.

I watched her for a minute and saw she hadn't changed much. Perhaps she was slicker, her shoes cooler, more expensive. I knew she had met with massive success, had seen her face staring out of every

Prada campaign and lots of DKNY ads. But I hadn't counted on running into her again, and very much doubted she would remember me. She wandered past with dragon-girl and I smiled, very shy, and looked away. Maggie stopped.

'Japan – wasn't it? But your hair . . .'

'I know. This was an accident . . .'

'Are you doing Chloë?'

'Just Gaultier. And some small designers out . . .'

'I would have thought they'd want you for Chloë.'

I took an Embassy from her crumpled packet she offered. It felt cool to smoke with her.

'Are you in Paris?' she asked.

'London actually. You?'

'New York, baby.'

'How is the baby – yours?'

'Not really a baby any more but I broke up with Mike so . . . but Roman is great with him.'

I remembered reading about this change of boyfriends in a story accompanied by grainy colour photos shot with a telephoto lens.

'I don't remember your name?'

'Justin. It's changed.'

'Okay. Bye Justin.'

And she was off to her next show. Two other girls, with a minor fragrance campaign, four *Vogue* editorials (one French, two British, one American) and a tycoon boyfriend between them, were waiting for her. All were toting large leather shoulder bags (fringed and studded) and I desperately wanted one. I also wanted two friends who would wait for me. Models always move in packs because they look scarier and taller that way, and you can pass the time in conversation, comparing notes on who is working for whom and where and how often. I stared after them and once again wished I was Maggie.

'What did you think of Gaultier's show? Would you ever consider implants? What's your name?'

A small and very perky American brunette with large breasts and bottom was beaming at me with perfect teeth. She waved a dildo in front of my face. 'Speak into the microphone – it's so loud back here. Are you getting this Dave?'

The cameraman moved closer, now about two feet from my face.

'I love your make-up, so dramatic. Did it take forever to do your hair like that?'

My hair was still carefully rolled in a forties-style wave. I could only shrug. I felt my eyes roll around in my head.

'This is Justin. Watch her closely. She is the Agency's new star.' Margutte had materialised from nowhere. Bookers always say that to journalists about any model, hoping it will become a self-fulfilling prophecy – if you throw enough dung on the wall, some will stick. The media have the power to make the superstars.

Margutte put a constricting arm on my shoulders and I thought I might collapse under its weight. He swept me away with a fixed smile.

Repeat After Me

Margutte had picked me up at the airport and driven me straight to my first fitting in the centre of Paris. As usual I didn't really know if Margutte was his first or last name. He was the head booker at the Paris branch of the Agency, and he had a mouth like a fish and blue eyes so pale they were almost white. He wore his leather trench-coat tightly belted and reminded me of a Russian baddie in a film. But he spoke English and I was only going to be in France for three days.

I was nervous at the fitting but tried to tell myself that Gaultier had already booked me for the show, so I didn't need to be. The orgasm photo in my book had clinched the job, according to Margutte. I prayed they wouldn't change their minds, that I was thin enough for the clothes and that they wouldn't see I wasn't sexy. Gaultier himself popped past once (short white hair, very large blue eyes), approved the design, smiled at me and was gone. The rest of the work was done by stern, dry seamstresses who spoke only French and wore only black. They terrified me: four clustered at my feet, kneeling steely-mouthed, pinning the hem of a massive (short) hoop skirt in black. They fussed silently around me like precocious children playing dress-up with an oversize doll.

Each 'look' (there were four) was recorded on Polaroids by a photographer, immortalising my scarecrow nerves and hungry rigidity.

Then I was whisked to two fittings for minor labels. They were watered-down versions of the first experience. After that, exhausted, starving and too nervous to ask for food, I was looking forward to a bed.

Margutte had waited for me, chatting. Now he drove me home.

We passed through high, wrought-iron gates and stopped at a gorgeous white house with baby orange trees by the door and a welcoming light.

'These are the model apartments,' he said in his heavy French accent. He bustled me inside, carrying my crumpled shoulder bag. The foyer was deserted, cool black-and-white marble. We climbed an elegant spiral staircase.

'Damn sight better than our London flat,' I thought enviously.

'This is Gerard's mother's house,' Margutte explained.

'Oh. Who's Gerard?' I thought I owed Margutte at least polite conversation.

'The owner of the Paris Agency.' He opened a white door on the first floor. It was close to ten and I was exhausted. We walked into a large room filled with bunk beds – eight in all, sixteen beds. All were full of young girls in their pyjamas. Margutte walked among the bunks and girls bent or stood to kiss him hello. I stared in disbelief. It was like walking into a greenhouse filled with warm, tender saplings quivering with breath. Or a supermarket filled with nubile girls, the colours seemed all pale-pink and blue. My black outfit felt crumpled and heavy. I was Gargamel in the land of the Smurfs and about as happy. Margutte gave me the address for the next day's show and bade me goodnight.

I got top bunk.

Underneath me a tall girl from Holland sat weeping. I really couldn't be bothered, but I tried anyway. Swinging my head down to look, I saw she wore pink pyjamas with a panda sewn on the top. My nightie was torn and covered with small red hearts. 'Hi.'

Her face was red, and her eyes were huge. So were her bare feet. I waited for her to speak but she just stared at me.

'I like your panda.'

She looked at it and started crying all over again. I pulled myself back up to my bed. Too much effort. A little later her head appeared level with mine. She was taller than I had thought.

'I am terribly homesick.'

The lights went out.

Panda bent closer to me. 'I miss my mother in Amsterdam. I arrived on the train on Wednesday afternoon.'

'You've only been here three days.'

'I'm so homesick and I do not speak French. Everyone is so hard and angry here. I'm frightened.'

I didn't feel much sympathy for her. I couldn't understand why she was crying. 'How old are you?'

'Nineteen,' she gulped. 'You?'

'Seventeen. My home's Australia. At least you can go back and visit your mum whenever you want. How long is it by train?'

'Four hours.'

I tried to keep my scorn to myself. 'Margutte seems nice, a bit thuggish, but okay. He bought me a hot chocolate on the auto route.'

I could hear her tears beginning again.

'He told me I have to lose weight. Everyone heard him.'

Now she had my ears and my heart. 'How much?'

'Five kilos at least. I can eat only apples.'

'Apples?'

'Nothing else. Apples for breakfast, lunch and dinner. Every day.'

Now I felt sorry for her. The nightmare of being scolded for your fat in front of skinny people.

'I'm going crazy – apples, apples, apples!'

'Well, he can't watch you while you go on castings can he?'

'He won't let me go on castings. He won't let me go anywhere. He keeps me here, with Gerard's mum, watching, watching me always. I can't leave the house. He comes to weigh me every day – twice.'

'How much have you lost?'

'One and a half kilo.'

'Shit. That's another two weeks in here.'

She began snuffling again.

'What's your name?'

'Anca.'

I looked at her. She would be pretty when her face calmed down – large features, slightly cow-like expression, but her height would make her desirable on the catwalk.

'Well, I'm going to sleep. I've got a show at six. It's Gaultier. The other two will be a breeze compared to that one.'

'You have nothing to worry about!' Her voice was loud and bitter. 'You are skinny – Jean Paul Gaultier takes you. You are *thin*.'

'Shut up!' came the cries from the other beds. Then 'you shut up' in five languages. I retreated to my pillow.

The other shows were tamer and smaller than Gaultier, with not as many people and no champagne. The rooms were stiflingly hot from smoke, hairdryers and hairspray. At Samurai Soyama I was dressed in bubblewrap and almost sweated to death. Then there was a focus on Renaissance sleeves for Nicolas Bernardesque, a show staged in a disused metro tunnel. Margutte was in the wings of them all, watching me. When I finished the last one, it was eight p.m. and my head felt like it might float off on its own like a little red balloon . . .

It came back to me on a velvet sofa somewhere above the Champs Elysées. I was watching a game show on television. Margutte was in a pretty kitchen talking to a man named Hervé, who was tall, tanned, blond and doing something with ice cubes. They spoke in French.

Alex, another booker, sat beside me. He was younger than the others, around twenty-four. He reminded me of Peter Andre.

Hervé brought our kirs on a tray and a vodka for himself. Only Hervé waving the tray in my direction told me I wasn't invisible. Alex flicked the channel to MTV fashion, and stared at the screen. The American reporter came onto the screen, followed by a huge close-up of my face, staring blankly at her. I gasped.

On-screen Justin rolled her eyes and blew her cheeks out with boredom and the men in the room above the Champs roared with laughter. I smiled. The girl on screen could not have been me. She was a real model, glamorous, cool, confident, savage. I would have been scared of her if I'd seen her at a shoot. It had taken the distortion of television to make me feel like a star. They cut to me topless on the catwalk for a second, then to Gaultier. I lost interest. Not so my companions. It was as if the glass eye of the television had given all the blind men in the room sight, and they began to talk to me.

'Bébé! You could be a supermodel. Look at that face.' Alex took my cold fingers in his. 'You must move to Paris immediately. We can make you a huge star.'

Hervé stared down at me with cold eyes. 'My family own Cartier.'

I looked back at the TV. A dog food commercial was airing: *'Bono, c'est bon'*. It seemed to unlock my first French words: 'J'ai faim.'

We'd been driving for what seemed like hours in Hervé's black Range Rover through the streets of Paris, stopping to pick up this and that person. Parking in a deserted road, we all climbed out. Hervé made for a blue door.

Entering, it was as if we had stepped into a Thai rainforest. The air was warm, moist and full of the sound of strange birds. Trees and ferns and flowers of every tropical kind flourished. A small man in Thai dress greeted us and we followed him to our table.

The restaurant was on different levels, with rocky outcrops flattening into natural verandahs, each with room for eight people and a table. The other diners were partially hidden by the foliage. A waterfall fell from fifty feet and a stream flowed by our table, carrying with it the odd flower. Margutte, Alex and Hervé were with me. Already seated at our table was a roundly pink young man with beautiful hands who I recognised as another one of the the Agency bookers. He was deep in conversation with a stoned-looking brunette. I had seen her lying on Hervé's billiard table earlier that evening but hadn't really noticed her properly.

She now revealed herself to be American and very thin. She ordered mountains of food but ate nothing. Well, to be fair, I saw her eat one small shrimp. She ordered a blue drink in a tall glass. The other three were explaining why I should move to Paris for my career.

'On dit que la perfection n'existe pas ... Mais ça s'en rapproche.'

'Did you understand that?'

'Hervé is telling you – they say perfection does not exist, but this comes close indeed.'

Out of the corner of my eye, I saw the American girl gulping down another blue drink, still talking.

'Your mother must have been a thief.'

'Huh?' Hervé made no more sense in English than he did in French.

'She stole the king's diamonds and put them in your eyes'.

'You will hear these things every day in Paris.'

Hervé said: 'Look at her – she doesn't understand.'

Why was I always 'her'? Had I lost my name again?

'Explain to her the Rough Diamond theory.'

'What Hervé is talking about is my theory on how to make girls,' Margutte began to explain.

I began to listen. I needed all the help I could get.

'American, English – all the agencies like to send their girls to Paris, even Milan if they have to. When in Paris, these girls go out to dinner and meet European men. The men here are still chauvinistic, they can make a girl aware that she is a woman. She feels beautiful and powerful, yet wholly dominated and very female. She feels attractive and strong, yet soft and delicate. She gets used to being watched all the time, gets used to the attention, she begins to acquire the polish and shine necessary to be a star. This is the charm of European men.'

I turned away before one of them could start polishing my diamond and forced myself to break into the other conversation.

'Hi.'

The booker smiled and said, 'I've seen you in the Agency. You are?'

'Justin.'

'I see. I am Olivier. This is Amy.'

The skinny American model stared right through me. I tore at my napkin as she took another gulp of her blue drink.

'Are you enjoying Paris?'

I blushed, grateful for Olivier's mercy.

'It's been quite a ride. I had the weirdest adventure today. I was looking for the show tent for Gaultier –'

'You did Gaultier?' The girl was suddenly alive again. I ignored her back. 'And they told me it was in a grand building by the Louvre. So I walked in through these double doors and headed for reception. There's this guy with a Hitler moustache sitting behind this massive ornate desk. He stands when I walk in and I think, how nice, they're expecting me. Anyway, I'm asking for Gaultier and he keeps shaking his head. He has this sort of Russian accent –'

Amy sank her fourth blue drink and started giggling. Her voice became high-pitched and strange and she seized my story, finishing it for me. 'And then he told me that this was the Estonian Embassy and that there was no Gaultier anywhere. Can you believe it?'

Amy screeched with laughter, and the booker giggled.

'And to top it all off,' she hooted, 'my top fell off backstage and I had to go onto the catwalk almost naked. The press loved it, though. They interviewed me for TV afterwards – you know, the perky American with the big tits and ass? She was asking me all these questions and waving a microphone that looked like a dildo in my face the whole time.'

They were both hysterical, Amy's thin glamorous arms draped over the booker as she finished her tale. He was enjoying her beauty and attention, her funny story. Somehow this girl had taken the place that was supposed to be mine. I should have been the one making Olivier laugh. She had stolen my stories – or was she me? That wasn't possible. Was I crazy?

The Agency had taken my name, L'Oreal had switched my look, and now Amy had stolen my stories. How long would it be until I had nothing left for anyone to take?

I played with my pad thai, not wanting to eat if Amy didn't. Hunger was weakness and immortals did not need to eat.

The other end of the table was still deep in French conversation. I looked back. Amy had disappeared.

The booker was calling out to Margutte, something about the cover of American *Vogue* and Naomi Campbell's new dog. I saw that Amy had fallen off her chair and was lying face down in the stream beside our table.

'Hey!' I waved my hand. 'Margutte!'

'Bébé, what is it? Don't shout.'

I pointed. Everyone looked at Amy in the stream, then kept talking.

'For god's sake. She's going to drown!'

The other diners were beginning to peer through the foliage. The booker reached down, grabbed Amy's bony shoulders and swung her back into her chair (she was not heavy). I saw she was breathing. Margutte and the booker continued their conversation. Amy opened her eyes and stared at me, head dripping wet.

'What is that?' I said at last, pointing at her drink.

Amy turned to the waitress hovering behind her. 'I'll have another blue elephant,' she said. 'I have an option for the cover of American *Vogue*, you know.'

Margutte was very pleased that French *Vogue* liked my face.

The editors had spotted me at Gaultier and squeezed in a small shoot before I had to return to London. He drove me himself, at seven in the morning, through the beautiful dawn-pink streets of Paris. I worked hard to keep my heavy eyelids from closing – I had only lain in my bunk for three hours, oblivious to Anca's sniffling and the muted mobile conversations going on under the covers in different languages.

Margutte was coaching me. 'Don't forget to smile, bébé, always. And be nice. Don't sit on the floor with your comic books – a little tête de mort, a little "head of death". Nobody likes that, and they must love you. This is a *very big chance*.'

My thoughts drifted off and landed in the branches of a passing chestnut tree.

Wouldn't you like someone to love you? Of course you would, but you think you might be incapable of loving, incapable of receiving love because you are so knotted up inside. But maybe the fashion world could embrace you as you have seen it do others. Perhaps you could become a fashion star and people would have to love you. They could become your family and call you 'chérie'. You could have a small flat on the left bank, one in New York, a tiny poodle and a large leather bag.

You know all the sycophancy is just pretend love, but the fashion-pack are so good at pretending that there's hardly a difference between the illusion and the real thing. Why shouldn't you believe the hype? As long as the cameras are trained your way, their attention will be too. Life is a dream you never wake up from. Nothing is solid, so does it matter that everything is a lie? Illusion is reality here, and reality only the image of itself. Do you think you could be satisfied with a life on the surface of things?

Yes, you do, don't you?

You want to be like Maggie and float around the bathtub of the world without touching the sides . . . Why don't you try it, become the image you project in pictures, become the girl you were on TV yesterday? They all liked you then. They all wanted to know you after that. Let go of thinking and feeling too much, let go of caring, let go of your self-consciousness, become the image, float through life and then you will be happy. Stop thinking, start smiling. Let go. Don't look back. French Vogue *will love you.*

'French *Vogue* will love you.'

Why did Margutte have to wear black leather gloves when he drove?

'And Jean-Luc is the best hairdresser in Paris – he will make you a star.'

'I hate hairdressers.'

Margutte glared at me with protruding Gallic eyes. 'Don't be difficult. Short hair will suit you. You have a beautiful neck.'

'He's cutting it all off?'

'Like a boy. But very soft.'

'But . . .' It was too early in the morning for my thoughts to rouse themselves. I could feel Margutte's gloves, cool and clingy like gorilla skin, closing around my neck. I remembered my resolution to Let Go. He swerved to avoid a milk truck. I shrugged.

'Whatever. Ça m'est égal.' People were always saying that and shrugging. I figured it set the right tone, whatever it meant.

The *Vogue* studios were enormous, beautiful, light-filled and warm.

Everyone wore black and most had greying hair. The fashion editor, Anne-Marie, swept in last of all, wearing a madly stylish pleated silk skirt, tiny, delicately pointed Marc Jacobs heels, a cashmere roll-neck, large pearls and a heavy lace shoulder caplet – all black. She was terribly thin and tall. The room spun to greet her; she waved a hand. 'Nous célébrons tous un enterrement quelconque.'

The crew looked at her nervously.

'C'est du Baudelaire.'

'Je connais bien, Madame.' Jean-Luc was smiling ingratiatingly. He kissed her on both cheeks.

'How were the New York shows, Anne-Marie?'

The stylist was trying to get in there now, coming up for her kisses. She too wore pearls, I noticed, as I stared in envy at the caplet.

'Les défilés de New York sont vraiment naïfs. Il faut que les stylistes, comme Racine, se mettent en scène au début, en disant: "Et alors j'en offre içi toutes mes excuses aux spectateurs intelligents."'

Laughter. They could have been speaking Jupiter for all I understood. But I let it go. It didn't matter to me what they were saying.

I stared at my face in the mirror and wished I were Anne-Marie, bon mots, pearls, ribs and all. She came over to inspect me.

'Jolie. Très jolie.'

They began to cut my hair and it settled like down on the black towels that covered me. I closed my eyes, feeling a failure of bravery coming on if I had to stare at myself any longer in the huge mirrors, a smooth blonde egg incubated by cawing black vulture-mothers. Eyes shut, I concentrated on the deep red photospots that fell like rain on the inside of my eyelids and for the millionth time sent myself elsewhere.

Short.

That was the predominant feature of my haircut to my newly opened eyes. A white blonde Fauntleroy, an upturned milk pudding.

I smiled automatically. Anne-Marie considered me in the mirror with her beady, black eyes. My indifference made it all easy and I wondered why I hadn't Let Go before.

'Jean-Luc, j'adore les cheveux. Patrice, moins de noir autour des yeux.'

Something about my hair, I think. Patrice hurried in with an eyeshadow brush to do her bidding.

Nobody asked me if I liked my new hair but they were all rapt and my hair hadn't been my own since L'Oreal anyway – why start worrying now? So I said very little and smiled very much. They called me 'charmante' and 'ravissante'.

André, the photographer, wanted Happy – I was laughing in most of the photos. It all came easily as I Let Go and brought the embroidered schoolgirl shirts and smocks to life as best I could. André had six assistants and had shot Helena Christensen the week before. I felt confident I was in the right hands.

There was wine at lunch in a bistro around the corner. There were also a few stares, but the staff were used to the fashion castaways tumbling in for lunch, and I felt protected by the *Vogue* editors and stylists who, like an army of grandparents, sheltered and terrified me at the same time.

I couldn't read the menu – the handwriting was awful and it was all in French. I pointed at 'boudin' when the waiter came. It rhymed with 'puddin' and I thought it auspicious (chocolate, vanilla, my haircut).

'Are you sure?' asked Jean-Luc.

I nodded. Of course I was.

'Le blanc, Justin. Le rouge, c'est mauvais pour les dents.' Anne-Marie pointed to her teeth, grimacing.

For a moment I thought she wanted to eat me for lunch.

Patrice leant over. 'Red wine will stain zee teeth.'

I poured white and drank a glassful in three swift swallows.

My food arrived. It was black. A huge, wobbling black sausage, with mash. I poked it with my fork. It trembled, then split open to reveal a dark red interior, like the inside of a cherry or a murderer's heart. Everyone was eating and I was starving. The mash was fine. I forked up the trembling dark mass next. It didn't taste too bad, didn't taste of much really. But the texture was horrid.

Jean-Luc raised his glass to me. 'I had no idea you would order blood sausage, ma puce.'

The puce hadn't either.

That night at Queen, the nightclub: the man hanging off the parachute nets in a kilt with a long plait had to be John Galliano. He lost his grip and dropped right on top of me, like a preying ape. An elbow caught me in the head and I tottered in my zebra stilettos, then went down. I didn't have the strength to get back up, just lay there on a velvet banquette and studied the footwear – delicate heels made of willow twigs and lambs' ears, calf-skin loafers in cochineal, motorcycle boots worn to bad-boy grey around the edges, knee boots in jelly-crystal green – stepping to the beat of conversation.

'Paris is Jazz'. Malcom McLaren's whispered ramblings about the sixties kept crawling into my mind. 'He wore black, she wore black – Jazz is Paris. And Paris is Jazz'.

The season of fashion shows always ends in Paris and there were parties everywhere. I had been to two that night already. Margutte dragged me along, tired and vague and I had completely lost track of who they were thrown by and for whom or what. Mind screeching with nervous static, I was able to focus only on details, fragments. Nothing was quite real, nor was it strange enough to be a dream.

Standing above me, a twig-girl with golden-brown skin, draped in a crimson dress slashed to the (pierced) belly-button, was gesticulating with two glasses of champagne in each hand, her wide mouth open. Her audience was a well-fed and fifty-ish man who smelt of Hermes orange-blossom water and gold. His variegated blue shirt-collar with white cuffs announced his field to be money, as did his deep tan. His smile was on her as the ice-cold contents of one of the champagne glasses landed on my head.

'That must bring luck', I thought, and touched my crown and dabbed damp fingers on my earlobes. Spilt champagne is always dabbed on earlobes – a superstition I could not remember picking up. I wondered if this counted as a baptism, and if it meant I could be re-named and accepted as the child of a more glamorous god.

I leant on an elbow – it was a miracle nobody stepped on me – and finished the last of my champagne, liking the idea of being reborn enormously. My body tingled with pins, needles and champagne bubbles. I had an uncontrollable urge to laugh as more champagne spilled out of Crimson's glass and onto me.

'Hey up there,' I called out, and tugged gently at the hem of her dress. Crimson and her audience looked down at me then continued talking.

'My name. Won't you give me a new name?'

Crimson stepped on my hand.

Wanting the attention of my new godmother I tugged harder at her dress.

A firm brown breast leapt out of her décolletage and lay quivering in silicone surprise. Both Crimson and Money looked at it before he took a waltz step forward, cupped the breast with a manicured hand and swept Crimson off, his mouth on hers.

Two hands gripped me under the arms and pulled me off the floor. Margutte was furious. 'Bébé! What the fuck are you doing like that?! What are you doing on the floor? That was Giancarlo Barbarelli – he practicalement owns Italian TV and you were lying on his feet like a dirty lapdog. Look at you!'

My arm hurt where he gripped me, but I couldn't help giggling. The tighter he gripped the more I giggled.

'Fucking hell. You're hurting me.'

'You are hurting yourself acting like this – and me. Act like a woman. Not a bébé. I want to see you smile and glide in the room.' He pinched my waist hard. 'At least there is no fat. At least that. I like your hair. But look.'

He clutched my cheeks and swung my face to the mirror.

The blue lights made me pale and accentuated the shadows of cheekbones too close under the skin. My eye make-up had smudged, leaving me with even darker circles under my eyes. Margutte's hands looked big and fleshy on my arm, like they might snap it with a twist. Champagne hair lay straggled and damp on my forehead, glowing white like a halo in the dark. My high-necked black dress merged into the background and left my head and limbs floating in the black room.

'You need to eat more.' He spun me so my shoulders were to the mirror. My dress was backless to the buttock cleft, my ribs showing as small blue shadows like the gentle markings of a zebra.

Matches your shoes, darling!

'Non. I like you toute faible. So fragile.' Margutte turned as Gerard from the Agency prowled past. 'Qu'est-ce que tu en penses, Gerard?'

Gerard stopped, tugged on my hair, stroked my cheek once, twice, lightly. 'I like her thin. But she needs to loose weight from her face.'

And he was gone.

'See?' I sneered. 'So chic to be wasted baby, don't you know?' and twisted my arm free.

Margutte grabbed the back of my head and pressed his mouth on mine, his groin into mine. It wasn't a kiss, it was a hot, wet suffocation. He jerked my head back by the hair and I yelped in pain.

'*Vogue* loves you and I will make love to you. But not yet.'

On my way to the bathroom I found an open bottle of champagne unguarded. I checked for floating cigarette butts (clear) and drank from the bottle as I walked. The basins were crowded with boys and girls doing drugs and their hair. I locked myself in a cubicle and sat on the lavatory lid. My temple was throbbing from Galliano's elbow, my arm from Margutte's love-grip. French, English and American voices crowded me from all sides. Paris was an intestine.

What would your blonde art gallery queen and her handsome king be doing now? Sleeping, perhaps, or sneaking soft kisses at the back of the bus. Doing homework? The planet Homework seems so distant doesn't it? You can just, with massive effort, remember red margins on blue-lined paper but absolutely nothing that you wrote on those pages.

'The brain is a muscle – it too can atrophy.'

I was no longer locked in the bathroom but perched on a red box marked 'en cas d'incendie, break glass'. I didn't remember moving but there I was, and I looked up to see who had spoken.

Tall man, dark eyes wilder than mine, but smiling. Olive cords, pale shirt, boat shoes.

'You're a civilian,' I said, surprised.

It was his turn to be confused.

'Never mind . . . what did you mean?' I asked.

He shook his head. 'It's the only possible explanation for the way so many people here behave. Their brains have dwindled to the size of Ivana Trump's diamond – considerable for a diamond, less so for a brain.'

The incident with Margutte was still fresh in my mind and I giggled. This man was English and his accent comforted me, so I accepted when he pulled out a bottle of Moët and popped it softly. I offered him some room on the red box but it was obvious it would not hold two, so he leant by me all night. I was rude to him most of the time – I felt hard and hurt and wicked on my red box, ready to set the world, and myself if necessary, on fire. But he didn't mind at all, seemed to quite like my aggressive replies. I didn't care either way, and I let him know that with every ounce of my teenage bravado.

Why he even stayed so long, I don't know.

'Are you bored? I don't need you to sit here you know.'

'I'm not bored. I'm happy here watching all the . . .'

'Models.'

'Them. The people. Such a funny world, fashion. I don't know much about it.'

He didn't need to tell me that.

'Then what are you doing here? I mean, this is a fashion party and you're not in fashion.'

He smiled again. 'I give lessons in English.'

He didn't ask me what I did – I assumed he knew or didn't care or both. I never found out why he was at the party. He told me stories about the mad people he had cared for in an insane asylum he'd worked in over the summer, their names, their mental illnesses, morbid obsessions. I was fascinated and grew relaxed under these tales of other people's demons. Then we talked of his and mine, and he listened to me carefully.

Six a.m. brought pale morning light and we were still talking. He was taking me home over the bridges spanning the Seine, and we were walking slowly.

'I often think about how many people have jumped from here,' he said. 'For love.'

I looked at him, trying to diagnose any suicidal tendencies but found none.

'Justin – you're fascinating, tremendous. Don't waste your mind, your life, with people who aren't real. You're special.'

162

'Oh shut up. Don't you feel like an old cliché?'

But it got worse. He knelt in the street and took my hand. I wasn't embarrassed. I wasn't pleased. I watched him, feeling detached as I did when I watched the drag queens feminising their faces in club mirrors. I was cold and wanted to go home.

'Justin, don't leave me.'

'My flight's in four hours and I'm not packed.' I yawned.

'Let me kiss you, please.'

'I'm going home,' I said, and walked off into the pink light. I knew better than to linger with a man deranged enough to think I was worth pursuing.

Like an actor in the bad movie that this was turning out to be, he got up and chased me, spun me around, held me close. I let him kiss me because I knew he needed to complete the scene he had set up for us on the bridge. My body made the right moves, trained by years of Hollywood movies. His kiss was wet and violent, his tongue another thrashing fish in a barrel. I didn't tell him his lips were kissing Margutte's leftovers, but the thought wouldn't leave my mind as he pressed himself on me.

I disengaged and agreed to give him my number in London. I wanted to get away, sure, but also he was more interesting than other men I'd met. He talked to me, not at me, and let me finish his sentences.

'Bye.'

I turned into the first alley I came to so that he would lose sight of me.

I had forgotten, it occurred to me, to ask his name.

I was slumped seedily on a plane with Jebbery Hoochey by my side. He had seen me dashing in circles around Orly as I looked for the departure gate, and persuaded the stewardess to seat us together.

Jeb was the last person I wanted to see. He wore a candy-pink shirt, unbuttoned as usual, a little too much gold jewellery, and his pale trousers set off his St Tropez tan. His aura was an offence to my morning-delicate senses. I told him so when appeared suddenly by my seat.

'Well, hello, to you too, Justin-baby.'

He slipped into the seat next to me, reached over and pulled my seatbelt far too tight. 'Now you won't go anywhere – Captain's orders.'

I loosened the belt. 'I need the bathroom.'

He tightened it. 'No you don't. We're taking off. Be a good girl and I'll get you a colouring book.'

'Get me some champagne. I *cannot* deal with you – or anything – this morning.'

'Are you flying incognito?'

He leant over and lifted my large black glasses before I could stop him. I squinted like a blind mouse as white light pierced my brain.

'Leave me alone!'

But Jeb remained where he was.

'Animal passions rage in you, I see little Justin. Underneath your milk and honey exterior there lies a feline wildness I'm just longing to explore . . .'

He was staring at my upper arm. The T-shirt I had pulled on (no shower, no sleep) didn't cover the purple bruises Margutte had left during our conversation. Jeb stroked them gently. 'So sexy – I'm jealous of the guy who left these.'

I ignored him.

'Sometimes –' he placed a finger on each mark and gripped hard – 'the pain can help recall the passion.'

'Get off me, Jeb. Keep your hands in your lap. I've had enough grabbing to last me forever. *I am not a toy.*'

I think that came out too forcefully, even over the roar of take-off engines. Heads turned to look. I stared back rudely and they turned away.

I wasn't much to look at – the black glasses covered the top half of my face, my lips were dry, swollen and cracked, my new blonde hair was matted in stale-champagne clumps and smelt of smoke. I was happy with my T-shirt because it was red and Iggy Pop had autographed it in black pen (left shoulder blade) backstage at some point in Paris that I couldn't clearly remember. Gaultier had given me the studded stiletto boots of my dreams, but they were almost covered by my denims, which were faded, too large and held up by criss-crossing belts. I was exhausted but spinning with adrenaline. I felt I might pop, or pass out.

'Would you like me to bathe you, Justin? The bathroom cubicles have room for two – I can vouch for that from personal experience. I could wash –'

'Jeb, why don't you flush yourself down the toilet? I don't want to talk to you.'

I was rude. I was childish. I was almost a child – seventeen – but I felt I knew the world and that it should be very afraid of me. I didn't know where all the anger had come from but I could feel it nibbling at my edges. 'I have become,' I decided aloud, 'unpredictable.'

Jeb laughed and handed me champagne I had not heard him order. We drank four half bottles before I passed out from fatigue. There were only fifteen minutes left of the flight but I dreamt of fat men with hairy hands holding me under the icy waters of the Seine with roses in their teeth. I awoke, pleased to see I had drooled on Jeb's shoulder. With skillful moves I evaded him at passport control, giving assurances that I would see him that night. But I found him waiting outside for me.

'I have a limo.'

'Of course you do.'

'I'm giving you a ride in. It's hot. You don't want to catch the tube.'

It was and I didn't, so I got in without a word. I had revived somewhat and lay back enjoying the cool leather interior. Jeb turned on the television and poured some more champagne. Lara O'Hara was on breakfast TV. Soon her wholesome face earnestly answering questions about diet and make-up had me cackling. There was nothing particularly funny about it – just Lara's vacant eagerness – but I was riveted.

Jeb pulled out his phone and got on with the business of being Jeb. He was in the middle of pre-production for *Dixieland Debutants: A Right Proper Massacre*. We stopped at Swiss Cottage and I stumbled out, leaving Jeb with a promise to dine that I did not intend to keep.

Inside, TK was in full flight, surrounded by pots of cheek colour, lip colour, eye colour, face colour, lash colour and every other sort of colour. She was making up a sweet-faced girl I had seen in the Agency a few times – a young Mia Farrow with ginger hair.

'This is Matilda.'

Matilda dropped her heavy, made-up eyes.

'Why are you doing her face?' I dropped my bag. 'Hey Matilda.'

'I've finished.'

Matilda stepped down from the stool and said quietly. 'I've got a casting ...'

'Cool – leave your make-up on and tell them I did it, okay?'

Matilda left without looking at me, head down. I didn't look at her either.

'So?' I asked.

TK was gathering her brushes. 'Like I said the other day, I've always been good at painting – and we watch make-up artists do us every day. I'm going to be a make-up artist. I'll do models and take their pictures, get a book together. We already know the photographers. It'll be simple.'

'Sounds good.' I flopped on the sofa.

'You smell awful.'

'Don't answer the phone. If it rings I'm not here. I'll ring Mandy later.'

'How was Paris?'

'I'm trying to change my life. I met a guy who likes my mind.'

TK raised a perfect eyebrow. 'He said *that*?'

'Sort of.'

'Is he for real?'

'He's not in fashion.'

'Promising then. A step in the right direction. He smart?'

'He went to Cambridge.'

TK seemed despondent as she packed away her brushes. 'Lara lent all these to me.'

'I saw her on TV just then.'

'Breakfast TV? I saw her too.'

'Everybody must have seen it. Good for her.'

'Pretty cool, in a public kind of way. She'll get a job out of it.'

There was a long pause as we contemplated the possible ramifications of an appearance on breakfast TV.

'Do you believe in the dream, Justin?'

I giggled. 'Life is a dream. Iggy Pop autographed my T-shirt and I worked for *Vogue*. It's all a dream.'

12
You Should Learn to Listen

Milan, 11 a.m.

Whoever had given him the cocaine hadn't done us any favours. Ly spun around the studio like a top, singing, 'It's L.Y.! Not L.E.E!'

One of the clients had made the mistake.

'Ly to rhyme with high! HY-energy. It's what they book me for isn't it, bitch?'

This last remark was addressed to Paul, the make-up artist. I wished Ly wouldn't bother the man holding a pointy brush near my eye.

Paul was dignified with greying close-cropped hair and a black turtle-neck jumper. Perfect nails on steady hands.

'Yes, Ly, you certainly have that.' Paul's voice was deep and soft, full of what I imagined was zen.

It was eleven in the morning but I had flown into Milan that morning and gone straight from Malpensa to the studio, so it felt much later to me. Ly might have been high-energy, but he had the focus of a faulty firehose. Six young assistants – all lean and pale with trousers slipping off their hips – had been raking a mountain of black sand carefully into the right shape for hours. The backdrop had been painted black and now the lights, bright blue halogen-type numbers, were going up. It wasn't what I had imagined when they had said 'Beach Baby' but then, beaches in England are rather dismal and at night, well, they might even look very much like the one in the studio.

It was a beautiful studio, huge, warm and bright, with its own cafeteria and white leather sofas. Outside, the fog was as dense as a concrete wall. I could have been any place except Australia.

Mandy was very excited; I'd had her on the phone from London three times already. The job was a campaign – advertising for a famous Italian label specialising in jeans – and the ad would go all over Europe. 'Big money, baby, and loads of face!' Mandy had said, over and again. She and Ly would either have got on like a house on fire or spontaneously combusted upon meeting. The thought of the two of them engulfed in pretty flames, still trying to talk, made me smile.

'Don't smile,' came Paul's soft voice. He was doing my lips and I had disturbed his perfect brush. I made a noise that I hoped he would interpret as contrition. He was a gentle man and I wanted to be nice to him.

Someone had hijacked the CD player and replaced Ly's 'Ibiza Summer House' with calming Moby-esque ambience music.

Ly had shot some beautiful campaigns, but it was always a struggle to achieve a balance between the control that would produce the magic, and unchecked bedlam.

Fourteen clients, representatives, directors and their assistants formed a protective circle and let Ly run free within it. They had worked with him before. Four stylists were buried in a rack of bikini tops, singlets and jeans, discussing at endless length the best combination. Studio managers and delivery boys from film and lighting houses came in and out, so that thirty people were buzzing about the studio at any one time.

And I was at the centre of it all.

It's easy to understand how pretty young girls can be transformed overnight into gorgeous despotic models. Thirty people running around you every day, catering to your every whim because they have invested thousands in your face and body and need you to be happy – talking about you, looking at you, touching you, smiling at you, kissing your tiny toned butt. And you're only seventeen. You haven't even finished school. And at the end of the day they hand you a fat pay cheque, thank you very much.

A man named Rinaldo, Ronaldo or Ranaldo was doing my hair, pushing my fringe up and back, letting it down, brushing it, then teasing it and starting over again. I felt as though it might just break off. I sat back in my plastic chair – wearing nothing but a navy-blue G-string because Paul was applying shimmering bronze to my entire body – and picked up the paper I had bought in London that morning. I lit a cigarette and concentrated on the cartoons at the back of the tabloid, then I started the easy crossword. I only ever managed six or seven clues but it had been a part of my ongoing – now apparently futile – quest for self-improvement. At every job, even after my ardour for erudite intellect was extinguished, I'd plug away.

Temptress, (5): VIXEN
Seat of learning, (10):

Today I stopped there and chatted to Paul instead, looking at myself in the mirror. I was still in the chair at two o'clock – four naked, motionless hours after I had first arrived.

Ly wanted to break for lunch *now* – he would not hear of waiting. And so, dressed in a white robe and towering gold heels, white hair shining, my body glittering with a fake tan, I followed the crew into the dining hall.

It was full. All the other studios were eating here. I saw faces I recognised as famous, including Naomi Campbell's in large sunglasses. Her table was frightfully glamorous, with a grizzled photographer and fashion doyens who could have been nothing but Italian, or perhaps French, all drinking champagne. But they got up and left soon after we arrived and I didn't have time to watch Naomi as much as I would have liked.

Ly ordered champagne and declared he couldn't eat a thing.

'Justin, darling, how dare you sit all the way down there. Come up by me at once. Paul – you can't have her all to yourself.'

As I moved to Ly, I realised that faces in the room had turned to look at me. Suddenly I realised that our table looked pretty glamorous too and felt a thrilling surge of power. I could engender desire, jealousy and despair as well, I held the power of immortality. I was high on it and nothing could touch me.

My movements became languid and my attention span shortened. I smiled less and sipped my champagne with a casualness that I had never felt even in my oldest jeans. One of my breasts peeked out, but it looked pretty and shimmered under the lights and so I left it the way it was. Ly lit my cigarette and I didn't even thank him.

In that instant, I belonged where I was, I was on the right side of the glass wall. I understood now what had transformed Debbie that night with R. I understood the power of fame.

The shots were supremely sexy. The stylists had settled on a tiny, white singlet, pushed up to bare my stomach, and a pair of tiny, white underpants.

'I thought this was for jeans?' I said, not really caring.

'It is, but we'll just have a picture of them in the corner. The whole idea is: "Where are my jeans?" That's the slogan.'

'Genius!' gushed one of the assistants, 'I love it!'

A group gathered to admire the end product.

'We thought it was sexier this way.'

'Sex is what sells.'

'Yeah. That's so sexy.'

Ly raced past and licked his lips at me. If he hadn't been gay, it would have been quite disgusting but I figured lewd must be okay if the guy was into men.

Shot after shot of provocative poses, teetering in heels on the mountain of black sand, bruised under the blue lights. The clients were loving it and Ly was mad, leaping around like a praying mantis.

'I want tragedy now, little Justin. Give me a look of torture. That's it. God, you are beautiful! Hand up to your face. Yes!'

The strobes fired and the world was surreal.

'Stick your butt out, that's it! You have the body of a little boy! The hair of a boy! You even have the name of a little boy! Justin! Fabulous!'

I wasn't really listening to what Ly was saying, but I knew he was pleased.

'Okay. Can we get some shots with the denim?' Ly waved his camera around and an assistant raced to reload it. 'Just in case. I want something Brooke-Shields-for-Calvin Klein-y but modern – that pre-teen sex thing.'

I was hauled off my mountain of sand and led to the make-up room. Paul checked my face and touched it up. I could hear the stylists arguing over jeans. I stood naked again, save for my G-string. Black sand clung to my skin.

Ly came in just as Paul went back on set to talk to the clients. 'That was great, Justin. God, you know? You're going to be a star!' I had heard that before but it still sounded good.

'Just look at yourself in the mirror.'

I turned and saw my skinny, brown body, my white fluff of hair.

Ly ran a finger down my bony chest. 'God! Even your bottom is like a little boy's.' He touched it lightly. I flinched and reminded myself that Ly was gay.

'You turn me on, Justin.'

Before I could move, I felt the weight of his body crushing my back. He pushed me over until I was bent over the make-up table. He had my bottom in his hands.

'I could fuck you up the arse like this,' he hissed.

I felt a hard, hot bulge through his jeans. He thrust his hips into me, hard and horny, his forearm on the back of my neck, holding me down. I was too shocked to cry out.

'Ly!' At the client's call he got off me and left without a word.

The stylist came back with the jeans. 'Justin. Put these on. Justin?' She snapped her fingers in front of my face. 'They're tight but they'll look awesome.'

'French, please,' said Lara carefully. 'I always prefer French.'

The manicurist swabbed Lara's perfectly square, unbitten nails with polish remover and began pushing the cuticles back with an orange stick.

It was Lara's day off – the perfect opportunity to catch up on a little grooming and exercise. As she watched the orange stick push back an nth of a millimetre of rogue cuticle on each nail, her shining blonde head drifted into thought.

She catalogued all she had consumed that day: *one cup of tea with skim milk; one orange, peeled; one banana, also peeled; half a bowl of raisin bran, with water.*

She placed a free hand on her belly. Flat. That meant empty; she could have lunch soon. Brown rice and a bowl of steamed vegetables around the corner at the organic restaurant with blonde pine tables.

She decided to buy a fillet of sole for dinner and make a fruit salad. TK would probably complain about the smell of fish in the apartment. Well, maybe if she ate some fish once in a while her skin would improve – but that wasn't very nice. Lara couldn't understand how those girls survived on French fries, ketchup and peas every night. The amount of grease was disgusting.

A handy mirror reflected Lara back to herself and she was pleased with what she saw. Grease never entered her digestive system so her skin was perfect. She had something of a Marilyn Monroe aura – a slinky, tanned Monroe, who never drank alcohol. Tomorrow she had a casting for an Avon catalogue, and her nails would be perfect. Avon paid well and Lara saved every penny.

Her mother had taught her well and Lara had been a good pupil. Mother felt modelling would be a wonderful finishing school for the already-finished Lara and a fine profession for a Virginian debutant. Until she found a suitable husband, that was.

Lara had 'come out' only two years ago and her triumph was still fresh: the lovely white dress, the cotillions starting at eleven in the morning, all the beaux in their evening wear, her dance card carefully filled and vetted by her mother. There were tea parties, watermelon parties, bowling parties and riding parties. Lara had been photographed by the local newspaper who had proclaimed her 'a peach' and said she'd revived the tradition of the Southern Belle.

Mrs O'Hara had sent Lara north to do the New York season, but Lara had been horrified by the loose morals and 'fast' behaviour of the young beaux and belles and had not stayed. Soon, however, she was spotted by an Agency booker in a nail salon and signed with the Agency the same afternoon, accompanied by her mother.

Mrs O'Hara clipped every photo of Lara from the catalogues, magazines and brochures and kept them, along with the ones Lara sent her from overseas, in a scrapbook – with captions. She was a good mother who sent Lara packages from home.

Only last week, Lara had received a professional portrait of her mother and father photographed sitting at the Steinway – well, it looked like a piano, but actually it was a cleverly disguised bar. Her mother had paid an extra fifteen dollars for the professional filter that 'softened' the photograph, but she still didn't look eighteen and her husband still looked bland and constipated. The photograph was enclosed in a paisley-print cloth frame Mrs O'Hara had made down at the Craft Centre.

Mrs O'Hara had also made four matching scrunchies and a Kleenex box cover in the same material and sent them along to keep the frame company. Lara's mother was very innovative and never wasted anything.

She'd even sent a headband, a handkerchief, three ribbons and a hairclip, all upholstered in the same paisley fabric. For a moment, Lara felt the weight of that paisley on her shoulders. Her mother's waterfall of red and blue flowers rushed across an ocean toward her. Mr O'Hara, immersed in his papers at the dinner table, seemed even further away.

Lara wondered if her mother had started drinking again – if she had ever stopped – but banished the thought. Mrs O'Hara was perfect, and such speculations didn't belong in the perfect head of a perfect daughter. Lara told herself she would do an extra twenty sit-ups at the gym that afternoon as penance. Plus her usual moderate run (444 calories burned an hour) followed by an hour on the rowing machine (600 calories).

She handed the manicurist her other hand and watched her apply the first coat of perfectly smooth, glossy polish to her naked nails.

You'll Spoil Your Appetite...

Vivienne Westwood, London, 8.52 a.m.

All the casualties were out for Vivienne Westwood. It didn't help that it was freezing, even though it was supposed to be spring, and everywhere translucent skin stretched over brittle bones, threatening to snap through. Rumour had it that Jodie Kidd had been sent home because she was too fat for the clothes.

'It's the post-rehab weight bump!' sniped Zander. I could hear his high voice taking aim. 'Happens to all the girls. They stop taking the drugs, start feeling the pain, start eating! WHAM. Fattyfat all over.'

'Fattyfat' was any girl whose upper thighs were wider than her knees.

Tia had escaped that fate. Simple really, don't stop the drugs. TK had pointed her out or I would never have recognised her.

'See Tia?'

TK was doing the show too, thank god.

'What? Who?'

'You remember Tia – the public service announcement thing?'

'Oh God, but –'

'I know.'

'Should we?'

We struggled up from the floor where we had been smoking up a fog with Frankie and Erin, two cool English girls with Storm. Tia was standing with Eugene from make-up, her jeans hanging loose from hips so pronounced they might have been a coat hanger in pantyhose. Her bare breasts were as full as a twelve-year-old boy's. She was smoking, of course, and drinking champagne. She turned her washboard back, ribbing gently.

'Shit.' TK stopped.

Tia's name was tattooed across her back in gothic script, thick and black, each letter standing five inches tall.

'There go her swimwear jobs.'

'I don't think she would get them anymore anyway.'

'Yeah. You're right. It's –'

'Insane.'

Tia turned. Her eyes were massive in her face, cradled in purple slings of fatigue and toxins. She stared vaguely, not focusing on anything, not even TK's face as we drew closer.

'Hey Tia.'

Tia smiled broadly. 'Hel-lo!'

Her eyes remained loose in her face and she started laughing. Eugene pulled her away to do her hair.

'She didn't recognise us, did she?'

I shook my head. 'Look, here's Mandy.'

Mandy was kissing Eugene and Tia with her big red lips. She waved at TK and me through the backstage haze and I could see her thinking about coming over, trying to make her feet cross the main room over the tangle of hairdryer cords and bags and feet. But she realised with a wobble that she probably wouldn't make it without incident and so waggled her fingers in apology. Her eyes were rolling around too, but with more mania than Tia's.

'Like she's going to be any help in this asylum.'

'Let's count the zombies,' TK suggested.

We tried, but it got too confusing and then Emma needed to finish my hair and TK was hungry.

I choked on a cloud of hairspray.

'Sorry darling, but there's just no way it's going to hold if I don't cover it. At least your hair takes well to teasing. V wants it all *huge*.'

'I don't think you can get it much bigger.'

'Don't you worry – it'll be a bastard to get out though. What do you have next?'

'Paul Smith.'

'Oh. You might have April. If it is, tell her I'm sorry about your hair.'

'Yeah. *Ow*.'

'Sorry.'

'Was Jodie really too fat?'

'You know how it is, Justin – she's gorgeous. I don't know.'

'No one does.'

A small blond man brought champagne and I sipped it through a straw. Kate, Stella and Shalom arrived – the big models got to come later.

Emma glanced at me in the mirror. 'Any cute guys?'

'Where? Huh?'

'In your life? Here? I don't know.'

'There are always guys around.'

'Yeah – but they're usually the wrong ones aren't they?'

'In Paris there was a guy after the shows. Not fashion. He took my number.'

'Well, plenty more where he came from – if he doesn't call you that is.'

'He was a little bit ... different ... maybe.'

'Is this hurting?'

'No, my head's gone numb ... mmm ...'

I couldn't remember what I was feeling or thinking or had felt or thought. I was tired and hunger had left me hollow. The cold and the fumes distracted me. I didn't even have the commitment to finish a sentence, let alone a life.

I set off to find TK for some perspective and almost fell over a small, white dog. Why were graffiti bags so popular this season? I wanted Kate Moss's winter coat.

Most embarrassing thing for you to do: go up to Kate and tell her it's only your second time on the catwalk and ask her to show you how to walk and pose. Then walk up and down the room in front of everyone, practising, regardless of what she says. Up and down the make-up tent, trying really hard and pouting.

Finally I spotted TK behind a chair. From the back she looked frustrated, hot and in the middle of something important. I sat on the chair and leaned down.

'You know Lara says she did a cover-try for *Vogue*?' I said.

'Can't you see I'm busy?'

TK was rummaging in a bag of mixed lollies.

'Can I help?'

'No. I'm looking for the cherry.'

I peered in as she searched.

'There it is!' Triumphant, she picked it out.

'So ... what about Lara?'

'Well, how many cover-tries have you done?'

'Yeah, okay, I know. But they haven't been for *Vogue*.'

'Do you know how perfect the picture has to be to get on the cover of *Vogue*?'

'I did *Just 17* and *More* and that other one.'

'I saw them. You are the Teen Queen.'

179

I giggled. 'Oh, yes, I am.'

'My perspective on this is not untainted with jealousy.'

'Mm, me too.'

'Look at all the zombie girls . . .'

'Megadeath.'

It was lunch-time in Soho and the pub was busy with suits. Creative suits, though. You could tell by the way they wore their jackets. I leant on the bar, my feet dangling off the floor.

'As a vegetarian, I find it offensive, that's all,' TK said.

'It's just a name – Shakespeare's Head – it must market itself as the thinking drinker's pub! It's not like they serve it to you on a platter with your pint.'

TK squealed.

'The eyeballs for cocktail onions, a bit of tongue to chew on.'

'Stop. That's so gross. I'm supposed to be focusing on my casting.'

'Where is it?'

'West End, just around the corner. It's Bumble and Lewis I think.'

'You're the only one who got sent to it.'

'Because I'm the only one who has the remotest chance of passing for twenty-five – not the greatest compliment – and I probably wouldn't do it except for the ten thousand pounds if I get it.'

'It's worth lying about your age for ten thousand pounds.'

'I don't mind the lying, I do that anyway. It's just that I usually lie down, not up. The Agency still think I'm twenty but I'll be twenty-three in a month.'

'I'll buy you a zimmer frame.'

'A what?'

'A zimmer frame.'

'Zimmer?'

'You know, what old ladies use to walk with.'

'A walking frame. Who calls it a zimmer frame?'

'Plenty of people.'

'Did you order yet?'

I shook my head.

'What do you want?'

'Just get me what you're having.'

Catching the bartender's eye was not easy. I stood on my tiptoes and leaned in.

'Two pints of lager, please.'

He set down two slavering bulldogs of pints in front of TK.

'It's fine for you, TK, you're going to an alcohol commercial around the corner. I have to turn up at Victor Victor's in Old Street for advertising – beauty, what's more. I don't know how they'll feel if I turn up drunk.'

'I just need to loosen up,' TK said.

I was watching a Spam of a man eat pork crackling out of a cellophane bag.

'He's cute.'

I giggled. 'Yeah, right.'

'Why are you laughing?'

'The pork crackling guy?'

'Not him. Over there. The guy with the glasses and the tweed jacket. Looks a bit like Johnny Depp. He really is cute.'

'Him?' All I could see was the tortoise-shell arm of a pair of glasses and the back of a sports coat.

'Shh. He'll hear you.'

'I can't see properly – is he doing a crossword?'

'Yeah. I think it's *The Times* as well.'

'He looks like,' I dropped to a whisper, 'an *intellectual*! He might have a fit if he hears there are *models* at the bar.'

'He'd probably think modelling was so beneath him.'

'Or something you do with clay.'

'What do you think he does?'

'He probably helps his consumptive uncle run a used gardening-books shop.'

'I think he's a writer or a scientist.'

'What would a scientist be doing in the West End?' TK reached into her bag and pulled out a maths book, dumping it on the bar, between the beers. 'I took calculus in high school. I was a maths brain.'

'Really? I'm impressed. I was a mathematical retard.'

'Now I do equations for fun, you know?'

I didn't know. I had never heard anything so alien and the fact that it came from TK did nothing to lessen the shock. I didn't know her anymore.

She opened up the book. The language was incomprehensible.

'What does that one mean?'

'It's really hard to explain if you haven't done it before.'

Her eyes went back to the book. I was left staring at the television. A Bacardi ad. 'Look, that could be you, TK.'

She glanced up, but went straight back to scribbling figures.

'Don't you need a calculator for maths?' I was bored.

'You can't do calculus on a calculator. I do it in my head.'

Crossword Boy looked over and saw us. He turned back to his friend, nonplussed. TK returned to her textbook and I turned to the television.

'Princess Di's on TV.'

TK sighed. 'I miss maths.'

I looked over. She had a pencil in her hand and her eyes were still on the book. This was serious. TK loved her princes and princesses – and Crossword Boy wasn't looking.

'You'd better go TK. You'll be late.'

She took a deep drink of her beer and stuffed her maths book in her bag. 'I've got to get to class.' She said it for Crossword Boy's benefit.

I played along. 'Okay then. See you there?'

I stayed to finish my pint and watch the Windsors. It was old footage but I missed my family and thought maybe I would like to have my own. Perhaps I could pick up some pointers. I wondered what it would be like for the girl who married Prince William but didn't think for a moment I might be her. Princes don't marry girls like me. My fairytale would end differently – with more wicked witches, less gnomes (unless I counted Margutte and his friends) and perhaps a rock and roll prince at the end of it.

'Do you believe the fairytale?'

I looked up to find Crossword Boy next to me, propped on his tweed elbows, eyes on the screen. Then I recognised him. The man from Paris. It had to be – the bridge at dawn! But he didn't seem to know me – perhaps he hadn't recognised me, maybe I was mad. In a panic, I turned back to watch Princess Diana, waving to the crowds. Neither her hair nor her tiara moved an inch out of place.

'Yes.'

'But she's dead.'

'That only makes the fairytale easier to believe.'

'Will you marry me?'

That shook my eyes from the screen. Crossword Boy was offering me the wilted pink carnation from his lapel. I refused to look at him.

'No, thank you.'

'Why not? We could get divorced straight after.'

'Why get married then?'

'I think you might like me.'

'You're not my type.'

'I suppose you're waiting for your prince, then. They come in all shapes and sizes, you know.'

'I'm not waiting for anything.'

'Not even my phone call?'

It *was* Paris. I shook my head.

'The tragic thing was, I lost your number.'

'I lost interest.'

'Where is your friend?'

'Calculus class.'

'You're students?' He seemed surprised. 'But I thought you were a – '

'A what?' I wasn't about to help him out.

'Well, aren't you … a model?' Even he had trouble saying the word. 'You are. I've seen your face.'

I turned back to the T.V. 'I hate questions.'

'Ask *me* some then.'

I looked down. There was a huge bag at his feet.

'What's in the bag?'

'Swords.'

'Liar.'

'For the dragons. Will you stay for another drink if I'm telling the truth?'

'Yes.'

'Promise?'

'Yes.'

He opened his bag and it was full of swords, long and thin and sharp, all unsheathed.

'Now I'm scared.'

'You promised you'd stay.'

'You didn't tell me you were a maniac.'

'I'm a fencer. What will you have?'

The barman was waiting.

'Vodka with soda please.'

'Sherry, thank you.'

I had to stay because I had promised. I thanked him for the drink, not feeling quite as brave as I had that night on the firebox.

'You don't know my name, do you?'

I wasn't about to let him win this. 'Paris,' I replied. 'You're Paris.'

'I like that. Paris Falconer. Won't you accept my carnation now that I have a name?'

I told him I didn't like carnations, and his was practically dead anyway. He promised to wear something else next time.

I wasn't sure there would be a next time. You couldn't just befriend people in a bar like that, or on the street. It was dangerous.

Don't Talk to Strangers

It was Jeb's habit to ring at least once a week. He called it 'checking in', I called it uncommitted stalking. Talk invariably turned to girls or boys or combinations thereof. And he always wanted to know who else called me regularly. I enjoyed teasing him tremendously.

'Ali rings me. You know, that Middle Eastern man with the scarred hands.'

'I know Ali.' I could hear the displeasure caught in Jeb's throat.

'I think he's a lovely man. He gives very good compliments. It's addictive.'

'Little J, he is not a lovely man, let me tell you that! And men like that want a lot more than conversation.'

'You mean men like *you*! You both ring up and do the same.'

'I am nothing like Ali,' Jeb sounded genuinely put out now, 'and I can't believe you think we're the same. He's a sleaze, I just pretend to be.'

I laughed. Obviously I had touched a nerve.

'Men like Ali only want one thing,' Jeb continued darkly.

'Oh, and you don't? Ali wants me to buy one of his fighter planes and have his babies. At least he's thinking of something more long-term than one night of Jebbery love.'

Jeb, for once, fell silent and I felt a teensy bit bad. I said, 'Anyway, you don't want kids.'

'You're right. I don't think I'd be a good father.'

'I can't even imagine you married.'

'Oh, I'll get married. I'm going to marry you.'

'After you've had every other girl you can get your hands on.'

'You'll be the only pure one left, and I'll marry you.'

'Because I'm the only clean pair of socks in your underwear drawer – what a wonderful proposal. I'll have to think about it.'

'Don't think too long. Once a girl's eighteen, she's over the hill.'

'And you think marriage is going to stop the ageing process? You're in more trouble than people think.'

'You'll have to get married someday. You should do it while you can still have any man you want. You're getting old.'

'Well, I wouldn't choose you, especially not after that revelation. Anyway, what if I want to have a proper career? I don't have to get married.'

'What would you do?'

'I don't know. Go to university, study art. Paint. Maybe in Paris. Meet a guy who admires my mind . . .'

Jeb laughed. 'I adore your mind, little J!' He roared with laughter again.

I began again, trying out this new image of myself on Jeb: 'I saw a great show at the British Museum. With TK. *Botticelli: Images* –'

'You shouldn't try to be clever. It doesn't suit girls. There's nothing better for a girl than to be a model. It's a great life and everyone aspires to it. There's nothing more worthwhile.'

'You're unbelievable.'

'I would have made a great supermodel.'

15
They're Just Jealous

I Let Go again and accepted an invitation from Paris. It was a stifling summer Saturday in London and the idea of punting conjured pictures of white flannels, strawberries and livid trout.

Paris arrived in a broken, bottle-green car and we sped through the green English countryside in its full, obscene fertility. For once, all was as it should have been. Paris wore white trousers and I had forgotten he was handsome. I saw champagne in the back seat and smiled all the way to Cambridge.

I was wearing my most winsome summer dress – faded pale-cream cotton with pink roses and capped sleeves. I liked the way it was a little too short and crept up at the right moments. I felt young and carefree, like I was supposed to.

My new hair and my summer legs made me feel pretty. I was almost famous thanks to *Vogue* and Ly's jeans campaign. I had money and an option for an editorial in Capri, and a television commercial in Iceland. But Paris loved my mind, he told me so.

'I love your curious little mind,' he said at the Stansted turn off. 'Tell me more of your "weird ideas". Do you write them down in that red book in your bag?'

I looked down. The corner of my *Book of Compliments* was showing. I shoved it out of sight.

'No, that's just silly – I write down anything nice people say about me. Dumb I know ...'

'No it's not.' He smiled at me. 'Tell me a story.'

I told him about a fat woman in fur I had seen in Paris. On her middle finger she wore the biggest diamond I had ever seen. I watched her disappear into the 'Dames' and my bladder made me follow. There she was, scrubbing the lavatory bowl with a brush in her diamond hand. When she looked up and suddenly saw me, her face had that ugly, naked look of shock. I felt her shame so acutely that I back-pedalled into the 'Monsieurs' out of pity.

To make sense out of what I had seen, in my 'curious little mind' I made her a cleaning woman. One day she won the lottery, was show-ered with money, bought luxury goods including a large Jacuzzi for two with power jets, but found herself strangely unhappy. With nothing to get up for, her life devoid of the lavatory camaraderie that had greeted her each morning in her leaner days, she spent much of her time eating. Every now and then, when her melancholy got too bad, she would leave her lovely apartment by the Bois de Boulogne and descend on the entrails of Paris. She would choose a café and sneak in to scrub its toilet, to bring back that feeling she had once despised and now missed ...

'You just plucked that from the air? How do you do that?'

I blushed with pride and shrugged.

'I wish I could do that. I mean, I'm a writer. I write poetry. I have a novel. But – '

'It's easy.' I blurted out. I wanted Paris to tell me more, help my vanity grow fat. Perhaps I did have some special talent locked away behind my pout and cocked eyebrows, something more to offer the world than a catalogue of sexy expressions.

But our drive was over and I could already feel the cool air of the river, and smell the dank water nearby.

Paris introduced his friends, who had names like Ricky, John, Boady, Woods and Billy. They fitted my summer tableaux so I paid these details no real attention. We pushed off from the bank and I marvelled that such a delicately built boat could hold so many hearty lads. A ginger-haired boy was poling steadily and the boat made no noise. Only the male voices disturbed the ducks.

I saw two swans. 'Aren't they beautiful!'

The moment, I felt, needed an expression of aesthetic sensibility. I took it upon myself to provide one but it glided by unnoticed, like the swans.

'What's the name of this river?'

They laughed. A boy with a large head replied. 'Funnily enough, its called the Cam. Cam–bridge. Do you get it?'

I thought it best to say a little less from now on.

'William, did you bring food. What's in the hamper?'

William perked up. 'Chicken sandwiches, egg sandwiches, salad!'

'Old boy!'

Soon they were all 'old boy-ing' each other loudly around the punt.

'Which sandwich did you choose first? The chicken or the egg?'

They all laughed.

'Christoph trug Christum, Christus trug die ganze Welt, Sag "wo hat Christoph Damals hin den Fuss gestellt?"'[1]

'But you permit yourself contradictions which are hard to reconcile with one another.'[2]

One of the smaller boys looked at me. 'At least there are still

---

1. Borrowed from K. Richter, *Der deutsche S. Christoph* as quoted by Freud in IV of 'Group Psychology'. The speaker has just finished Freud's volume 12, *Civilization, Society and Religion*, and is keen to share his knowledge.

2. He has just read the same book but prefers section 9. In 'The Future of an Illusion'.

some things which are plain to see – evidence of "physiological feeble-mindedness".'[3]

I felt that maybe I too could be intelligent, or at least clever. I smiled at their comments to show my potential.

You could be happy like this . . . is that what you're thinking?
Maybe this world could save you from fashion. Will they share
it with you?

'What about a pingle[4] at the hamper?'

'If you drop it –'

'Your aposeopetics[5] aren't going to work with me!'

They brought out the food. I ate a little salad, drank half a glass of champagne – there wasn't a lot to go around so I refused more. The boys ate noisily, ignoring me for the most part, for which I was grateful. They were so strange. Were they for real?

'Where did you go to school?' one finally asked me. He had on a straw boater of the kind private schoolboys wear in Australia. Even I felt this was taking it too far.

'Australia.'

'Ah. A convict!'

I smiled. I had heard that joke every other day.

They seemed pleased with this, with themselves, with talking about school, and I didn't have the heart to ask why it mattered. Weren't they sick of school?

The day remained beautiful. A motley punt slid by and the puntees stared enviously, I imagined, at us. I posed languidly, drifting like a fairy and ignoring them, completing – I hoped – the perfect tableau our

---

3. This is a very popular book. Phrase *ibid*. Women said to suffer from a lesser intelligence than men.

4. The action of eating with little or no appetite.

5. The act of deliberately leaving a statement unfinished to imply a threat.

boat made on the river. Suddenly the attention of Paris and his friends turned to me.

'Where did you go to university, Justin?'

'Aren't you American? You could be.'

'You do know, of course, that Cambridge is far superior to Oxford in all respects, and we take our studies rather more seriously.'

'I've heard it's far prettier, too.' I agreed in a hurry, although I'd seen neither town and only one stretch of river. I was keen to eliminate 'my life' from the conversation.

'We debate for a lark – I speak in the Cambridge Union. For example: Curd, is Darwin a philosopher? Many people are confused, but he is a scientist above all else.'[6]

'Don't be so naïve, Roger! Don't be so na-ïve . . . na-ïve.'[7]

'You're better off entrusting yourself to myomancy[8] than Billy's intellect!'

My concentration focused on a ginger-haired boy who was rooting through the picnic hamper for uneaten sandwiches. A Chinese duck wrap with plum sauce and an egg and bacon sandwich emerged. He took a large bite from each, but the egg and bacon won out. Horrified, I watched as he fed the duck wrap to the ducks.

'That can't be good for them!'

'They love it – look at them feast like Tereus[9]!'

The ducks were quacking in delight, calling to others to come and join in.

'Intus habes, quem poscis.'[10]

---

6. Roger is regurgitating a discussion heard one sleepless night on BBC radio, partly digested.

7. Nick is frustrated here by his inability to pronounce a perfect diaeresis.

8. The art of predicting the future by studying the movements of white mice.

9. Tereus was unwittingly served a dinner of his own children by his angry wife Procne.

10. *The one you want is with you now inside.* Procne answers Tereus when he calls for his son.

Much laughter.

'I think that's cruel,' I said quietly, because I was afraid of Ginger, with his large teeth and stout appetite.

Ginger giggled. 'La crudeltà può essere molto divertente.'[11]

'We only despise wickedness in others because we don't understand it.'[12]

'Well, what about you? What do you do?' asked Nicky or Solly or Sam. The boat rocked gently on the river. I thought for a moment and decided not to answer. I smiled and shrugged instead. Billy or Martin or Johnny or Paul moved in closer and the others began to listen.

'What do you do? You haven't told us.'

I looked into their expectant eyes, freckles, noses. I knew from their faces that Paris had already told them . . .

'I model.'

They leant back satisfied. Correct answer, first-class honours. I was relieved.

'That must be very stimulating.'

My heart sank for a minute, then bobbed back. *The Lightness of Being Justin. Let Go.* I tinkled the way I imagined an Edwardian puntee might have tinkled, lightly, with little expression in the eyes.

'Do you think you could explain for us what exactly models *do*?'

'I've often wondered the exact same thing myself, Chris. What is it that models do? I always thought they stood around having their pictures taken all day not really *doing* anything, but perhaps we'll learn something today.'

'I'm sure Justin has a lot to teach us. We're dying to hear. Tell us about the life behind the face – it must be fascinating.'

---

11. *Cruelty can be very amusing.* There is no reason for the ginger boy to express himself in Italian. He chooses to do so on the basis of a gap year spent in Rome.

12. The speaker has mis-remembered a quote from his book of Oscar Wilde's witticisms.

'I'd also like a short piece on make-up. Lipsticks, mascara, that sort of thing, model tricks to make me as beautiful as you.'

'Oh, Derrick – remind me to renew my *Vogue* subscription when we get back to London. Aren't you in *Vogue*?'

They came from all angles, confusing their quarry.

'I heard it was French *Vogue*, Patrick – quel chic ma chéri!'

I deeply regretted having told Paris about *Vogue*, deeply regretted being born.

'Does it take a lot of intelligence to be a model?'

Ginger spoke louder than the rest. 'Anyone could stand there in their clothes. I could be a model! It doesn't exactly take brains.'

He had neglected to consider looks, but I kept quiet.

'You're basically a prostitute – that's what a model is. A whore sells her body and isn't that what you do?'

'Has this always been your life's ambition?'

'Oh pity her. Maybe she can't do anything else. Be merciful to the poor dumb darling!'

Their laughter frightened away the cannibal ducks.

'You must do something else, or are you a vegetable? Do you just lie there and let people look at you?'

Paris lifted his head a little. He had remained silent all the while. I brightened as my knight turned to speak. He would be able to tell them all, in that funny, footnoted language they spoke – in a way they could understand – that I was indeed special, yet modest; that they shouldn't ask me too many questions but rather take his opinion of me on good faith. And he would finish his speech with a sharp, humorous, put-down from which they would rise dusty and bruised.

Paris smiled at me reassuringly. 'Yes, Justin, we're all curious. Why don't you show us that book of yours, the red one in your bag. There, I can see it from here.'

I was trapped. I thought about quickly, neatly slitting my throat – bleeding red all over their whites – but the Marks & Spencer picnic knives were plastic. I turned like a disco dolly but everywhere I looked, pink faces looked back.

Nick or Teddy or Pete went for the leather book protruding from my satchel. This morning I had thought the day looked ripe for new compliments, ones that would help me change my life as soon as I could find a quiet corner to transcribe them.

The hand that snatched the book opened it and began to read out loud. '"Book of Compliments" – I can't wait for this! Here we go: "You make my loins quiver!" You took that as a compliment? You're dumber than you look!'

That had been Mick Jagger when he had found out my age.

'"You have a face men would go to war for!" This is unbelievable!'

The reader struggled to be heard above the mirth.

'Who says these things? And who writes them all down in a book?!'

'"You've kept me sleepless since I first saw you". Look at the way she spelt "tellement envie"!'

'"Your father must have been a thief." It gets worse! Here's another French one: "on dit que la perfection n'existe pas – " Well, it certainly doesn't in your French spelling – she's spelt "Ça" with an "s"! "I'm going to make you a star." That's not even a compliment, it's a statement of intent.'

'Here's a good one – it's in bold too: "You're my dream girl!"'

Paris was laughing. They were all laughing, and gnashing their teeth, their eyes folding into skin.

Dream girl! Dream girl!

They were chanting and laughing so hard they had to stop poling, and the front of the punt nudged the muddy bank. Shame consumed me as I leapt from the punt in mortal terror. My feet skidded and I slithered into the river, waist-deep in dirty green water. Two swans flew at me, obviously feeling I didn't belong in this world, and chased me as I scrambled up the bank, clutching tree roots. The swans, spreading their huge wings, beating them, brushing me with menacing air. The water soaked my dress, and my knickers and nipples were plain to all.

'Just like Leda[13]!' they shouted from the punt. 'There's one for your book!'

More laughter. Would that choking, animal sound never stop?

I collapsed on the bank.

'Bye, bye, Leda!'

'Bye bye, Dream Girl, bye bye!'

'Happy days, Dumb Girl!'

I couldn't even look at them as they drifted off. Something heavy hit me full in the back. I thought I would vomit the Marks & Spencer salad I had picked at, but could only gasp. Jimmy or Jolly or Brian or Todd had thrown my book after me in a fit of compassionate hate.

The red leather burned with colour on the green grass and I couldn't bring myself to touch it.

Dumb Girl. What's the point? So many compliments of so little use if one snide word can outweigh them all. And you know what? It serves you absolutely right for having a book like that in the first place . . .

I thought I might burn the book. Then I knelt on the grass and vomited. An elderly professor on his walk stopped; I assumed he was a professor because he too fitted the picture: spectacles, suede elbow patches, corduroy trousers. It seems I was the only one who did not – muddy, red and crying.

The professor watched me impassively. 'Are you a member of the university?' Clipped, perfectly rounded vowels.

---

13. Leda was raped by Zeus who had taken the form of a swan.

I must have looked blank as he tried again. 'Are you a student?'

'No.'

'No?'

'I'm a model,' I said, this time with weary resignation.

'A model of what?'

'Nothing. Just a model.'

'You have to be a model of something. A model is a scaled-down version of the real thing. Are you quite sure?'

'Quite.'

'That makes you an impossibility.' Satisfied, he strode off.

It's a sorry sight, you know, when a shrunken muddy thing sits sobbing, especially if it's wearing only one shoe. Are you sure this is your life? Perhaps you are the inferior twin, the formless parody of a brighter, stronger, more beautiful you, one living in a parallel universe.

When you try and step out of the shadows you find you can't. You end up slithering down a riverbank, weeping in shame, vomiting in the grass like a sick cat while an old man denies your right to exist. That's what happens, that's what happens when you want too much, because you are someone's underbelly: soft, vulnerable, mostly invisible, covered in mud, and slightly damp . . . And you will never have the strength to roll over, to make that massive inversion, swivelling until you come out on top.

Can't you at least be dramatic in some way? Grow alien cheekbones, lose fifty pounds, stretch yourself two feet, cover your skin in freckles? You're far too ordinary to be interesting and the world is plain enough without you.

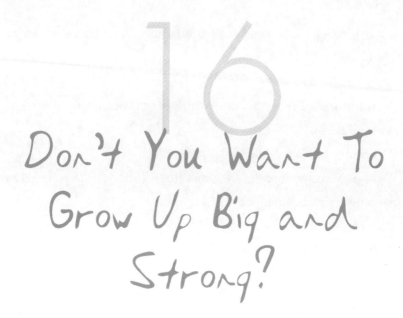

16
Don't You Want To Grow Up Big and Strong?

What do you say to a girl who's just become a superstar? 'Congratulations' seems inadequate when she has fulfilled a model's highest aspirations. How do you think Cinderella's coal-scuttle friends greeted her when they first saw her on the arm of her prince, dressed in her fancy gown? 'Gee, I'm so happy for you?' 'You must be so excited?' 'It couldn't have happened to a better person?'

Fact was that all four of us felt it *could* have happened to a better person. We may have been jealous if any one of us had pulled off a similar coup, but we would have also been genuinely excited for the lucky girl.

But Lara O'Hara?

She had always been far too perfect. She was the model model, the template for us all, and now she'd hiked up the standard even further.

Lara had the self-assurance we all lacked, you couldn't call it arrogance. I think we all suspected that she would be the one to break through to stardom, and we resented the fact that it all seemed so natural to her. Celebrity was expected; it had arrived promptly at the right address and appointed time, bearing a tasteful bouquet of flowers.

Lara never stumbled. She was above that. We were offended.

We knew she wouldn't gloat, that she would be smiley and *sweet* as ever. We wouldn't be able to hate her for wallowing in her triumph or trying to lord it over us. She had robbed us of even that simple pleasure.

Her victory was one for the other side, and a loss to ours. We would now have to put up with extra-reprimanding stares from the Agency when we didn't blow-dry our hair for castings, when we didn't wear neat, coordinated outfits, when we didn't eat carrot sticks for lunch and get manicures and bikini waxes between jobs.

We were pretending not to be waiting for her to come home, but we were. It was a Sunday and we had nothing to do but sit around and talk about Lara. Our ears pricked when we heard her key in the lock.

She smiled over our heads and placed her bag neatly by the door. Four copies of *Vogue* under her arm. 'Hi, guys,' she said brightly, as if nothing had happened. I was bent over the sink, trying to set fire to my *Book of Compliments*. Despite the nail varnish remover that I had poured on its cover, it was refusing to do more than smoke around the edges. The smell was atrocious.

TK knew nothing of my boating disaster. I had been too ashamed to share it, even with her. I had told her Paris was not my type, and I'd fallen in the river. She had believed me.

'Hi, Lara,' I said and wondered who would broach the topic first. Our silence might be construed as jealousy. Of course we *were* jealous – but we would never have admitted it to her.

My money was on TK. She looked up from the calculus books spread before her, wearing reading glasses that I did not know she needed.

'We saw your cover Lara.' I was right. 'You're a star, babe.'

Lara smiled sweetly and put the magazines neatly on the table, face up. 'Thanks, TK. Gilles is just so great to shoot with – I guess he could make anyone a star.'

Gilles? He was *Gilles* now? And she wasn't allowed to refer to *herself* as a star – only we were. Way out of line.

When your high-school teacher walked into a noisy classroom and announced that everyone was staying back that afternoon for talking, Lara was the girl who put up her hand and said, 'Excuse me, Miss Forrester, but I wasn't talking.' And she would have neatly completed spelling exercises to prove it. When the school bell rang, Lara would have quietly packed her bags without a trace of smugness in her big, blue eyes and walked out to meet her perfect mother.

Lara O'Hara was the ultimate goody-goody, and that was reason enough to hate anybody, whether in the pre-school playground or in a model flat in London.

Lara had her own answering machine. She slipped over to it (neat black stretch pants) and pressed play.

Beep.

'Lara, honey! We're *so* excited about your cover! You look *so* gorgeous! It's George, baby. Call us when you get this – the phones have been going crazy for you. Donald Trump called asking about you! It's the most amazing –' *Beep.*

Her booker. Almost as voluble as Mandy but obviously a lot more sane if he could get her a *Vogue* cover.

Beep. 'Lara? Hello? Are you there, honey? We're so excited about the news on *Vogue* magazine. Your mother and I want to know if we'll be able to get copies at the Mall – she's told every –'

Lara fast-forwarded that one. We forgave her that, everyone's parents embarrass them.

Beep. 'Lara! George again! Prince Albert of Monaco's secretary just rang! He loved your *Vogue* cover! He wants to invite you to his birthday dinner at Catch this Thursday! Honey, call me back – there'll be so many fabulous people and he said they'll send a limo so not to worry yourself about – '

Beep.

We didn't need to hear any more. That beep said it all. Lara moved into her own apartment two days later in a better post code, with all mod cons and the key to a common garden. She had moved up in the world.

Despite our disapproval, later that evening we could all be found at a party given by the Agency in Lara O'Hara's honour. It was a last-minute thing, the *Vogue* cover having spun off a Revlon contract and a Ray Ban campaign in the one afternoon. Lara O'Hara wasn't just a superstar, she was practically a millionaire.

The limousine cruised up as all good limos should – at least it had the discretion to be black. The Agency had alerted the paparazzi so that they too could share in Lara's good fortune and let the tabloids spread the Word to the Bored. Five or six stocky men with heavy cameras were ready to shoot the new superstar and their loose stances indicated, quite rightly, that they did not anticipate much opposition from their prey.

TK and I paused a while, a few steps back from the club entrance, and watched for the shining whale to disgorge its Venus. We didn't want to move in case it looked like we wanted to share Lara's fame, and make claims on a friendship that had been tenuous at best and certainly wouldn't stand the glare of the spotlights.

'So she's the first.' TK's face was lit pink by the lights, tiny pink bulbs spelling out the name of the club: 'The Royal We'.

'To make it, you mean?'

'She's a supermodel and her path to glory is paved.'

'Do you think any of us will make it?'

'Who cares?' TK turned her eyes to me – she had rimmed them with black and they looked huge. 'It's not really up to us at all, is it? We can't just decide to work really hard one day and make it. Everybody else's eyes determine our future.'

'I hate being so goddamn powerless!' That came from me with too much violence – the punting mud still stuck.

'Me too. We need ... Oh my god, look ...'

Lara was emerging from the limo, and living up to expectations. A long, long, tanned leg slid out first, Manolo Blahnik sandals adding inches and delicacy. Then we glimpsed her animal frame, perfect skin, small shining blonde head and large shining white smile. She was pure gold.

The paparazzi fired and she moved in black-and-white slow motion in the strobe of flashes. It was a cliché and it was awesome. Lara was gracious as she played the part of the movie star she would undoubtedly one day want to be. Fame had already rubbed off her edges and she looked different in a way that had nothing to do with her new dress or professional make-up.

The chauffer held the door proudly, claiming ownership as his car disgorged this jewel, while a black-suited minder paved Lara's way. That is what a little fame can do, why we all chase the dream. Lara would never have to ride on the tube again. She had become untouchable.

'I know what's going on inside her head,' TK said.

I laughed. 'One Weight Watchers can minestrone soup, 20 calories.'

'Flute of champagne, 40.2 calories.'

'Smile. Shoulders back. Chin down. Careful, step.'

The paparazzi disappeared inside – there were rumours of Naomi, Angie, Erin, Karen, Maggie. Flashes, smiles, jewels, breasts, flashes. TK and I followed in the wake of the strobe-storm.

I collected four flutes of champagne from the open bar and handed

TK two. We made our way over to Debbie, who was wrapped around some guy's arm.

This particular guy was wearing a black suit, although it was summer, and he had a hearty, emphatic blandness that distinguished him as an American. He was about thirty-five but you could tell he was confident he could pass for twenty-five. His longish hair was sun-streaked in all the right places, but the accompanying deep tan did little to hide the fact that he was not very handsome. He was laughing loudly, his eyes half-closed, his mouth open, capped, white teeth shining like hotel bathroom tiles.

'Jesus, I hope Debbie isn't mistaking him for anyone who matters.'

'R.'s away – he's probably her walker. He looks familiar, do we know him?'

TK laughed. 'We know them all. Standard model hound come shallow-man. He's some writer – LA, I think, maybe New York – somewhere like that. Writes semi-popular books about rock stars and models and such.'

'Does he know what he's talking about? His books – are they any good?'

TK raised her eyebrows slowly one at a time, and shrugged her shoulders.

'Ooh,' she trilled, 'I'm just a poor little model – I can't wead or wite!'

'Oh, god. Another one.'

'Yep.'

'Justin!' Debbie had a habit of screaming when she was merry. She detached herself from Tan Man and swayed over. 'Drink up, girls, it's party time.'

'We're doing our best, Debs.'

Tan Man sauntered over, unable to resist the allure of three scantily clad models at a champagne trough. He snatched a full glass, turned and whispered in Debbie's ear.

She giggled. 'No, silly, they're models – I live with them.'

She leant in. 'He thought you guys might be scientists or something. Isn't that funny?'

She thought so.

'Hilarious.' TK's eyes were narrowing dangerously.

The man stepped in with his free hand and smile extended. 'My name's Kort.'

I stiffened and took my cue from TK who pretended not to notice the hand.

'What?' The music was too loud for TK.

'Kort.'

'Dork?'

'Kort.'

'Why would any parents call their kid Dork? Don't you think that's mean?' She smiled. 'I'm sorry. I don't mean to offend.'

Kort smiled widely and bent in, eyes shining malevolently at me this time. 'And you?'

'Pamela,' I said.

'Pamela. So what do you do, Pamela?'

I looked at him and waited. Refusing to take the bait.

'Don't tell me you're . . . in politics. No . . . a surgeon perhaps, or a tax attorney.'

'I'm a model.'

'A model. Surprise, surprise. Can't you girls do anything else? Is the allure of standing for hours in your underwear having your picture taken *that* strong?' He laughed, pleased with his wit.

'Tell me, Dork, this is a model party – a party for a model, thrown by a model agency. What are *you* doing here?'

Kort was still smiling at me but the lustre had gone out of his eyes.

'I'm a writer.'

TK took my arm protectively. 'That must take up a lot of time,' she said, smiling sweetly.

'Yeah. It's my passion, my life, you know. The words just flow. I do have a quirky way of getting inspired though – I'm quite famous for it. I live all my characters so deeply I sometimes lose my own personality. And that's pretty hard to do, big personality and all.'

'Oh, it sounds terribly exciting and clever. Who do you write about?'

'Modern angst. Relationships, romance . . .'

'I asked *who* you write about, not what.'

'Umm, rock stars . . . models.'

'But I don't undewstand!' TK put on her Tweety Bird voice again. 'If you despise us so, how come you spend your whole time witing about us and twying to sleep wid us?'

Dork forced a smile and slithered off with the oblivious Debbie. TK later succeeded in setting fire to the back of his jacket and he had to be doused with an ice bucket before being bounced by the minders for unauthorised self combustion.

Debbie bounced too – right into the arms of a rapper called WhyteBoy.

The billboard went up over Oxford Circus. There could have been no more visible place than that. Crazy Ly's photos for the 'where are my jeans?' campaign had turned out better than I had imagined and the Agency were excited. Mandy was going nuts and the Round Table – the scary bookers who made a point of never remembering anyone's name – had taken pains to learn mine.

My billboard self was about twenty feet tall and I shone copper in the blue light of the fantasy night beach. They had chosen the denim shots in the end, the white underwear proving too provocative for its own good. The slogan was still 'where are my jeans?' but it now made very little sense because, legs apart on the sand, I was wearing a very tight pair. I was brushing my white hair away from my face, lips slightly parted.

Powerful and sexy. The kind of girl I would have envied. It felt so strange looking into my own huge eyes.

'At least it's a turn away from the horrible heroin-chic look. Justin looks strong, beautiful, healthy and happy. That is the picture of a girl who is in control of her own destiny. You can quote me on that.' Serena Blonde, the head booker, flung her headset onto the booking table. 'The bloody media are always up in arms about our girls being poor role models – and when we give them one that is positive, they're still unwilling to see it from that angle. I think she looks beautiful.'

Mandy came over and hugged me. 'Of course she does!'

'What are they saying?' I wanted to know.

Mandy looked at me. 'It's nothing my darling! Just the usual stuff!'

Serena came out with it. 'They're saying that the girls are just as thin – the only difference is now they are tanned, younger and richer.'

'It's true,' I said. 'They're right. People see the billboard and they have no idea – no *fucking* idea – what it's all really like. They just believe what the industry sells them, and what it sells them is a big bare-arsed lie.'

Suddenly I remembered Ly, felt his breath on my neck, his skinny hardness. It made me want to scream at the bookers how disgusting they all were, with their sudden interest in me, their fake concern, their greed. I wanted to explain the frustration – the horror – I felt at the thought that hundreds and thousands of people passing through Oxford Circus would look up and aspire to be *that*. All those intelligent girls allowing themselves to have their desires shaped by a handful of art directors and a mad photographer who liked to dry-hump his young models in the arse.

The words wouldn't come.

I felt the weight of disapproving stares from Mandy and Serena, before they were quickly replaced by beaming smiles. Serena spoke first. '*Sky* mag's booked you tomorrow for a young-sexy thing. I'll give you the details when you check in. Editorial rates though.'

'When are you going to get a mobile phone, Justin?' Mandy whined. 'Surely you can afford one now – you got twenty thousand pounds for the billboard. We might need to get in touch with you suddenly. We'll pay for it up front if you need us to.'

'I wouldn't know how to use it.'

'Now you're being silly.'

'I'll think about it.' I walked away from the booking table. The reason I didn't want a mobile – and TK felt the same – was that we could think of nothing worse than constantly being able to contact, or be contacted by, the Agency. If we had mobiles, the best excuse for lateness/missed castings/not checking in would be taken from us.

'Will you wait to see Terry O'Marney?' Serena again. 'He'll be in at three and he really wants to meet you.'

I nodded and went to find TK, who was sitting on the floor at the back of the office.

'Oh my god.'

She was reading an *Evening Standard* while she, also, waited to see Terry – the photographer from American *Bazaar*. 'Just simply gorgeously AMAZING,' Mandy had explained.

'You won't believe this. The girl's nuts!'

'Debbie?'

'Not this time.' TK handed me the newspaper. The headline read: 'Oh, oh, Daddy-oh!'

Ageing rocker Mick Jagger has done it again. This time it's a Croatian beauty who claims she is carrying his love child. Eighteen-year-old Cristina Gojanovic, a Zagreb-born stunner, shocked fans today by going public with their affair. 'I don't want any money from Mick,' said the voluptuous vixen, who is with the Agency in London. 'I just

want him to know it's his baby and I want my baby to know who
his father is.'

This latest disclosure ends any hope for a reconciliation ...

There was a grainy reproduction of Cristina's composite card next to a picture of Mick on stage in a tiger-print shirt. I couldn't believe it.

And at that moment, Cristina walked into the Agency, accompanied by a tough-looking boy in leather who I guessed instantly must be the boyfriend she was always ringing. The bookers clustered around her, demanding details and trying to figure out how to turn the situation to their best advantage. Cristina detached herself from the group and came over to us, boy in tow.

'When did you get back? I thought you'd gone home to Croatia?' I hugged her.

'I did. Then I come back – with Milos.'

We shook hands and I saw that Milos couldn't have been more than twenty, despite his muscular build.

'So, what's all this about a baby? Is it true?' I asked.

Cristina nodded. Milos beamed and rubbed Cristina's belly. 'Mick and I are the daddy,' he said, 'Mick Jagger of the Rolling Stones.'

'I've heard.'

'From the night in the bathroom,' Cristina said. 'Remember?'

I hadn't been able to forget.

'So it worked?'

'Yes. It worked.'

I was skeptical, but kept my opinions to myself. 'Well, you must be happy. What do you think, Milos?'

Cristina turned and spoke lovingly to Milos in Croatian. He beamed again. 'Angie, ain't it good to be alive! And I am so proud wild horses couldn't drag me away. You catch your dreams before they slip away – we're dying all the time, if you lose your dream you lose your mind.'

Milos had obviously learnt his English through his idol's lyrics. It lent a romantic slant to the whole situation.

'Anybody seen my baby?' Milos was laughing now, still rubbing Cristina's belly.

I wanted to ask Cristina if she was sure it was Mick's baby, and not Milos's – the timing was out, but the couple seemed so happy that I didn't want to spoil it.

'So, where are you going to have it?'

'It will come in five months. I want you to be godmother to my baby.'

'Me?'

'Yes. You helped me make it. I want you to be godmother.'

I accepted the honour. I had never been a godmother before and it made me feel important.

'You should go home, Cristina, to Croatia. Have the baby where your family is. That's what I would do.' Just then I was called to go to my casting. 'I'll see you later. Nice to meet you Milos.'

'Goodbye, Ruby Tuesday!'

Later that week I found myself in a large studio in Angel. The grey cold outside made the white walls inside glow brighter. I stood at the window staring at the grey concrete of the street and the dark grey limbs of the trees below. Slicked black with rain, they reached up and waved their twigs in the wind like mad, hungry children. I welcomed the bleakness. I wanted the wind to blow harder, to punish the insolent trees with their starving arms. The more dismal it was outside, the more pleasure I took in being inside, away from it all. It made me feel fortunate.

Alice, one of the make-up artists, was powdering a male model's chest with a pink pouf. His shaved chest was glowing under the hot studio lights. She took out her eye-shadow palette and brush and chose a taupe brown. Benny was a young man with a serious jaw and a deep cleft in his chin, of which he was particularly proud. He was exceedingly handsome, star of aftershave campaigns for Armani and Hugo Boss. Alice was shading in his pectorals with the eye-shadow, giving Benny's sculpted body a little more definition. Benny flexed obligingly.

I stood by the window, waiting for Alice to finish.

A harried editor's assistant came over with a leather vest. 'Benny, sweetie, will you put this on when you're done with Alice? Robert wants to shoot you next.'

Benny looked at the vest. 'Is that leather?'

'Yes.'

'I can't wear that.'

'What do you mean?'

'I won't wear it.'

'But . . .'

'I won't wear it.'

The editor's assistant scurried away with frightened eyes. She reappeared with the editor two seconds later, a handsome blonde woman of about forty who used the halogen lights as an excuse to wear enormous sunglasses indoors. Her motto was 'If they made sunglasses for teeth, we wouldn't need plastic surgery.'

'What's wrong, Benny? You won't wear the vest? This is what we booked you for.' She was gentle, careful not to upset the talent. She knew from experience that tear-stains aren't easy to cover with make-up.

'Look, I said no. Call my agency – whatever.'

Editor and assistant went to confer with photographer. Benny turned to Alice. 'You have to have principles. And I'm against leather.'

Alice was finishing his last abdomen muscle. 'Animal cruelty?' she asked.

'No, I eat meat. It's for my image. I look stupid in leather, you know?'

I lit a cigarette and watched the smoke curl in the air then cling

to the window pane. The best way to light smoke is from the back –
then you get those clearly-defined wisps snaking around your head
like Medusa's snakes. Snakes scared me.

*You know what Freud has to say about that, don't you? You're
afraid of snakes? You're afraid of sex. You say you can't get a
boyfriend, but it's because you don't want one. You are afraid
to tell anyone you haven't had sex and you're afraid to do it. You
think people will laugh because you are paid to project sex
and desire and lust, but have never experienced it for yourself.*

*That's why you cringe when people talk about sex, why an
occasional look of confusion crosses your face when a photographer tells you to 'think sexy'. What passes through your mind
when he says that is colours, Sharon Stone, red lipstick on bruised
lips – you feel some vague sense of empowerment that never
makes it past the look in your eye.*

*Don't you think that if you really wanted to you could sleep with
someone? You don't need to do anything ridiculous like standing
on Old Street in your underwear, waving at lorry drivers – just
hook up with Jeb or Ali. Benny's right behind you . . .*

*Your skin is crawling – you're cringing at the idea. Yet you
are intrigued by it, by the unknown. How can you not be when
the whole world revolves around sex, and you're on the outside,
looking in?*

*Turn around to the male model behind you. While everyone is
standing around, confess to him that you are a virgin and would
like to be de-flowered by him. Right here, right now. Ask him
humbly and sincerely and blush a little so people know you're
not kidding.*

I found an *Evening Standard* and went to sit on one of the sofas
along the wall, next to TK. It was one of the few times we'd been

hired on a job together. My make-up was done and I was wearing a small, leather bikini under a bathrobe, waiting my turn to be shot. Strobe flashes were popping and Radiohead was playing on the studio sound system. Everyone was smoking.

I could hear Robert from across the room. 'Yeah, great. Great!' Then, 'Give me sex. That's it. Sex! S-E-X. Yeah. That's the face, baby – come on! You're beautiful.'

Robert actually said those things. They were clichés but they seemed to come naturally to him, and they also seemed to work.

'Work it, baby. Work it. I love it. Yeah! Love it, love it. Sexy!'

I looked up. Benny was bare-chested, posing in front of a wind machine.

'Give me manly,' Robert was coaxing him. 'I want tough, rough. You're a mean mutha fucka!' Benny swung around and looked over his shoulder, clefted chin lowered for maximum exposure.

'Take my picture!' he scowled.

Robert went wild. 'I love that. Great! Again.'

Benny jumped around and brought his fists up in an imagined black American gang insignia. 'Take my picture!'

It came out: 'Tayk mah pitch-uh!'

I put my paper down. 'What else does he think he's here for?'

TK laughed. 'It must be even harder for male models to do that stuff. So uncool – and they don't even get paid as much as girl models.

'Take my picture!'

I looked over again. 'He doesn't seem to be feeling too badly about that.'

Benny was wearing a fur coat over his bare chest and had a tall milky blonde tucked under one arm.

TK nodded. 'He feels *very* cool. If only his friends could see him now.'

'Oh, but they will.' I said. 'That's the whole point.'

We broke for lunch at four. Everyone was famished. A buffet had been set out along one wall. TK and I stood beside Benny and watched him pile four chicken breasts on a paper plate. TK picked up two drumsticks. 'Would you like some chicken?'

'I've got some, thanks. I'm on a protein-only diet.' He went and sat by the blonde.

'Do guys watch their weight?' I asked TK.

'Sure they do. There's been a crop of boys with eating disorders since those Calvin Klein ads came out ages ago.'

'The ones with Marky Mark?'

'Yeah. All the guys have to be super-buffed and cut.'

'I guess it's the guys' turn to feel the pressure.'

'At least we don't have to work out, we just have to be skinny.'

'Unless we want to be Lara O'Hara.'

'No one can be that perfect.'

'I don't even know where there's a gym in London.'

TK reached for the bread rolls. 'I used to sing in a band in high school. It was called Ghost Dog, and I had this great hair, all over one eye. I only sang back-up, but I was pretty good. I used to do this eighties dance ... it was cool.'

I took a cheese and cress sandwich from a pile.

TK went on. 'I should start singing again. You could play an instrument and we could have a band.'

'I hate sandwiches.'

'I didn't even think about it at the time, but we were pretty famous. I just, you know, hung out. I was sixteen ... I *loved* singing. Maybe I should take classes.'

Luis the Portuguese make-up artist with the golden curls took TK by the arm. 'TK – let me touch up your lips.'

They went off to the mirrors. I raised my sandwich to my lips and sniffed. I had developed a very bad habit of sniffing everything I ate on jobs. More often than not, the discovery was not pleasing. Taste and smell are often worlds apart. The alfalfa in my sandwich smelt of underarm.

'Are you almost done, Justin?' Robert was behind me. 'We're ready to shoot you.'

'Sure.' I tossed my uneaten sandwich into the bin and followed him onto the set.

17

Don't Talk With Your Mouth Full

Debbie called one afternoon after a long absence somewhere exotic and announced that she would deign to dine with us in the evening. She gave us strict instructions: the locale had to be unfrequented because Debbie had a pimple on her nose. TK and I chose an Indian restaurant with a grand name that belied its décor. The Rose of India was carpeted in worn red velveteen that had absorbed a thousand smells. Pictures of "satisfied customers" with greasy hands and flash-bulb eyes sat proudly under plastic by the door.

Debbie arrived half an hour late with a purple pashmina covering all but her eyes. A madwoman in purdah. We'd taken a table near the window. She glanced about, then hailed a waiter.

'We'd like a table in the back, please.'

The waiter appeared disconcerted by the talking shawl. 'This is a very good table,' he replied.

'That is not a good table. Kindly seat our party in the back.'

There was a gold mesh curtain separating the back of the room from the front, a sort-of VIP curry-corner. The poor waiter scurried over, cleared the lager-and-limes off the table, and TK and I were moved with our drinks.

It was only once she was comfortably seated, with her back against the wall, that Debbie greeted us.

'You have to insist on the best! Oh, you darlings. How have you been? You both look so pale.'

Debbie, of course, didn't, having just spent a leisurely five days in the Caribbean. Or so we guessed, judging by the beautifully tanned hand she waved in our direction.

'You should really try and get to St Barths – it's a gem of an island. R. and I stayed in Bobby De Niro's house. It's gi-normous, but he only uses it one weekend of the year. He lets R. stay there whenever he wants.'

We smiled crookedly, not knowing if she was smiling back. Debbie had collected a few fancy words since we'd last seen her. I'd never heard her call anyone 'darling' before, and 'gem' was never part of her vernacular. The old Debbie would probably have said 'neat'.

'How's the pimple, Debbie?' TK brought it up.

'I'm taking time off until it gets better. I suppose I could take this off, seeing I'm among friends.' Debbie lowered the pashmina.

She had a large red spot on the side of her nose. The scowling whitehead of pus threatened to erupt at any moment. I wondered if it would be rude to ask her to put her shawl back on.

'It's stress, all stress.' She hushed her voice to a whisper. 'By the way, it's Caprice now.'

'What is?' I thought she was using a medical term, some awful jargon for gangrene.

'My name,' continued Debbie, 'it's Caprice now. I changed it. R. said everyone in the movie business changes their names. Don't you just adore it?'

'Caprice?' TK looked nonplussed.

'It means "whim" – very European, don't you think?'

Debbie beamed at us. She'd had her teeth bleached. They gleamed like Swedish furniture.

'Great.' I said and reached for the menu. I decided against ordering the creamy white raita.

There was a sudden flash of light, the kind we knew well. A flash-bulb flash.

Debbie/Caprice shrieked and snatched at her shawl, rushing to cover her face. Her elbow knocked my beer over the table. Turning in fury, she set upon the source of light. 'For god's sake! You people are animals! I'm on holiday, leave me alone! No pictures!'

The photographer stumbled in shock and fell on his back, taking the gold mesh curtain with him. The waiter rushed to help. All eyes and ears in the restaurant were on us, the slap-stick show at the back. The poor man was groaning and cursing in Hindi, tangled in the gold curtains.

TK turned to Debbie. 'I think you killed the poor man.'

'Those bloodsucking paparazzi get what they deserve!' She was trying to shout and rearrange her shawl over her nose at the same time.

TK peered down. 'Um ... Debs? I think he's the restaurant photographer.'

The café we took refuge in had greenish lighting and was deserted. We had been told the Rose of India did not welcome 'our kind' and that we should 'seek customer satisfaction elsewhere'. We were starving. Debbie was quiet all of a sudden. She didn't protest when we walked in. She didn't ask to change tables – covered as they were in oily plastic cloths – or complain about the film of grease that coated every surface. The radio played gently in the background and TK sang along with jerky, sideways head movements that were neither chiropractic nor dance-related.

'Running just as fast as we can ... I think we're alone now ...'

TK was making up for time lost since the demise of Ghost Dog.

A matronly woman with large pores and a neatly pressed pale-green pinafore took our order. I wanted scrambled eggs, TK ordered poached, I suggested fried for Debbie.

She shook her head gently. 'I don't eat fried.'

'Have scrambled then, Deb – I mean, Caprice.'

She nodded. The matron bustled out and returned with plastic mugs of hot, dark tea. We lit cigarettes.

'You've got to laugh about it. You weren't to know,' I said while I tried not to laugh.

'It is pretty funny,' TK smiled.

Debbie didn't say anything.

'The poor guy. I can see the headlines now: "Capricious Caprice in Curry Caper".'

'"Hullaballoo at Vindaloo",' I put in, delighted with my inspiration.

'"Titty Tart in Tikka Masala Trip-Me-Up"!'

We giggled while Debbie sat in silence.

'You *are* looking quite titty these days, Caprice,' TK observed, looking at Debbie's bosom.

'I know. I had them done . . . last month. Before . . .'

'You had surgery?' I was astonished.

'I can't believe you had surgery! What are they now – D?'

TK and I, flat-chested girls, were very interested by the swelling of Debbie's bosom.

'CC cup.'

'That's a good size,' TK said.

I didn't know what to offer as a post-op compliment. 'Pshaw! That's a humungous pair of hooters, love', didn't seem appropriate, although I was sure there'd be lorry drivers on the Old Street route who'd disagree. Caprice was hard to miss – her breast was now almost the size of my head.

'Why'd you do it?' TK was always more direct. 'You were working a lot anyway . . .'

'I did it right after all the publicity, then it sort of died off . . .'

'So are you getting more jobs now?'

'Yeah. Lots of swimwear and men's magazines. I'm on the cover of *Loaded* next month. I make more money.'

'You don't sound very happy – did it hurt?'

'What about scars?'

'Do people stare at you in the street?'

'What did the Agency say?' That was my question.

'I bet Mandy was chuffed – she's been hinting about it to me for the last six months. I told her no way, José. No offence, Deb.'

Debbie looked up at us, with tears in her eyes.

'I did it for R. He likes big-breasted women.'

She was sobbing now. TK and I felt uncomfortable, as if we were responsible for this deluge of snot at the table.

Our eggs came. The matron didn't give Debbie a second glance. The café looked like the kind of place where a lot of people came to cry.

'He left me.'

I wondered briefly how many times the walls had absorbed these very words, those same bitter tears. I reached over my eggs, all jumbled on the plate, and took Debbie's hand.

'He told me he liked big breasts. I got them done to surprise him, when I was in New York – before the trip to St Barths. When he saw me, he made fun of them, called me his Playboy bunny and started slapping me on the ass in front of his friends . . .'

Her tears plopped into her eggs.

'When we got back, he told me he wanted to take a break. That we were too young for serious commitment.'

'The guy's over forty, for Christ's sake,' TK exploded, along with her tomato sauce (she was American and liked tomato sauce on her eggs). 'What does he think he is? A goddamn spring chickadee?'

Debbie reached in her handbag and pulled out a tabloid.

The front page was a huge photo of R. and another woman. It had been taken with a telephoto lens – the image was grainy and confused – but it was definitely R. I think what hurt Debbie most was that the girl was unmistakably flat-chested, and a brunette.

'It was taken outside Claridges ... we used to stay there if we wanted a romantic night in the city.'

There there you're better off without him a girl like you could get any man she wanted there are plenty more fish in the sea all men are pigs you deserve better than that have a good cry it'll make you feel better I'll get you a cup of tea ...

The walls oozed platitudes but TK and I didn't know what to say. We remained silent as our eggs cooled on the table. There *was* nothing to say. I could only hold Debbie's hand.

18

It's Rude to Whisper

It was Monday morning and I was out on castings. Sleet was falling and I couldn't remember where I was going. My brain had been numbed with cold and boredom. I'd suffered too many icy grey roads, location vans, hungry days, stale cigarettes, bad coffee and freezing nipples, feet and hands.

I found myself wandering into one of those enormous chain-store pharmacies – probably Boots – and roaming the aisles like Hamlet's ghost. The cold had numbed my feet so I felt like I was floating, past the bandaids and baby oil. I could not remember who I was – I barely remembered my name, and when I said it out loud it sounded wrong, as if I might be lying to myself. I pulled out a composite card from my bag and stared at my face, my vital statistics.

In nine days I'd been to Athens, Milan, London, back to Milan and now London. I felt bleached by the fluorescent lighting in so many airports and aeroplanes.

What are you doing in a London pharmacy with white blonde hair and a bag full of pictures of yourself? How has this happened?

Last time you looked, you were hating maths class in a summer country ten thousand miles away.

I picked up a box of hair dye. L'Oreal. My blonde head was on the front. Hundreds of small boxes with my face on them, all staring at me. This was not a mirror. I looked far more serene in the picture than I did in real life. My hair had been smoothed for the ad, ends curled under, and I saw they had airbrushed the blemish on my chin that had caused so much consternation on the day of the shoot.

Where was everyone when I needed an anchor? TK was in Paris and the Maldives doing an editorial for *Jane* and an ad for hair gel. Debbie/Caprice had gone to LA in search of TV work. Lara O'Hara's tantalising life drifted down to me from all angles like confetti – magazines, pictures, industry gossip, a perfume campaign – but even she was out of town.

Back outside on the streets everyone was moving with purpose, one way, the other way – they had places to go, people were expecting them. They seemed to know where they were going and what they wanted. A lady in a Burberry raincoat looked smart. She was probably on her way to work, leaving her lovely little flat in Westbourne Grove, small dog and basil plant.

Why can't you be her?

'I don't know.'

Because you're an idiot!

'I know.'

Did you call Mandy?

'Yes.'

And?

'I don't remember – I didn't write anything down. I'm taking the day off.'

A canvasser with a clipboard stopped me. 'Let me ask you a question about your hair.'

I wanted to bite her.

You're wearing a beanie – tell her you're bald.

'I'm bald,' I said and brushed past her.

You could go and buy a pair of trousers – in there.

'Okay.'

Blue? Grey? No, brown – no, pinstripe! Here.

'But they're for children.'

Oh, I'm sure they'll fit you. You've been disappearing lately so I don't think you need proper clothes.

'They must make pretty big twelve-year-olds . . .'

That woman's staring at you –

'Everybody always stares at me. Who cares?'

You have no idea where you are, do you? There is nothing right now that you can say is true, or real.

'I am what I look like.'

Well then, it's easy: just get some new clothes – buy a Burberry raincoat and everything will change for you.

'But what if I don't want a Burberry life?'

What is it that you want?

'I don't know, but I wish the future would stop rushing in to crush me. I want to stop time while I figure things out. It's like my future has been condensed into tomorrow, or yesterday. I can't explain. I keep trying to seize the instant, but it keeps slipping away . . .'

It's your greatest fault – always accelerating time in your mind until things are dead before they begin. Your lives are lived in your imagination before they have had time to be born.

'No. I think I just want to be famous. It would be so much easier then because people would always be telling you what you're like, where you are, how you look, who you're with. If you got confused, you'd just have to pick up a tabloid.'

But the trouble is, fame is like love. You can't force it. But one is much more worth having than the other.

'Which?'

Finally I phoned Mandy and wrote down the address she gave me in my diary.

'Honey, it's up in Kentish town, Oseney Crescent – you know the studios! Pamela's a great photographer! She'll love you!'

I groaned. So far away and I was so tired. But I got myself to the casting. A shoot was in progress at the same time. Emma the make-up artist was there with Miko the stylist and Zander was doing hair.

'Hello lovey!' he said when he saw me.

We chatted and I told them I'd seen the Acropolis a couple of days ago. 'It's amazing to think what it must have been like in those days.'

'Oh, I know! Such culture!'

'Divine!'

'You know what else is divine? Those toga things they wore – with the purple – '

'I think the purple was Roman – '

'Gorgeous! So Versace-before-Versace.'

I realised then, with Zander's words, that I had become a cliché too. I wasn't reading *War and Peace* but I might as well have been.

I waited for an hour to see Pamela, to be told that they were looking for a girl with very dark skin, black hair, preferably Asian.

I rang Mandy – I was cross. She flipped through and looked at my chart. 'Oh, sorry darling! But it's good for her to see you anyway, you know! So she gets to know your face!'

She didn't give me a chance to complain. I wouldn't have minded, but it was the fifth such 'mistake' Mandy had sent me on in the last month and they were rarely conveniently located.

Caprice bought a motorcycle and started taking drugs. This remedy for heartbreak may have been rather obvious, but that had always been her problem. She acquired a dangerous edge, or the semblance of one – and even the bookers were scared to say no to her. She was working less and turning up two hours late when she did. The clients complained about her bad behaviour, but they loved it at the same time. She fulfilled their idea of what a successful model should be: very tall, very blonde, very thin, with large breasts and a famous ex-boyfriend, a notorious past and leather trousers. She was living out their stale fantasies.

I was in awe of her pain – if that is what it was – but it didn't take her long to find the drummer of a famous band (Trayler Trash) and seek solace in his tattoos. Pain, like weddings, apparently made you very unoriginal.

I envied the colour she had injected into her life, for living a cliché so completely and wholeheartedly, and envied her the boy. When Caprice showed me the winged heart she'd had tattooed on her chest, and told me that Shrimp had a matching one, I considered a tattoo myself. I wanted a heart like Caprice's, I thought, then realised I had no one who would match it.

With all the love – or what passes for it – in the world, the fact that I was without even the inkling of a prospect made me feel pathetic. Cold nights in front of the television, swaddled in flannel pyjamas and a scratchy blanket were no one's idea of glamour, least of all my own.

'Will you lend me some cash, Justin-baby?' Caprice asked, looking hard in studded denim and tight, white leather pants.

'How much?'

'Fifty.'

'I can only give you twenty.' I was pretty certain I would never see the money again and twenty pounds was as much as I would give to someone for play money. 'How come you're so broke? All the lingerie ads? The LA stuff?'

'The Agency won't advance me any more money until the clients pay, and I've spent the rest.'

That meant Caprice was probably out around ten thousand pounds. The Agency would advance her that much, I was sure, because her name bobbed in and out of the paper. I could only ever advance three thousand.

'I have to borrow money to buy food, for god's sake. It's criminal.'

'But you don't eat,' I reminded her.

'The Agency doesn't know that. What if I did eat? What if I had to buy food?'

'Ten thousand pounds buys a lot of sandwiches.'

'Nine thousand eight hundred and fifty-two, actually.' She went on: 'And if you include clothes and cigarettes ... fucking tightwads.' She sat staring at her shoes.

I wanted to help her. 'Go into the Agency with Shrimp. Get him to help you give the bookers hell in front of everyone. I guarantee they won't refuse.'

I smiled to myself. Unleashing the fury of Caprice around the booking table would be a tiny revenge for me – and almost certainly would get Caprice her money, especially if she was accompanied by her star-on-a-stick.

'Do you think that would work? I'm totally mad enough to go nuts on them.'

'Just be super-loud, and don't be afraid to throw stuff. It makes a convincing argument.'

'I'll pick up Shrimp on my bike.'

She slammed the front door on her way out.

'Hey Mandy, it's Justin. I'm just checking in for tomorrow . . .'

'Baby, I'll be right with you! Let me just get your chart sweetie! Oh, darling, beautiful! You have a lovely shoot tomorrow – just a half-day for Rimmel but it'll be gorgeous! Five hundred pounds. Isn't it awful out! We've had such a day in here I can't tell you! We almost had to call the police! That's ten a.m. so you can sleep in a bit. Hang on while I look for the address . . . Old Street Studios, you know where they are. Things were smashed! Serena almost jumped out the window! Caprice came in with the drummer from that band – '

'Trayler Trash.'

'Yes. He's gorgeous – all rock and roll and really famous! He's much smaller in real life, though!'

'His name is Shrimp.'

'Caprice just went crazy, darling! She started screaming that we had stolen her money! And she pushed over that lovely barrel of filtered water – you know, the one in the corner near the fake plant?! It went everywhere. Little Dean had to stop her from shoving the fax machine onto the floor!'

'What did Serena do?'

'She tried to pretend it wasn't happening! But then this Shrimp grabbed the telephone receiver from her ear and jumped up on the booking table! How he managed that in such tight leather pants I will never figure out. He started swinging the phone over his head like a lasso, screaming, "Show me the money!"'

I tried not to let her hear me laughing.

'Serena wanted to call the police, but the drummer had her phone, and before she could get to another, the entire booking table tipped over and crashed to the floor!'

'Did Caprice get her money?'

'Well, yes! In the end Serena just handed her a wad of cash from her own bag, the accountant having gone home hours before. It was frightful – but terribly dramatic! Both of them shouting and carrying on! Caprice looked fabulous! Fringed leather pants!'

'How Spinal Tap of them.'

'Indeed, sweetie, we're all lucky to be alive! Anyway, got to go, honey, bye, big kiss! Mwwah!'

'Bye, Greg.' I wanted to see if she'd notice.

'Bye-bye, Justin-baby!'

She didn't.

19

You Should Be Grateful!

The first two, even three times I was pinkly flattered. Who wouldn't be, coming home to a mass of white roses the size of a tractor wheel sitting on the middle of your bedroom floor? But after a fourth, fifth and then sixth bunch in as many days, the feeling turned into an icky, cold creepiness and I took to subconsciously washing my hands whenever I saw flowers. I didn't even tell Jeb about them – though he would have writhed with jealousy at the thought of another man paying me extravagant attention.

But yes, I did keep the roses. They were overwhelmingly beautiful and the sight of them blooming in a crush at the end of my bed fed my vanity. To someone, I was worth the extravagance.

It bothered me, however, that the someone was Ali. I had told him many times that romance was not to taint our friendship. I had first said it over a cosy tea at Browns, when the log fires and damp woollen smell of my first London winter had made me think of gentle domesticity and marriage, and of how comfortable I might be as the second half of a whole. I had even wondered if I might grow old in London, ever feel like I belonged among the English and their fog. I heard my future self clipping my vowels and announcing: 'Hello dahlings, potty at mai haise,' with a toothy grin. But I knew that Ali was not a man I could ever feel at home with and I told him so. Rather abruptly. The minute he sat down.

'You look all rosy, Ali. I already ordered tea.' I sat up straight, legs tightly crossed.

'Darling Justin, I kept you waiting,' he said, smiling his soft smile.

'Not a bother. *Friends* sometimes keep *friends* waiting.' I took a breath. 'I've been meaning to say to you, or tell you, that you know we are just friends and only ever will be friends. Never more, but that doesn't mean I don't think you're a wonderful friend.'

I blushed and was glad when the waiter put a silver, tiered platter in front of me. Ali watched closely as I ate a cucumber sandwich.

After a pause, he said, 'Of course, Justin, it will always be only as you wish,' sent a tiny bow in my direction and chose a salmon sandwich.

I told him again a few months later over a gin and tonic at the Ritz (wearing a diamante tiara and borrowed pale-pink dress, velvet heels).

Then again at a dinner at The Ivy. Crammed between two art dealers and a comedian, I told him without artifice, in all seriousness, but carefully, so no one would hear, that there was nothing romantic between us.

I explained myself again in the private box at Albert Hall, watching Elton John perform wearing a pink, plastic suit. I told him twice, on the telephone, late at night, after the first roses appeared.

Each time he calmly said he respected my wishes. He seemed to understand. He never did anything to make me feel that he had other ideas – except the roses kept arriving.

So I decided I would have to stop seeing Ali, that his intentions were somehow not entirely honourable. He was tall and handsome, always beautifully dressed, but he was also forty-three and so old enough to be my father. And he was quite probably an arms dealer.

After nine days, the roses stopped. I breathed a sigh of relief and concentrated on keeping tabs on which girls were shooting what editorials in London. The weather grew even colder and I dreaded days where I didn't have a booking and had to roam the streets on moronic castings, begging advertising people for work. I preferred the inanity of studio conversation to the pain of walking winter streets.

Four days after the roses stopped, the first box arrived. It came early in the morning, hand-delivered from Browns. I was still at home and I was almost too afraid to open it, sure that it was either a bomb or a ridiculously expensive gift. I wasn't sure which scared me more.

Just then, the front door opened of its own accord. My heart leapt in terror and knocked itself senseless on my front teeth. A matted blonde head appeared on the shoulders of a red leather jacket. Caprice. She was home so rarely these days TK and I had all but forgotten she lived with us.

'You gave me the fright of my life, Caprice.' I still wasn't used to calling her that.

She looked at me through a tangled fringe, her eyelids at half-mast.

'Where have you been?'

She flopped her string-bean body onto the musty, green couch. My eyes flicked to her black, leather boots, covered in a rash of gold studs. So rock.

'Shrimp ... they were playing Wembley. We partied on after ...'

'Must have been a good party.'

Caprice shrugged. 'Trayler Trash are at the Dorchester penthouse.'

When the band was on tour, all the members insisted on sleeping in the same set of rooms – almost invariably the Penthouse (animal house). Shrimp always looked so goddamn sexy on stage – his skinny body in tight, leather pants and old, ripped T-shirts. Caprice shed her jacket like a skin. She wore Shrimp's gig shirt underneath. She took that off as well and lay back bra-less, covering her face with the T-shirt.

'He just smells of sex – it drives me wild.'

All I could smell was beer, body odour and cigarette smoke, but the T-shirt was very cool: tomato red, faded and thin, with the words 'kneel down before me' scrawled on the front. I would have been disappointed with anything less. Rock stars had images to project and protect.

Caprice lit a cigarette with a diamante-studded lighter and looked at me over her large bare breasts that jutted firmly from her chest, the silicone stopping them from lying down to the side. The effect was eerie. 'Am I not fucking sexy?' she demanded, her voice hoarse.

'You're sexy.' She was.

'How much sexier can you get? I'm better than Barbie for god's sake.' She threw the lighter onto the floor.

'What's wrong?'

'Groupie bullshit.'

I turned my package over in my hands. I had almost forgotten it.

'I got a parcel.'

'Who from?'

'Ali.'

'Diamonds?'

'Too big.'

'Haven't you opened it?'

'There's a note.'

'Read it. Open the fucking parcel.'

I read the note: '"Darling Justin, it's cold outside. I hope this may keep you warm. Every day I see you on the billboard, and I can think of nothing but your sweet countenance. Yours in worship, Ali".'

That damn billboard – that's what had triggered this! Caprice made a gagging noise, but I wasn't listening.

I opened the package and its contents would most certainly have kept me warm. It was a heartbreakingly beautiful hooded dress in angel-white pure cashmere that fell to the floor and skimmed the body in all the right places. Wearing it, I'd feel like a Czarina sitting high on a winter sled fleeing slavering wolves through silver birches in moonlight.

'Look.' I held it up. Caprice was asleep. '*Look!*'

She opened one eye. 'Cashmere. Expensive. Returnable for cash but probably worth keeping. Unless you're short. Intentions are serious enough, but it's harder to tell when the guy's loaded.' Her eyes closed again and she began to snore softly.

I couldn't allow myself to keep it, wouldn't even let myself try it on – more than once. I covered Caprice with a blanket and left her on the sofa rolled on her side, just in case she did something rock and roll like vomit in her sleep and choke on it.

I took the dress back to the store and got a cash refund. It was as expensive as I had feared, and it took me a while to find a gift of exactly the same value to send back to Ali. I did not want to offend him, but this was an extravagance I could not condone. I chose a solid gold cigar cutter, manly and well-crafted but not personal or overly thoughtful. I included a note that thanked him, but explained that I could not accept his generosity for we were merely friends.

Another box arrived the next day, gold embossed red leather this time. Inside, a Cartier watch lay in wait. Again I returned the gift. Finding something of equal value and wholly impersonal proved a bigger challenge this time. Finally I had to settle on a massive Italian leather sofa which I hoped would inconvenience him enough to make him stop sending me gifts. I had it delivered with a note begging him to stop, saying it was exhausting and upsetting me.

But the next day was heralded with yet another box. This time I fired the box back unopened (despite ravenous curiosity) with another missive that told him he must stop the nonsense or our friendship would cease.

No couriers came to the house the next day.

20
You're Too Old to Believe in Monsters!

Every now and then, without warning, the world would change speed. I called it The Great Melting because everything seemed to run together – days, weeks, faces, jobs. I was preoccupied with my future but could see no way forward. I would suddenly be overwhelmed with the sense that I was turning turgid circles and the river that was my life seemed as dank and brown as the Thames.

This was not the sharp and glamorous life I had imagined for myself. Sure, there were parties and playboys and drugs and photos and fabulous clothes, and I was a part of it all, but I did not feel the way I looked. I did not have the hard confidence that should have gone with my appearance. The lazy voice, the dirty jokes, the men, the fearless power were absent. I was empty inside and I did not know what to fill up on.

Floating this way and that, caught in another Melting Moment, I bobbed in the crowded streams of London from one casting to the next, one job to another. There was a shoot in Barbados. I remember a pink hotel, and that the photographer was a small, nut-brown man who invited me to his room to smoke pot. I rode a horse – or was it an elephant? – through the sugarcane fields onto a white sandy beach, then there was a mad rush for a plane to Paris.

Was it Paris? I was groggy from in-flight champagne but it was definitely that funny circular airport and there were bunnies on the runway. I remember a cold soundstage and a warm dining room where they served red wine with lunch. Someone left flowers in my hotel room. I think I was there for a television commercial – my feet grating in my shoes, still sandy from Barbados.

Home to London – it almost felt like home – and scrambled eggs, tea and drizzling clouds. I read the tabloids on my way to a shoot. Yet another bomb-scare on the tube – paramilitaries with tanks above ground because the IRA had made threats. Everyone just wanted to get to work. Another job out in the countryside on a cold, cold day with nothing to eat but a packet of crisps. I wore jeans with bullet-holes, and stood in an abandoned garage. The photographer kept saying, 'Stand very still, this is a slow exposure.'

Then San Diego. 'Big Money,' said the Agency. Too young to drink in the States but sank six margaritas – how was I going to handle these strange people sober? There's a handsome Japanese photographer – I think he was handsome – did I flirt with him? I can't remember really.

Another windy day on the beach. It's been so cold lately. My nipples burn from being constantly erect with chill. It's ten degrees, cloudy and I'm in a bikini. We're slow and lazy in the van, we have to wait so much and I am so, so bored. I draw pictures of the sunshine I cannot find.

Then I'm posing on a highway. Another bikini. I am suddenly scared someone will kidnap me. Cars stop and shout things but I can't listen or I'll start crying. In bed that night, I'm lying on my back when the door opens slowly. Victor Victor, the photographer, comes to my bed. I pretend to be asleep and see what he does. The blanket lifts off my feet. His warm, dry hands take hold of my ankles and part my legs slowly, afraid of waking me. I feel his hair on my thighs. What's he doing?

Fingers pull my panties aside. Now I am scared. I feel that I have to wait for something to hurt before I can scream. I'm so scared I can't move. Something warm and so soft is flickering between my legs. It doesn't hurt but I don't know what it is – it's not a hand, or a finger. It keeps flickering and now I know what it is and I am so ashamed I want to die. Leave me Victor! Leave this room! He does, although he still thinks I'm asleep. I know he has a wife, and I cry for a while.

Next day is business as usual. 'LDC, baby. Locations Don't Count. No talking about last night.'

Back in London I feel safer. I will never go to Victor Victor's studio again. Jeb is at a party full of half-drunk vodka bottles and half-drunk models. I sit on his knee and we laugh and laugh, but I can't remember what was so funny. On my left, Steve Martin tells me I look like a toy. On my right, Warren Beatty says he wants to buy me like Barbie. More laughter. Jeb is jealous but he has no right to be; I'm sitting on his knee. Someone gives me cocaine with a tiny silver spoon. It's almost Christmas again, but I don't want to think about that. The Rolling Stones are on their way to the party.

21
Hold Hands When You Cross the Road

'But sweetie!! You just need a nice cup of tea! I'll make you one! Come on now! Sit down here!' Mandy patted the space on the leather sofa next to her.

'Mandy, I need more than a cup of tea.'

'A drink! What do you want?! I've got vodka!'

She did too, in the bottom drawer of her filing cabinet.

'Or there's gin, or a bit of rum left over from that hideous party the other week when Dean threw up on that Algerian photographer! Oh no, sorry, that's all gone! Time to re-stock the emergency cupboard! I'll put the kettle on, honey! You're tired, you're stressed, you're hungry, but it's all good! Paul Smith loved you and he's thinking of using you for the new fragrance launch and –'

'YOU'RE NOT LISTENING!'

' – it's being shot by Thierry –'

'I DON'T KNOW WHAT'S GOING ON!'

' – most amazing pictures of Kate and –'

'I DON'T EVEN KNOW WHAT DAY OF THE WEEK IT IS! Mandy, I need a routine! Girls my age need a routine! Discipline! THIS IS JUST IRRESPONSIBLE!'

Mandy stopped talking. I had stolen her exclamation marks and she was lost without them. The rest of the Agency took no notice – we were down the back and they were used to hysterical outbursts. I think I scared Mandy into listening. This wasn't part of the Great Melting – this was meltdown.

'Baby. Tell me what you want to do. What can I do to fix this?'

I felt suddenly sheepish. 'Maybe ... some time off ... away from things,' I mumbled. 'Maybe if ...' I stopped and watched Mandy's hot little brain spin into overdrive:

London - Justin = less jobs for Justin

Less jobs for Justin = less money into the Agency = less commission for Booker

Booker's salary dependent on Justin's jobs $\therefore$ London - Justin = salary < normal

'Baby *no*!! You can't leave now! You're doing so well – if you go away now you'll lose your heat!'

'If you don't book me out, I'll quit. I'm not kidding. I need to sleep and grow and eat and SLOW DOWN.'

Mandy re-did her sums, taking the new data into the equation. There was almost an audible ka-ching! as she came to her answer.

'Baby! I've got it! *New York!*'

We both checked her sums.

Work in NY = temporary absence vs permanent absence

temporary absence = long-term investment

t = 0 : work in NY $\rightarrow$ t = 1 work London

So: London (Justin) t = 1 > London (Justin) t = 0

Even my poor maths brain could follow her logic. New York tear sheets would raise my fee in London and get me more work, thereby turning my absence into a long-term investment in my career for the Agency.

'How about it, baby?! I'll book you on a flight now! DNA loved your book – they saw it last week! I'll call Celia!'

'I don't know Mandy – New York is scary and scary is the last thing I need right now. I – '

'Maggie!!' Mandy jumped up and grabbed Maggie just as she walked through the Agency door, looking very cool in long, navy cords and a huge leather belt, trilby over one eye. I glimpsed a black Mercedes plus driver idling outside.

'Justin's off to New York – it's her first time!'

'Is she with DNA?' Maggie sounded bored, tired.

'Yes, baby!' Mandy was practically jumping up and down. 'It's the best agency – you know that! Their girls did all the Versace – '

'New York's cool, Justin.' Maggie spoke slowly, ignoring Mandy.

I would have done anything for her just for that. 'Is it scary?' I asked, feeling shy, silly, babyish.

'No. It's awesome.'

'Cool.'

'I'll watch out for you.'

'Cool.'

And she turned away to talk to Serena.

Maggie had calmed me, reminded me of my priorities. I was a model and crazy travelling was what models do. And I was cool – I wanted to be cool. Maybe New York would make me like Maggie, give me the swagger, the poise, the icy glamour with the rough edge that I craved. I could make money and grow up fast.

'So, do you want to go tomorrow?! Dean, book Justin on a flight tomorrow, darling! No, wait! Day after – you've got an important casting for TV tomorrow. Oh! I'll miss you, sweetie, but take care of yourself and don't forget to eat! You can always come back if you hate it! You'll have such a good time!'

Seeing Maggie outside, easing into the backseat of her waiting car, decided me. 'I'll check in later Mandy,' I yelled as I left the office. The electric window of the Merc went down and Maggie stuck her beautiful face out. 'I'll give you a lift to Swiss Cottage – you're in the model flats, right?'

I got in.

'I'm on my way up there anyway, working with David for Piaget at the Old Street studios. I'll be in New York in two days. I've got an *ID* shoot tomorrow. Mandy's a nut. But New York is fun.' She scribbled her number. 'Call me Sunday morning, not too early. I'm shooting with Mario Testino on Monday – I might be able to get him to see you.'

Mario Testino was the holy grail of photographers as far as I was concerned. The stars in my eyes blinded me. I was in love with Maggie.

New York was where Things Happened and I was on my way there with a suitcase full of hackneyed expectations. Before I left TK gave me a tape to play on my Walkman – she always made fun of my ancient cassette box when everyone else had MP3s, MDs or at least CDs. 'That's so eighties!' she'd say, but from TK that was also a compliment. She made me promise to listen to her tape only once I had landed in New York.

'Or I'll get really embarrassed. It's lame, but anyway … so you won't miss me.'

'I love it. I'm going to be nervous, so thanks.'

TK was jealous, and told me so. 'New York is where the money is. You'll be a star, I bet.'

'There's no way –'

'They'll love you.'

'You should come with me.'

TK said she'd ask the Agency. 'But I'm supposed to be going on a trip to the Seychelles for Tropicana. And besides, DNA don't want me, and I need the Agency to pay for my flight.'

'If you came over we could go shopping – we never do that in London. We only ever go to charity shops and markets and Top Shop. I'm cashed up and you will be too after Tropicana. We'll go to The Plaza!'

'That's a hotel.'

'Well, whatever. We could get an apartment – just us two – be free. Money is freedom. I'd love to have amazing clothes. We should spend more money on clothes. They're an investment, really.'

'What? In our future?' TK raised a sarcastic eyebrow and smirked at me.

'Well, yeah. Our lives. Something like that.' Why was TK trying to burst my bubble?

'We don't really have lives though, do we? Not real ones.' It came out so bitterly that I became defensive. *My* life was going to change for the better, even if TK didn't want to believe it.

'Well, I do. I have a life and I'm going to New York to get a better one.'

It was as close as TK and I had ever come to an argument.

I decided she was jealous that I was going to New York and leaving her behind. But I didn't understand it. I would never completely understand TK. People either loved or hated her; they either thought she was amazingly beautiful or just didn't get her look. She was curious and gentle and hard all at once, and she never stopped surprising me with her personas and the scraps of stories from her past. TK seemed to have no single personality of her own but merely the possibility of many types. The more I knew her, the more elusive she became – she had no centre, no hard red dot of truth. The true TK surrounded her like the seeds of a dandelion.

TK's voice was in my ear as I jolted around in the back of a cab, hurtling towards the forest of skyscrapers that I recognised as Manhattan. My fingers had gradually relaxed their hold of the door handle but they remained resting there in case I needed to leap out of the moving car. I had seen enough American movies to know that New York City cabbies were notoriously unpredictable. Mine, happily, did not speak to me but rather sang along to very loud reggae, sweating despite the cold. I watched him closely through the Perspex partition (in place, I was certain, more for the safety of the passengers than the driver) for signs of mania but his madness seemed to be restricted to his driving. Feeling slightly seasick, I listened to TK's words drifting through my headphones.

'... *New York once, when I was sixteen – sent by my LA agency for some job. I was scared of the photographer because he was so hairy ...*'

The cab rumbled over the Hudson River, and I felt a thrill of pure excitement.

'... *miss you. I'll have to make friends with some of the baby faces – the milk drinkers – in the agency I suppose ... like that Matilda. She's cute, I like her hair – very* Rosemary's Baby. *She doesn't say much and she's not cool ...*'

Everything I saw from my window was new to me and yet I had seen it a million times. Every cab, fire hydrant, police officer, fire escape, old diner, gas station and coffee cup had featured in so many films that the drive became surreal. The city seemed to have imitated itself, to be a false stage for its inhabitants. Nothing had ever so faithfully lived up to my expectations as my first encounter with Manhattan.

'*Oh, I forgot to tell you about Shelli – this girl I met the other day on that catalogue shoot. She was terrifying. About thirty, really tall and skinny, blonde, but her face was old – you know, scaly. She was doing the mum's bit and, god, I so don't want to be modelling when I'm –* '

The model agency managed a huge warehouse-type building in

Tribeca. It was a Jebbery Hoochey wet dream of pretty, feathered birds caged in brick, all singing into their telephones. At least we got a room each – there were about five of us to a floor with three bathrooms but only one kitchen. Models need bathrooms but most can't be bothered with kitchens. The house wasn't full but the girls I saw looked scarier and much more grown up than the girls in Paris or London. A couple smiled at me on my way to my room but no one bothered me.

Too shy to stay in the house but too bored to stay in my room, I left the building with trepidation.

'... be careful, J, because New York City's funny. You can be walking along and everything is fine and then you turn down one street and you're suddenly in a really bad area. And you're so blonde ...'

I didn't stray far from the building on that first day, a Sunday. I couldn't tell if it was a bad area or not – certainly there were no trees – but I followed a mother with a stroller who was just too pregnant to be a blood-thirsty gangster in disguise. We came to a diner and I went in and ordered.

'... you've got to order waffles. They're amazing. I miss American food when I think about it. Have a milkshake – maybe strawberry, no, banana, and get ice cream ...'

The diner reminded me of Tokyo and my meals there so long ago with those distant, homesick American models. I wasn't homesick. I hardly thought about home. But I thought about Maggie and after I'd eaten my pancakes made by a rude, fat man in an apron I went to call her.

The movies had taught me to leave a tip on the table and shown me what New York payphones looked like. TK's voice on my Walkman kept me company as I wandered about, a little more confident about crime levels in the area after spotting Robert De Niro badly disguised in a baseball cap.

When I called Maggie she invited me to dine with her 'and a few friends' at Le Caprice that evening. I wandered back to the warehouse and picked through the jumble sale in the suitcase I had yet to unpack. What would I wear in this stony, grey city? I wanted diamonds and black suede but I had nothing like that.

I had to settle for a second-hand, pale-pink leopard-print dress with weird white ankle boots I had borrowed from TK more or less permanently because they were too small for her. It was cold and nothing was going to induce me to wear strappy heels.

'... *I saw this great, weird pair of shoes the other day in the Oxfam by the Agency. I'm really into the whole fifties thing – my hair is quite fifties. They're purple tweed, sort of, with a pale grey ...*'

TK's fashion mantra was soothing. Whenever I was frantic and stressed out, I liked to pick up a magazine and read the text that accompanied the editorials: 'Balenciaga corset dress, eighteen hundred pounds, shoes by Gianfranco Ferre, diamond anklet from a selection by Butler and Wilson, belt – model's own ...' It was as comforting as a lullaby.

I knew that Maggie was cool and rich enough to have her own apartment that she shared with her little boy who, I had forgotten, was called Ford. She told me: 'It's a solid all-American name, blue-collar to the hilt, like me. And at least everyone knows how to spell it. I've had to chew-proof all my furniture. Roman is so good with him.'

I wanted to meet Roman, see Maggie's apartment, step into Maggie's life. She was living proof to me that a model life could be just that. And she was working with Mario Testino the next day. She invited me to call into the studio to see her, and he would look at my book. I was beyond thrilled. Mario, or any big photographer for that matter, could transform a model's life. If they chose you for a big campaign or an important cover, the doors of Babylon would swing open for you and your face would be your fortune, your insurance against a life of mediocrity, poverty or obscurity. I feared mediocrity most. I had technicolour dreams that I needed fulfilled. My eighteenth birthday was drawing closer as the days grew colder and, with it, my use-by date. I needed New York to make me, to justify my life with wealth and glory.

'... *I want someone to go on weekend holidays with, who knows stuff about trees, and history. I want to read the papers in bed and have lots of kids and Sunday afternoon walks like my parents . . .'*

I turned TK off. Her vision was not mine and it was intrusive. It didn't belong to my version of life now. I was invited to dinner with Maggie in New York – and I felt hard and cool. On the move and on the make.

Lascari, the head booker at DNA, was at dinner that night. I had met him at a party in London and he was the one who had asked for me, although I wasn't terribly pleased to see him. Squat and tanned, he shone as if he was lacquered from head to foot, and I marvelled that he hadn't died of dermal asphyxiation. His smile was too wide and his eyes too close together, their simian gaze lingering for a few beats too long. But Maggie seemed comfortable with him. They kissed and Lascari hugged her as if the fifty-two hours since he had last seen her had been fifty-two years.

'Honey, angel, you look ab-so-lute-ly stunning!' His voice, sliding through his even teeth, sounded as slick as he was. Maggie did look stunning in a short, silk, kimono top worn under dirty denim, the jacket setting off her lovely face and proclaiming her attitude, which did not, since my brief re-acquaintance with her, seem to have diminished one bit since Tokyo. She kissed me on one cheek, confusing me for an instant (I had gone for two). I hurriedly recalled my wayward lips and was placed at the table between Roman and Lascari.

My face felt hot and I had to concentrate on keeping my twitching fingers still. I didn't know where to look or who to talk to. In my brief career I had learned to hide my discomfort well, but this was New York and something in the air made me more nervous than usual.

Lascari ordered white peach bellinis and I soon relaxed. He had the same predilection for ordering my supper for me as Jeb had, but Lascari did it with less charm and was all in all a bland, if highly perfumed, dinner companion.

Perhaps I had expected too much, expected too much to be different, but by the main course (swordfish) only glances at Maggie saved me from total boredom. She was in deep conversation with one of Madonna's ex-boyfriends and they were just out of earshot.

'So true! Blood everywhere –'

' – horrible pain.'

The snippets that drifted my way were too tantalising to bear so I tuned into Lascari and Roman.

ROMAN: The amazing thing about working with Saul is his profound perception of what it means to be in an existential vacuum where the *self* becomes *elf* and you lose the true nature of your identity . . .

LASCARI: You're so right.

ROMAN (taking no notice): . . . and become one with that metaphorical darkness. It's a darkness that is very familiar to us all – especially me. (Roman spreads his hands wide and gives a deprecating beam at no one in particular.) You might remember certain events at the beginning of this year . . . (pauses to sip water)

LASCARI: The piece in *People* magazine . . .?

ROMAN: Drinking is different to alcoholism. Alcoholism is a disease. I had to recognise that it was not my fault that I turned to drink, and to put myself in the hands of a higher power.

LASCARI (taking a sip of his water): Oh. You too? Which meetings?

ROMAN: I like midnight meetings in Soho.

LASCARI: I've never seen you there, but I usually go on weekends.

ROMAN: Well, I'm only on my fifty-sixth day – I'm still going every day.

LASCARI: Are you sharing?

I began to wish I had brought TK's tape with me. Luckily Maggie and her dinner partner, who seemed to be having a better time than the rest of us, ordered more wine. As only three of us were drinking, there was plenty to go around. I tried to remain unselfconscious, wedged between two reforming alcoholics, as I accepted another glass. Strong eyes followed my glass.

ROMAN: I had issues with my rage.

LASCARI: Oh, me too. And my parents.

ROMAN: The amount of damage a parent can do to a child is staggering. I mean, I see even with Maggie's little boy, Ford, that . . .

I wondered about my parents. I had left a message for my mother, telling her I was going to New York and was working a lot. She had left a message saying she was excited for me, to have a good time and that she was working a lot too as there was a small group of frogs in northern New South Wales that . . .

I pulled out my pouch of tobacco and made myself a neat cigarette. I had begun rolling my own (after much practice on the kitchen table first, to get ready for public display) since I had seen a cool black girl in roller-disco denim doing it at a Levis casting. I was proud of my lighter, which said 'Cherry Tree Ranch. Best Little Whorehouse in Nevada'. TK had brought it for me from a shoot in Las Vegas for a modern interiors magazine doing a neon feature. No one at the table noticed my cool lighter but a waiter came rushing over. It couldn't be a no-smoking problem as Mickey Rourke's table next to us were at it like a bushfire.

'None of that in here!' he yelped as he slid to a halt, addressing Lascari.

'They're smoking,' I said, pointing to the next table.

'No drugs in here. I'm sorry sir!'

I had to laugh. 'It's tobacco. It's not weed. Here, smell it.'

'None of that here. Tell her to put it out,' the waiter said to Lascari.

I held up my pouch for his inspection, saying, 'Smell it. It's tobacco. I roll my own cigarettes.'

'Tell her to put it out!'

The waiter was treating me like a vegetable and so I started behaving like one. I stared at him blankly, feeling suddenly in control, interested at last in something that was going on at our end of the table. It wasn't until Lascari turned to me and said, 'Honey, Justin, maybe you should put it out,' that I slowly, deliberately, ground out my cigarette.

Ignoring the waiter, I spoke loudly to Lascari: 'Why couldn't he just have spoken to me directly? I mean, why did he have to say "tell *her* to put it out" as if I'm a pet or something?'

Roman spoke to me for the first time. 'They're trained not to talk directly to film stars. Jennifer Lopez's assistants aren't even allowed to look her in the eye.'

'I'm not a film star.'

'It's all the same – you're not a civilian so they don't deal directly with you. They go through your agent.'

I accepted Roman's explanation with grace but preferred my own reasoning – that the waiter saw me as an ungovernable pet, a yapping blonde chihuahua, and had appealed to the face he thought owned me. To reassert my undomesticated status, I rescued my unsmoked cigarette, re-lit it with my whorehouse lighter and enjoyed it far more than the conversation around me.

The second act of the New York evening had as backdrop a club in the West Village rumoured to be patronised by Leonardo and Russell. It joined other dark, glittering clubs in the big cities of my life, strung together like jewels on a velvet rope looping between continents. The drinks were 'reassuringly expensive', in Lascari's words, but I wasn't paying. I had my mind set on the neon pink cocktails I'd seen on my way in . . .

I knew that another way to change your life was to get a famous boyfriend, and here I toyed with the idea as there were many famous guys manning about in dark shirts and toffee-lensed sunglasses. But for some reason famous men never tried to pick me up. They smiled and flirted and turned me around with their expensive hands, admiring my moving parts, but I was never taken home to be played with. And tonight, while I could see two famous actors and a minor rock star of about the right age, I noticed their eyes were already taken by two blondes and three brunettes at their table (all models). So I decided it was better to ignore the men and make my own way to the top. Men could come later – they would have to. Famous people always had boyfriends.

I evaded Roman's long-winded forays into amateur psychology and sat as far away from both him and Lascari as I could. The night, like so many others, folded in on itself. I wanted to change tables, be sought-after, glitter and flicker, laugh and call young actors by their private nicknames. A cliché slunk into my mind and danced there like a cheap whore: 'So close and yet so far away'.

I got tipsy, received compliments from Lascari, shared my rolled-up cigarettes with Ethan Hawke and accidentally surprised two chi-chi sisters (blonde, Uptown money) doing cocaine in the bathroom.

'Evening ladies,' I laughed, but they slammed the door in my face. 'Terribly, terribly sorry but some of us actually need to pee!'

I didn't care about anything anymore, especially not a pair of over-dressed heiresses with blow-dried hair who were so far from London cool. One of the actors I saw that night did, however, remind me of Taber John. But I hadn't remembered him for so long my mind was unused to his name and unable to hold the thought for long.

It was two years since I'd left Australia and it felt like a lifetime. Taber John belonged to a world I hardly remembered, where my name had been Justine and I had lived in fear of detentions. I couldn't decide whether I felt sorry for that girl or whether I despised her, so I preferred not to think of Justine at all.

The next day I went to meet Mario Testino, handsome star-maker. He was shooting Maggie at a studio warehouse in the meatpacking district. She'd said, 'I can't promise he'll even like you but at least you'll meet him – he's into your sort right now.'

My sort. What was that? I was keen to go along and find out.

I amused myself while I waited for Mario by drawing a moustache on Claudia Schiffer. One of her covers, tatty with wear, sat on the studio coffee table. I had just started on the ends, making them curl like those of a Turk, thick, black and bushy, when I was interrupted.

'That's one of my covers.'

It was Mario, standing over me. I tried to cover my work but it was too late and I got black pen all over my arm.

'Sorry.'

'So, do you have a book?'

He sat down and stared at me. His eyes were very dark under black brows, and they remained fierce but still, like poisonous water. I fumbled with the straps of my bag, conscious of looking a silly fool, and handed my book to him. He hadn't taken his eyes off me yet and I was getting hotter. I didn't even attempt to comment on the book – make the usual apologies, explanations, describe pictures to come and options for future work – and Mario, although he turned the pages, kept his eyes on my face almost the entire time. Not knowing where to look, I watched him turn the pages, seeing myself flick by in clear plastic sheaths. So many poses, so many faces. When I looked up the studio mirrors caught my embarrassment, and everywhere I turned,

I found only myself. Make-up mirror, page, dressing mirror, page. I felt dizzy with narcissistic disorientation.

Mario broke the spell by handing back my book. 'Nice book. But all the photographers you've worked with don't seem to see anything but baby or sexy-doll. Your book's very young.'

'I know.'

At least he was speaking, but he was burning me with those eyes.

He put me against a wall and told me not to pose. That is a dreadful thing to be commanded to do by a photographic god, and it didn't help that Maggie chose right then to emerge from the dressing room to join the other few pairs of bored eyes following Mario's every blink.

I managed to go limp and think of my hunger. Mario snapped off three quick polaroids and showed them to me. I had come out blank, soft and paler than usual, a spot on my chin glowing. I looked cooler than I felt – still young, but not innocent, and not a doll.

'They look like me.'

The minute the words left my mouth I realised how stupid I sounded, but I meant it – they were the only pictures I had seen that actually looked like I felt.

Mario smiled for the first time. 'That's why I'm good.'

He gave the shots to one of his many assistants and moved away. He was replaced by Maggie, insanely good-looking in a tight denim jumpsuit that would have been impossible on anybody else.

'Hey! So, did he like you?'

'He didn't say much. Just that my book's young.'

'Where are you going now?'

'I've got a casting on 29th Street, then down to the Agency.'

'If you come back here I'll walk to the Agency with you. I've only got two shots to go. It won't take long.'

I have to confess I felt rather smug at my next casting, which was a cattle-call for Maybelline. The money would be good but I almost felt too cool. These clients were sure to be the kind who couldn't see past the pretty-punky baby. I wished I could tell the room full of bored models that Mario Testino had just taken my picture, and that I was hanging out with an almost-supermodel, but instead I sat quietly and pulled out my charred *Book of Compliments*.

'Nice book', I wrote, then attributed the compliment (such as it was) to 'Supermario'.

Two hours later I was called in to see the client. Trying to replicate my Supermario moment, I gave them my 'I'm too cool' stare but somehow it just wasn't the same. They barely looked at me, and pored over my book. The photographer put me against a wall (the five-thousandth flash-bulb firing squad of my career) and shot a polaroid which didn't come out. Well, that's not exactly true. The wall, the edge of the carpet and the top corner of a door came out perfectly, but I was missing. In the spot where I had been standing, there was only white wall. The photographer was dumbfounded. He looked at me in absolute horror, fear even, and quickly crumpled the polaroid before the clients could blame my transparency on his faulty eye.

In a shocking effort to smooth it over, I forced a laugh: 'Looks like there's nothing left of my soul to steal!'

He didn't get it, or at least didn't appear to. I didn't think it worth explaining my interest in the fear of certain Aboriginal Australian tribes. He took another shot quickly. We both looked frightened, me in the picture, him in the flesh, and I was sent on my way.

Out the door, I wished I had asked for the faulty polaroid, then realised it wouldn't prove a thing. Anyway, it was something I supposed should be kept secret; incidents of invisibility were not desirable in a potential supermodel.

I was still thinking about the strange incident as I walked back to meet Maggie. I remembered times when people had said, 'Oh, sorry, I didn't see you there!' or 'Oops, I didn't notice you by the sofa,' or 'What are you doing, popping up out of nowhere!' I had always thought it was just their unwillingness to incorporate glasses into their 'look', but perhaps I *was* occasionally invisible.

No matter, you have more important fish to fry.

Maggie left the studio looking cool in tight Earl jeans, heels and a Louis Vuitton bomber jacket. It was good I was chewing gum because otherwise my jaw would have dropped. Maggie was hot, I could see that, but it was the jacket that put me over the edge. It was silky gold on gold, lined with hot pink, and had her name embroidered on the back. It shone under the streetlights like all the treasure in the world.

'Nice jacket.' My voice cracked with desire.

'Marc made it for me for the show last season, then gave it to me. I don't suppose there was anything else they could do with it, seeing my name's on the back. But it's quite groovy.'

'Quite.' I couldn't take my eyes off it as we made for Canal Street in long, swift strides, my legs having to hop-skip every fifth step to keep up.

The jacket said success, it said 'I have friends who are famous designers', and it screamed money and cool and who gives a fuck. I had to own a jacket like that one day. It was my golden fleece.

Maggie was telling me about how Ford's first word had been 'baby'. 'It was so cute,' she went on, 'the way he said it. I want to get home and see him.'

We were walking by the Canal Street basketball courts when five black girls came towards us. 'Are they homegirls?' I whispered.

Maggie laughed. 'I guess so.'

They were truly splendid. They had long hair worked into fantastic braids and twists, and wore shiny shell suits in white, gold, black, red, and fluorescent yellow. Even their nails were amazing – five centimetres long, airbrushed and studded with tiny diamonds. Their ears, fingers and necks were loaded with gold jewellery and they wore expressions like fierce bulls. I had never seen homegirls in real life and felt thrilled that they looked exactly the way they did on MTV. I was also pleased to have Maggie by my side.

They passed us leaving a trail of scent, and I stole a closer look at the girl in the white shell suit. She had the longest nails and they were painted perfectly in white with a black lightning bolt down the length of each and a single rhinestone at the tip. Her hands were enormous, her wrists circled with thick, gold bracelets, but the ring on her middle finger was the most enormous of all. I managed to see it was a solid-gold crown with three points – the logo of King, the massive fashion label.

'Amazing,' I was about to say to Maggie, 'how people now wear fashion label logos as jewellery,' when suddenly that logo was flying toward me. The three points flashed once before crashing into my face with the force of a falling brick. There was hot light in my head, white hot pain, then warm red, then total black.

Someone was throwing apples on the grass, overripe apples into long grass. They fell in fruity thuds not far from where I lay. Perhaps they're falling from a tree, I thought. I could sense animals nearby, moving about and feeding on the apples, crunching through taut skins and grunting in pleasure.

I couldn't see the animals – I think my eyes were wide open but I couldn't see anything, not even stars. I could feel hardness against one cheek and knew I was lying somewhere. I was curled against something hard and straight at my back and felt comfortable, but knew I couldn't move away.

Now the brutal stench of piss was there too, and with it the pain. A steel tennis ball was lodged in my cheekbone and it was burning hot and throbbing. I wanted to cry but I couldn't see anything at all and my eyes wouldn't throw out any tears. Then a shower of stars, or sparks, began to fall like a waterfall of fire. I could see it was beautiful but the pain was consuming me. Soon the sparks faded. Light began to dawn and I lifted my head.

Maggie was lying beside me in a pool of blood so red I didn't think it was real until I saw two policemen running towards her. She wasn't moving and her gold jacket was gone.

At the hospital I told the policemen everything I could remember: the flying crown, the braids, the perfume – Angel, by Mugler, now that I thought about it. They said I was fortunate. The first punch had knocked me down and out, and I had rolled in a ball against the side of a mailbox in the dark. The girls had forgotten about me. The man at the taxi stand, the one who had called the police, had seen Maggie struggling with the girls, yelling and fighting back. But it was no good. The girls had become angry and punched her. When she fell to the ground, they had kicked her.

I tried to explain to the policemen that I had heard apples falling and had recently been afflicted by bouts of invisibility. 'That's what saved me, don't you see?' But they merely said they hadn't found any apples at the scene, and that I was definitely not invisible.

The hospital wouldn't let me see Maggie straightaway. They gave me an icepack and told me to come back later. The models at the flat were either out somewhere, or getting their beauty sleep. Without even turning on any lights I fell into bed, icepack pressed against my now-numb cheek.

The mirror's was the first opinion I sought when I awoke the next morning. It told me that I looked like shit. My eyes were rimmed by dark circles. The swelling had gone down, but I'd been left with a purply-red imprint of a crown, detailed and raised, right on the crest of my cheekbone. My fingers brushed over it in horrified awe. No way concealer was going to cover that.

'Don't let Ford see me like this, please.'

I nodded because I couldn't speak. Lascari had sent a huge bunch of pale peonies and I fixed my eyes on them, on my hands, anywhere but Maggie's face. What flesh was visible was swollen and red, but bandages covered most of her head. I described the flowers because her eyes were swollen shut. Her eye socket had splintered, her jaw was fractured, the bridge of her nose was smashed and there were cuts – Maggie was never going to look the same again.

Why does it always seem to be the model whose face is disfigured in a car accident? It's not, of course, but we only ever seem to hear about it when it is. When a model's face or body is damaged, she dies. Maggie had been killed in the attack, Ford's mum had survived.

'I'm afraid you can't stay much longer.' A young nurse brought in more pale peonies and put them by the first.

I read the card: 'These are from Roman.' He obviously used the same florist as Lascari.

Roman was in LA filming his new movie, he was going to fly out to see Maggie as soon as there was a break in filming. His note said, 'Get well soon'. Did he know there was never going to be a 'soon'? He had rung the nanny and told her what had happened so she was looking after Ford until Maggie's mum arrived from Ohio.

From a payphone in the hospital corridor I rang DNA and asked for Lascari.

'Honey! Oh God! We're just crazy in here right now – are you okay?! Were you with Maggie last night?'

'I'm fine, I just got punched in the face. I've got a big welt on my face . . . but Maggie –'

'Justin, I know! It's horrific. The hospital rang. I can't even bring myself to think about it. She was so beautiful.'

'Are you coming to the hospital?'

'I sent her flowers this morning. I can't possibly come down, Justin!

It would upset me too much to see her like that! I just want to remember her the way she was when I knew her.'

'She's not dead, you know.'

'Are you coming in today? Let's see – yes. You've got a twelve o'clock with Michael Sword. He wants to see some new faces – I think he'd like you. He's a very good photographer, does loads of big campaigns.'

'But my face –'

'Come in anyway and we'll take a look. It's not permanent is it?'

I took a cab door to door. The fear I now felt of walking down any street, even during the day, threatened to paralyse me.

I stared at my face in the lift mirror on the way up to the Agency. The welt was a deep red now and my whole head ached. The lift doors opened and I closed my eyes.

'Oh my god!' Lascari jumped up from his swivel chair when I walked in, making all the other bookers turn. He examined my face so closely I felt the air from his nostrils.

'Justin! Don't move.'

Confused, I obeyed as he snatched something from the table and – FLASH – took a snap. 'I've just had the most brilliant idea!' He turned to one of the junior bookers. 'Katie! Courier this ASAP to King, mark it "attention Yves", he runs all the campaigns. They are going to die, I'm telling you! Michael!'

A handsome, scruffy man had just arrived.

'Look at this!' Lascari dragged me over to Michael. 'Isn't it genius? Dreadful, but genius.'

Michael refused to join in.

'Yves is going to love this, don't you think?'

'Is it real?' Michael stared at my cheek.

'Yes! That's the best thing! Yves is trying to funk up their image, give King street cred. It'll make the most amazing campaign – top Kate Moss in Calvin! I've sent a polaroid up. Katie, has that gone yet?

Look!' Lascari snatched the photo up before it went into an envelope. In it my eyes were half closed but the purple-red crown was plain to see in bas-relief.

'Powerful, I agree,' Michael conceded.

Lascari dropped it in an envelope. 'Get it off to them. Now!'

Katie scurried away.

'We'll get you to shoot it, Michael. Today – no, tomorrow!'

'Let's do a few shots this afternoon. I'll get Yves to come by and look at them, see if it's working. I've got a studio for today anyway. I'll cancel the portrait of Hilary – do her instead. I think they might go for it.'

'I think they'll adore it. You shoot the pictures, Justin gets amazing exposure, King gets a great campaign – everybody wins!'

How could Lascari talk of everybody winning on the day Maggie had lost her face? I didn't want to think about their plan. It was monstrous and yet it made perfect creative sense.

Horrified as I was, I wasn't going to refuse. Three o'clock found me at a studio in Chelsea Piers.

'Leave the dark circles, it's edgier that way. Even out the skin tone around the nose, but don't touch the welt. Perfect. No, leave the inflamed bits red. I like it.'

Yves, a very tall man, arrived moments later, and stalked around the room wearing black. The polaroid had indeed lit his fire and he wasn't a man to waste a perfect opportunity. I still hadn't said a word but people were saying I must be in shock. I was, I suppose, but not about the attack.

Michael concentrated on perfect lighting. 'I want it bare, clean, bright. I want to see every detail, every pore, every broken blood vessel. Get me a filler!'

His assistants scurried around.

Yves stood over the hair and make-up, and the stylists, giving orders. He had decided that the concept would be most effective for his new line of unisex underwear – singlets, panties, tank tops and so on. I was photographed wearing various pieces of underwear, though most of the shots were taken up close, just head and shoulders.

'I want to capture that pugnacious look in her eye, like she's just picked a fight. I love it!' Michael raved, completely hooked now on the idea.

I felt like picking a fight. I couldn't believe these people. It was all so wrong but it was happening anyway. Lascari was hanging around watching.

'Okay, now give me a really angry face. Pretend you're just so angry with everything!'

'I don't have to pretend!' I snapped at Michael.

'Great! Perfect! More like that.'

I stormed off when he finished the roll. My eyes had filled with tears and I wanted to hide.

Lascari came running over. 'Justin, honey – what's wrong? Is everything okay?'

'Everything's *not* okay, Lascari. This is weird. Maggie's in hospital, I've got a bashed cheek and you're all – '

'Justin, honey, it's *business*.' He spoke slowly as if to an idiot. 'It's just good business. Now get back there and let Yves and Michael make you a star.'

Then he patted me.

Maggie's face was in the evening papers. They had used an old shot from her comp card, the one with the Canadian *Elle* cover that had made her so sought-after in Tokyo. They quoted Lascari: 'It's a tragedy, a real tragedy. Maggie was such a lovely young woman.' I knew he'd be wishing he had able to give them a better picture.

'Are you going to buy that paper, lady? This isn't a library you know!'

A wave of rage broke inside me. I wanted to leap at the man behind the newsstand, yell something awful, punch him. Instead I threw down the paper in protest, my tears hot with frustration.

The new *Cosmo* was out and, in a wicked twist of fate, Maggie's face was on the cover, smiling, her hair blown back by a studio wind. The cover image had a life of its own that had nothing to do with Maggie – who she was or what she was going through. Would her face continue to appear in magazines, on covers, for months after her attack, taunting her? I knew she had an editorial for *Bazaar* coming out in February, the cover of *Mademoiselle* for spring, and her Piaget ads would go up around town soon back in London.

Her fame lived wholly outside her now. Maggie the model had moved on into a different time scale – not quite immortal, but not subject to common time either.

Lascari rang me the next morning. 'I've had Mandy on the phone. She's so excited for you! You know they're going to use it? Yves showed Roland King this morning and he went ape. They're going to bring it out in the New Year. It's going to be *huge*, honey! You're going to be a – '

> The King is dead! Long live the King!
>
> Happy now? You've got what you wanted – but what about Maggie? Maybe it was your hunger for fame that made this happen. Did fortune take from one to give to another? There is only room in the spotlight for a few at a time. Maybe fate bumped her to make room for you. Did you kill Maggie?

'Lascari, I want to go home.'

Lascari let me go back to London because he knew I would leave anyway and, anyhow, it was almost Christmas so things would be quiet until New Year. 'Promise you'll come back after New Year, sweetie!' he said. 'Have a great Christmas –' but I hung up and began to fill my suitcase with the clothes that were lying around the room like withered skins.

22
Look Before You Leap

It would have been the perfect occasion to wear fur: almost Christmas, and snowing. The streets were still their usual oily black but by midnight the hard stones of old London had been put to bed under a duvet of undisturbed snow. Only the bare, black trees remained, standing out like pubic hairs on crisp linen, but beautiful nonetheless. A white mink would have suited the night.

Instead I chose my rhinestone tiara, ankle boots and a white dress adorned with blood-red hibiscus flowers (borrowed from TK). The cold bit my legs to my crotch but it was a Christmas party and no time to dress sensibly. Caprice and TK strode alongside me, the span of our collective strides easily eight metres as we powered through the streets, breath escaping white and hanging suspended like the promise of a steam train around the next bend. We felt just as unstoppable.

Caprice lit a Capri (the Newports had been dumped along with her old name). She had no compunction about smoking as she walked. I, on the other hand, always felt like a street-walker if I lit up outside and was never tempted, no matter how cold the night.

Caprice had lost even more weight and become even blonder. Her breasts seemed bigger on her thin frame and I worried she would fall forward under their weight. Her face was pale from the strain of too many late nights and a fresh break-up. Shrimp had decided that monogamy was bad for his Rock Dog image and that Caprice had to learn to share or get the bat out of hell out.

'Whose Christmas party is this anyway?' she asked.

'Arabs,' TK said.

'Rich ones?'

'Do we know any other kind?'

Caprice's laugh had lost its film-star tinkle and become throaty and lewd. It ended in a cough. 'Jesus, Mary and Joseph,' she doubled over. 'It's been a hell of a week.'

'I thought you and Shrimp were going to get married – what with the matching tattoos and all,' I said.

Caprice lifted her top and exposed a breast, oblivious to the possibility of causing a Piccadilly Circus. 'What tattoo?'

There was a large red rose on her chest under which you could just make out the letters 'IMP'. She inhaled deeply and sighed, as she always did before imparting one of her great insights. 'Men want to fuck lions and marry pussy cats.'

I think TK and I were expected to stop and gasp, but we were late, and Caprice's weary wisdom drifted onto the footpath and lay dead among the snowflakes.

Ali sent a launch to the dock to pick us up. I hadn't heard from him since the 'gifts' debacle and I was nervous. I tried to tell myself he might not even notice me at the party, that he might have forgotten all about me. From the banks, the river swirled with cold and dirty danger. Perhaps it was the river, perhaps the snow, perhaps thoughts of Ali, but I felt uneasy. I was tempted to make an excuse and bow out, but it was almost Christmas and I didn't have the energy.

'Just don't leave me alone with Ali, you guys,' I said wearily.

TK squeezed my arm. 'Relax. There'll be loads of people there.'

Caprice was chuckling. 'I hope Ali's brother's there. I'm dying to meet him.'

A uniformed sailor helped us on board, his eyes lingering on Caprice's 'smile'. And then we were speeding through the freezing black air toward a huge white motor yacht. Cheap pop music wafted across the Thames and in the background Tower Bride hung suspended in a garter of lights like an unimaginative – yet wholly attractive – snow-dome pastiche. I smiled and thought of the executions that had happened there in the Olden Days.

'I thought Ali and his friends were Muslim – why are they having a Christmas party?' I asked.

'Who cares?' Caprice called over the rushing air.

By the time we reached the boat even my teeth were cold.

The first face I saw was Ali's. He was standing at the stern railings in an enormous fur coat, smoking a cigar and patiently watching the launch draw closer. He was surrounded by friends – or bodyguards, I couldn't tell – all male and all in fur. Together, they formed what looked like a shifting woolly mammoth without tusks. I thought about how many furry creatures had given their lives for Ali and his friends, conveniently forgetting that earlier I too had coveted the idea of mink.

A ladder was lowered and Caprice, TK and I climbed aboard. Ali greeted us with his usual graceful charm, then turned to the man at his side, a pointier, younger, harder version of himself. 'You haven't met my brother yet, have you?' I held out my hand and the man took it. 'Call me Ishmael,' he said, his eyes burning with a fury that his gentle handshake belied.

'So nice to meet you,' I said, then turned back to Ali, trebled in size in his coat, and thanked him politely for inviting us to the party. I didn't mention the flowers or gifts.

Ali made a little bow and turned away. Good, I thought, he seems to be fine. I did notice, however, Ishmael eyeing us as we crossed the aft deck. To hell with them all, I thought.

Caprice was pleased to see that standards were being upheld. A gently swinging chandelier hung above the aft deck and the open deck had been sheeted in clear plastic and warmed with heat lamps. A few brave ladies had shed their coats and were showing shoulder a nd a lot of gold lamé. Middle-Eastern house music started playing on hidden Bose speakers, and it was perfect that the first familiar face we should see was Nellee's.

'Are you responsible for this?' I was feeling brave – nothing much to lose if you're a loser.

Nellee smiled. 'Do you want to dance with me, sexy?'

An ululation burst through the speakers. I imitated it for a second, eyes on Nellee's, then turned my back on him and accepted a glass of champagne.

Caprice, TK and I clinked glasses. Caprice's chipped at the impact, but she drank anyway. 'Merry fucking Christmas, girls.' She downed the whole glass, then spat out a shard of crystal flute. The glass drew blood from her lip. 'Live a little, then die a little, babes. Tonight, I'm falling in love.' And off she went to mingle in the crowd and seek out husbands.

I felt Nellee's lips on the back of my neck and turned.

'Where's Jeb?' I asked. Jeb's joking flirtation was the best way to keep others' more serious intentions at bay.

Nellee looked away, raised his glass and drank deeply. 'How should I know?'

'Don't pretend you don't travel as a pair – I never see you apart at parties.'

'Why do you want to know? He's a bad man, Justin.'

'And you're not, Nellee? Better the devil you know.'

'I'm a devil now?'

'Don't mistake the insult for interest.' I smiled. 'Are you sure you don't know where Jeb is, now that you know I'm not here for you?'

'Try the big front cabin – it has a bar and a hot tub.'

TK and I made our way around the bar, carefully avoiding a lubricated Mandy and her posse of models.

'She should just put them all on leashes and feed them a goddamn tidbit.' TK's mood had soured since she'd spotted Dirty Boy chatting to a brunette in crochet. 'Mandy takes them everywhere. She doesn't feel comfortable unless she has her models around – people don't want to know her except as a procurer. She's so sad.'

'We were her pets once, don't you remember?'

'But not like them. They're really lame – Lara O'Hara wannabes. We were never that limp.'

'Or uncool.'

'We'll never be proper models, with manicures and hair.'

'Thank Christ for that.'

'There! Do you remember him?' TK pointed toward Mandy. She was enveloped in a male.

'"Take ma picture!"' I giggled in imitation – it was the male model Benny.

'I've heard they're having a scandalous fling. He's ten years younger than her.'

We accepted another glass of champagne. 'Let's go find Jeb,' I suggested.

The passages of the yacht seemed to go on forever like Alice's Wonderland. The boat was big but people jammed every inch, and each room had its own vice on offer. It's funny how human indecency has the presence of mind, no matter how depraved the action, to organise itself.

The first room we passed was full of pungent smoke, strong as a beesting; the smell of cigars. Inside, there were only men and none were speaking English. The next cabin held an even number of boys and girls snorting lines of speed off the smooth finish of the dressers. A couple was fumbling on the bed, giggling.

Further along a cabin housed a large Italian (I could tell by his shoes), stripped to his waist, who was sweating away beside an open porthole as two girls in garters and nothing else kept him company. Their smiles gave them away as professionals. The man had his fingers inside the girl in front, twiddling them with fat satisfaction, as she ground her hips in simulated pleasure. The other girl was rubbing her breasts up and down the man's spine. None of them paid us any attention.

The next cabin was leaking steam. 'Bingo.' I threw over my shoulder to TK. She had stopped and was staring straight ahead down the corridor – at Dirty Boy, who had his mouth on the crochet girl as she leant against the wall.

Dirty Boy felt her stare and opened an eye. He winked it at us, his mouth never leaving its lippy pillow, then turned his back. TK was rigid and white. She stepped past the mashing couple and opened the cabin door. We were welcomed with moist warmth. There was a spa on a podium with only two people in it. One of them was Jeb, the other Nellee. There were no girls.

'We were just talking about you!' Jeb smiled at us through the steam.

'Sure.' TK was not in the mood to be flattered.

'Really? Nellee was just saying how nice it would be, how utterly divine it would be, if two gorgeous goddesses were to walk in and join us in the tub right now. And here you are.'

TK scowled and I smiled. She wouldn't hear compliments, but I liked them.

We sat on the edge of the tub.

'How did you get down here so fast?' I asked Nellee.

He popped a fresh bottle of champagne from an ice bucket and lifted his eyebrow mysteriously. We toasted the holiday season.

'Why have you two still got your clothes on?' Nellee demanded. 'Get in the tub – we're making soup.'

'In the water, while floating on the water – what could be more romantic?' Jeb was never short of 'romantic' ideas.

'I'm not sure it's romance we're after,' I said. 'I think you guys should talk to the girls we saw two cabins back. They seem to know what they're doing.'

TK smirked. 'Right.'

'Don't be spoil-sports,' said Jeb, 'live a little and get into the tub. I swear we won't touch you.'

'Right.' TK again.

Jeb looked up at me. 'I swear.'

I glanced at Nellee.

'He swears too. I'll kill him if he scares you.'

I took another sip of champagne and TK took off her dress. 'Why not?' She slipped into the tub, still wearing her underwear. 'Why the hell not?'

Jeb held my hand. It was hot and wet, but not unpleasant. TK was giggling. 'Come on, Justin – it's so warm in here.'

The bubbles tickled my nipples. There was no way I was taking my underpants off, but my breasts were public domain, having been shared with the readership of at least two Italian magazines, so they were bare. My knickers were of the large, seventies-style cotton variety and unlikely to arouse any lust in their own right.

The water was warm. I let myself relax. Everyone in the tub was keeping their distance. The champagne was making me happy and everything was good.

I felt a leg against mine, but it was smooth and hairless and I knew it was TK's. Safe. She looked over at me while reaching for the ice bucket. 'It's five days till Christmas,' she said, pouring us all more champagne.

We could hear the soft popping of champagne corks on the deck.

'Merry Christmas in advance, TK,' I said.

'Merry Christmas in advance, Justin,' TK said, and leant forward to kiss me. She went for my lips and took them into her mouth. She held them there for a beat and I felt it would be impolite not to respond. Plus, it felt soft and warm. We kissed each other Merry Christmas and a Happy New Year in advance.

The boys liked it a lot. Nellee and Jeb clamoured for their kisses. Jeb went for TK and Nellee had me in his arms. He smelt and felt good as he lowered his mouth and kissed me. I think it lasted a while and it wasn't bad, although a little too enthusiastic and with a little too much tongue.

Then we swapped. Nelle took TK and I turned towards Jeb. He stopped and looked at me. 'Best for last,' he said, but didn't move. I didn't either. Then he came closer, and kissed me softly – once, twice, three, four times.

'Merry Christmas then,' I whispered.

'I wish it could be Merry Christmas for ever,' he whispered back.

TK and Nelle were still kissing, TK now on top of Nellee. Jeb didn't move back, but neither did he move forward.

'I've wanted to make love to you from the minute I saw you.'

'Stop it, Jeb. We're flirting buddies, but being half naked in a hot tub with you blurs the line, so stop it.'

'I mean it. You're so sexy. I want to take care of you for ever. You could be my baby – my rock and roll baby – and nothing bad would ever happen to you. Let's make love. It's almost Christmas and I think I love you.'

'Jeb . . .'

'Justin, baby.'

He hadn't moved yet and it gave me confidence. 'I'm not one of your girls, Jeb. I don't do that. I'm not like them,' I said, but Jeb was looking very handsome tonight and I was charmed but also terrified. I didn't know if I wanted to get out of the tub, or stay in it forever.

'Baby . . . it'll feel so good.'

'Jeb, I've never done it before.'

'You're a virgin?'

I looked away quickly enough for Jeb to be able to assume a definite yes.

'Oh, Justin, doll-face,' he said as he grabbed me. 'You have no idea the effect you have on me. But if you don't want to, we won't. There are plenty of other things we can do. But I would be honoured to be your first.'

'I'm out of here.' But I couldn't move.

Jeb kissed me on the lips, then on the neck, up and down until I could no longer stand it. I could actually feel a pain running from my neck to my belly that turned everything in between to mush.

He pulled away. 'I want to kiss you all over. May I?'

I shook my head.

'Just close your eyes and let me kiss you somewhere, once.'

I shook my head again and drew my legs up.

'Justin – you trust me, don't you? A little bit?'

'Okay.' I closed my eyes, nerves jangling, and waited. I felt his lips come to rest on my exposed knee. I smiled in relief.

'See, that wasn't so bad, was it?'

Nellee and TK were still kissing among the bubbles. Jeb reached for the champagne. He had a tattoo of a black scorpion on the inside of his forearm. It had been blurred by time but this only made it look more ominous. He put his arm back in the tub and drowned the noxious insect. 'Tell me something, Justin.'

I hated it when they said that. 'That's not going to come off.' I pointed to his tattoo.

Jeb just looked at me. 'You're a little nutty, you know that?'

'Utterly.' I pulled myself out of the tub with as much haughty dignity as I could muster, my briefs sopping and saggy.

'Why are you leaving?'

'Nutty people don't have to answer why. It's one of the great advantages of insanity.' I turned to TK. 'Are you okay here?'

'Yes, babe. Anyway, there's no way I'm stepping outside right now. Not with *that* in the hallway.'

'Fair enough.' I dripped into the bathroom, pulled my dress over my wet pants and left the room.

I wandered the hallways, hoping to find Caprice or someone I knew. I looked and felt like a rat drowned in warm alcohol. I hoped my coat would hide the wet patch around my crotch that had rendered the dress transparent and might – to those uninitiated in hot-tub conundrums – look like the aftermath of a rather embarrassing accident.

The music reverberated through the walls and I could hear the thump of dancing feet on the deck above me. The narrow halls were filled with people moving in one direction then the other, and I was carried through the bowels of the boat like digesting food. The thought made me feel ill and I decided I needed air. I clawed my way up to the aft deck and wandered unsteadily to the bow.

The night air revived me, the cold cutting into my lungs with a satisfying thrust. Snow was falling heavily. Tower Bridge was hazy now, and more beautiful for it. I leant on the railings, oblivious to the snowflakes that came to rest in my hair, and breathed in the night.

Almost the New Year. I hoped I could make a New Beginning.

I thought of the days stretched before me, clean as the blanket of unsullied snow that was settling over the city. I felt tears well hot in my eyes and tumble down my face. The snow, the lights and the champagne were making me emotional.

Cry, you stupid fuck. Cry for all the days you've frittered away on empty nothings. Time is flying by and you're just sitting there watching. What are you doing with your life? You're a fucking model – and not even a great one at that. You've got wet pants and frozen nipples, your tiara's askew and you've come to the party in a borrowed dress. What happened to all your ambitions? You're just a dumb model with nothing to say who's too scared even to lose her fucking virginity. When are you going to grow up, get a life, and put yourself in charge?

From now on, it's over. You've thrown away all that you were given and you've given up on yourself. You're a hollow, worthless shell, old at almost eighteen. Serves you right. This is your punishment. Go inside and find a booker from a big agency. Tell him or her that you know you should have been a supermodel by now because you're prettier than all the other girls, including Giselle, Naomi and Kate. Then get on a table and start to strip off, all the while yelling, 'Isn't this the most beautiful thing you've ever seen?' Then stand naked in front of everybody, and start crying.

The weight of a warm hand on my shoulder made me start. I turned around. Ali. The present shot back into focus. This wasn't good.

'Justin, what are you looking at to make you so sad?'

I wiped the tears away quickly, sure that my nose was red and, for once, not caring. 'Nothing. I was just going inside.'

I stood to move but Ali blocked the path. 'Are you having a nice party?'

'Quite, thank you. You know, I really must find Caprice.'

'Of course. We will find her together.'

He took me by the arm and walked me aft. I'll admit I was a little afraid. Being on Ali's territory gave him an edge that I wished he didn't have. We were walking towards Ishmael and two furries. Ali called out to him. Ishmael shouted back something in what I imagined was Arabic. What he said sounded harsh but it might have been the unfamiliar-sounding language.

'I really must find Caprice now,' I blurted out, and headed for the cabin entrance. No one came after me and I began to relax. I roamed the hallways once again, looking for anybody I knew. Finally I came to an open cabin door and found Caprice.

She was the only girl in the cabin and I knew she was happy. That's the way she liked it. She was lying on her side, feet up, body propped on an elbow. A tall, immaculately dressed Arab gentleman was tending to her, alternately holding a flute of champagne to her lips and stroking her blonde hair. He was dressed all in white. 'Goddess,' I heard him murmur under his breath, 'I worship you.'

Caprice smiled lazily up at him. 'Imran.'

She saw me in the doorway and beckoned me in with a queenly gesture. I saw at once that she had become Cleopatra, and that she felt the role suited her perfectly. She proffered a hand and I wondered for an instant if she meant me to kiss it. I stared at her outstretched fingers. She fluttered them lightly and raised them to her mouth in a lady-like yawn. 'Justin, darling. Sit with me.'

She didn't move her feet, so I perched awkwardly on an armrest. 'Are you having a nice time, Caprice?'

'Splendid. Imran's been such a prince – which he almost is in his native land. Isn't that right, Imran?'

'I am cousin to a cousin of the prince, yes.'

I smiled. Ali had told me that there were hundreds of royal princes in the Middle East so Imran's blue-ish blood didn't impress me quite as much as perhaps it was intended to.

'That's great.' I turned to the prostrate Caprice. 'Have you seen anyone around – TK, Jeb, *anyone*?'

Caprice smiled. 'I've been far too preoccupied here with Imran.

I'm sure they're … around,' she said, waving her hand in tiny circles that I knew she had learnt from watching the royal procession on television. I had watched it with her and we had practised waving like the Queen. I backed out of the room.

A body crashed into my back. I lost my balance and felt someone grab my arm. I was propelled along the corridor, my feet dragging on the ground, confusion everywhere. I was conscious only of being surrounded by fur, thick, warm, brown fur. Ali again.

But the person pulling me toward the state cabin was not Ali, but Ishmael. I wanted to scream but the party was loud, and I wasn't sure what was happening. The state cabin was at the farthest end of the boat and there were no people there. Ishmael dragged me in and sat me heavily on the bed. His eyes were flashing with anger. I glanced over at the door and saw two hirsute henchmen blocking it. Ali was nowhere to be seen.

'You ungrateful little whore.'

Ishmael literally spat the words down at me.

'How dare you? How dare you –' He was so angry that he couldn't finish his sentence and his accent had grown thicker with rage. 'How dare you refuse my brother? It is unheard of!'

I had no idea what he was talking about, but the power of his anger kept me frozen to the bed. I tried to argue: 'I didn't refuse him, I –'

Ishmael raised his hand and hit me. I saw red and black and felt as though my face had been struck by an axe. There was ringing in my ears and my cheek burned. I was too shocked even to begin to cry. I thought, ridiculously, that I should have turned my other cheek. Ishmael had hit the same one that had been smacked in New York.

My mind spun like a kaleidoscope into a thousand fragmented thoughts.

Ishmael was talking again, softly, his fury drained by the blow. 'My brother courts you, and you refuse him. He wants you, and when a man from my family wants a woman, she cannot refuse without dis-honouring him. If you insult him by refusing again, I will kill you.'

He stepped softly to the door.

'You will stay here. Tomorrow we go to Saudi and you will come with us. It is useless to weep, your fate was decided at birth.'

With that he left the room and I heard the door lock behind him.

For a moment I wondered if this was real: the party, the boat, the threats, the champagne, the hot-tub, the furs, the snow, the pain. I went slowly to a mirror, lit Hollywood-style by soft light-bulbs. My cheek had split just enough to release a little blood and it was swelling fast. This had to be a dream, or *Days of Our Lives* – situations like this didn't happen to girls like me. This was a horror story told by cross-legged girls in hushed tones at castings on rainy days. This could not be real. I suddenly longed for the more manageable danger of Jebbery and his hot tub caresses.

I crept to the cabin door and put my ear to the polished mahogany. I could hear the muffled noise of the party outside but couldn't tell if the ruckus was muffled by the door or by the thick fur coats of Ishmael's henchmen standing outside. They had trapped their white whale – though I was more like a faded goldfish with a lump on its face, caught in a plastic baggie.

I tried the handle on the door – tried to shake it – but it was heavy, solid and immoveable. No one but the henchmen would hear if I screamed and pounded, and I didn't want Ishmael to come back. There had to be a way of attracting attention. *The boat is full of people! There is a party going on, for goodness sake!*

I looked around the cabin. I had to breathe and be calm and breathe. The only furniture was the enormous black bed in the centre of the room and a small, gilt coffee table. On it was a telephone. I leapt over to it, my mind already dialling. Silly Ishmael! But then I saw the handset was missing. I searched the room – under the bed, behind the bed, in the desk drawers – but there was no sign of it. Fear began to creep up my neck. I fought it off.

There's no way TK will leave the party without looking for me ... before the words could form in my head, the splinter of hope vanished. I realised how simple it would be for Ali to say I had become upset and gone home in a state. Why shouldn't TK believe him?

I kept thinking this might be a joke – but no one hit that hard for fun.

Keep busy, keep calm, keep looking for a solution, keep breathing ...

The windows. This was a luxury motor yacht and there were none of the tiny round portholes found on most ships. These windows were wide, square and tinted. Certainly more than wide enough for my hips. I flung myself at the catches and tugged. The window wouldn't budge. I yanked with all I had but it wouldn't move. I tried one after the other, my desperation growing with each failed attempt. The staff of crisp white sailors had seen to it that all hatches were battened before the ship left its moorings.

Catching sight of a small door disguised in the patterned fabric walls, I ran and banged it open. A perfect black marble bathroom, complete with gold taps. The light didn't work but I could see a window over the sink – and it was open. But just a crack.

I pulled and it slid easily. I wanted to laugh in relief as I leapt on the sink. Then I became conscious of the size of the window. Small. Very small. About the size of a magazine. I would never fit. I stared at it, willing it to grow but it wouldn't.

Through the window I could see lights on the shore, safe and welcoming, shining steadily, oblivious to my plight. I had another idea. I returned to the main cabin and began turning the lights on and off, hoping to attract attention. I knew I should be using Morse code but I had no idea what order to do the dots and dashes. I flicked the light-switch up down up down up until the bulb blew, and I was left in darkness.

I waited a moment but it was Christmas time and there were flickering lights everywhere. No one would take notice. They wouldn't even be able to see me from the water if there were no lights in the cabin. Tears were gathering like storm clouds but I couldn't let myself cry. I knew what was waiting if I didn't get out – every cliché about Arabs, harems and veils crammed into my head at once. I had visions of heavy black burquas and stone courtyards as deep as wells, snakes, tattooed faces and eerie wailing.

Terror didn't truly grip me until I heard the first of the motor launches start their engines. It must have been about three-thirty and they were beginning to ferry party-goers back across the river.

I flung myself at the door and beat on it with my fists, screaming. I don't remember how long I screamed, or who I called for or how loud, but no one heard me. The door remained firmly shut. It was then I realised that a life in Saudi Arabia as one of Ali's women (I was convinced he would have more than one) was not only a possibility but a distinct probability. I thought of my parents' shock when they learnt of my relocation. They would not be allowed to discover that I had been taken unwillingly. They would believe that I had gone of my own volition with complete disregard for them. It was the memory of their faces that split my heart. I suddenly became angry – furious – that someone thought they could do that to my parents.

Before I knew what I was really contemplating, I was kneeling on the marble sink again, straddling the gold taps. The window was still tiny. I reached for the soap – expensive stuff from L'Occitane that smelt of orange leaves – and wet it under the tap. Being a young skinny model had got me into this, and I was determined it would drag me out. I shed my coat and shoes, and peeled off my dress and knickers and put them outside the window. I began lathering my entire body with the soap, trying to cover myself with as much of it as I could. I soaped the window frame as well, rubbing vigorously until there was hardly any soap left. The smell of orange leaves was overpowering and my skin was burning despite the freezing cold. All I could do was stick my head through the tiny window and pray my shoulders could follow.

I reached my arms over my head like I did backstage at the shows when tight dresses refused to come off. I dove at the window as if it were a pool and stopped short. There was a fierce tearing pain in both my shoulders – but they were out. Just. I wriggled forward, ignoring the agony of the sharp sill pressing on my breasts. A few more wriggles and my outstretched hand was able to grab onto the railing outside. I pulled the rest of my body through with less difficulty and stood on the dark, abandoned deck like a featherless bird. I slipped my dress on and struggled – in an absurd act of modesty – with my tangled knickers.

I hooked one leg over the railing and perched there, listening for voices. All the guests had gone home or on to other parties and the boat was quiet. Big Ben struck four in the morning – the witching hour. I looked down at the dark rushing water then through the flurrying snowflakes toward the shore. I hadn't considered this bit yet – couldn't believe what I was thinking of doing . . .

The Thames is a notoriously dangerous river. The tides and currents make it difficult to navigate and there are always tree branches and other debris sailing down at speed. There was a very good chance I wouldn't make it.

I hooked my other leg over and rested my feet on the tiny ledge overhanging the water below, both arms stretched backwards, hands clinging onto the rail behind me. I leant forward into the darkness like a gargoyle, eyes closed, breathing the deadly cold dark, then stepped lightly into air. My feet found nothing for a second then my body hit what felt like concrete.

I scissor-kicked violently like I had been taught in water-safety classes at school. My head barely went under, but the weight of the

freezing water crushed my breath and any cry I might have made.
I knew I had to move my numbed limbs at once, and was counting on
years of swimming training to take my body through the motions as
I headed for shore. But, as I started breast-stroking like a solitary
tadpole, I saw the lights on the bank slipping by sideways. The current
was strong – much stronger than I had imagined.

I bobbed and fought, spitting filthy, freezing scum, my mind blank
with adrenaline. No fears, no hopes, just a primal instinct that kept
my arms and legs pushing forward. No way could I survive more than
ten minutes in this water –

Don't think you idiot, swim!

As I scrambled, fortune produced an eddy that drew me toward
the shore faster than I could ever have swum. It was low tide and the
boggy glut of the river bank was showing, covered in a light sprinkling
of white.

My knees hit the mud first. It took me a split second to realise
what I had bumped into. The glug was soft and velvety, and compara-
tively warm. I tried to stand but sank up to my knees and fell. I turned
onto my stomach and grasped at straggly reeds for help. They kept
pulling out and breaking but I clutched and snatched, refusing to give
up, until I had pulled my way in over the sludge. Reaching a rickety
wooden jetty, I hauled myself up with the last of my strength.

I lay in the snow, spread my limbs lazily and stared up into the
falling snowflakes. My hands had been torn open by the reeds and
were bleeding into the snow. I saw myself from above – a snow-angel
leaking red flowers on white snow. Curious, I thought, they match
the flowers on my dress.

Loud shouts, a bang and laughter reminded me that I shouldn't
remain where I was. I struggled to my frozen feet and staggered along
the slippery jetty past quiet, dark houseboats. No one was on the road
as I dragged my filthy, bleeding body along.

Autopilot was guiding me to the bright lights of the Kings Road. This is familiar – I know that bar. The doorman, his name's Rory, or Toby...

As always, a big crowd was leaving, while others were pushing forward to take their place. I headed for the velvet rope stretched across the doorway. 'If you're not on the guest list ...' I muttered. People parted for me, turned and stared, stopped yelling at Rory or Toby. I opened my mouth to give my name and my legs collapsed like a paper floor. I was falling through time and space and I heard my name from oh so far away ...

I felt warm breath, strong arms, a beating heart. I think I lifted my head to see who it was, but I couldn't see anything. It was all black. My eyes were closed and I didn't even know it.

Then I heard my name, repeated over and again in a voice that was not Ali's, so I let myself fall into my saviour's mercy.

Once
  I was
    a Cherry
      Tree

The words came floating down, accompanied by a soft melody. I listened a moment then opened my eyes a crack. The room was bright like a room can only be with a fresh fall of snow outside the window. I was surrounded by a warm, light softness and thought for a moment I was in heaven.

But it was only a bed. Somewhere the radio was on – I heard an English voice read out the traffic warnings in a calm, steady voice. Reassured, I lifted my head. Jeb was asleep on an armchair in the corner, bent like an old rose, still wearing his suit, an empty bottle of champagne and two full ashtrays keeping him company. Jeb's infallible model radar had found me in the dark.

My pillow was stained with the rusty brown of dried blood, and my hands were bandaged. I could see mud under my fingernails.

Can you stand?

I found I could.

Jeb's closet lent me a pair of man-trousers and a thick woollen jumper I knew he wouldn't miss. I borrowed a pair of bedroom slippers and left TK's hibiscus dress hanging muddy in the bathroom.

I slipped out without saying goodbye. Sometimes there are too many things to say in a single morning.

I ran into Nellee and TK out parading last night's conquest in a street not far from Jeb's flat. They blended well with the rest of the throng in the sunshine. I would have liked to avoid them but I found myself bearing straight towards them. Cuddling under Nellee's over-coat they walked past without seeing me. To check I still existed, I glanced in a shop window for my reflection. I looked like a violent lunatic.

The cut on my face had dried to a crusty scab on an otherwise milk-and-honey cheek.

The Agency will not be pleased.

Jeb's clothes were small for a man but hung loose on my frame, and the bedroom slippers, which had looked respectable in the privacy of Jeb's rooms, were unmistakably bedroom slippers, and four sizes too big. I was stooped forward, with my shoulders throbbing in pain, muscles torn from my dive through the boat window. My eyes were rimmed with black fatigue, bruising, hypothermia and old mascara. But the shop window showed me I didn't look fat, even in the baggy clothes.

Think how close you came!

I tried to still the voice, but it wouldn't shut up.

Think how close you came last night – yet you're still obsessed with how you look! You're almost dead, but you're thin. Thank fucking Christ for that! You really are a moron. You think you're better than those other girls – the models who obsess about their appearance – but you're just as bad. The reason you don't worry about your weight is that you don't have to. But you're always checking. Those department store mirrors where you can see your bum – you don't leave them for hours.

It's not cool to give a shit about the way you look – so you affect not to. You don't wear make-up, you don't wear fancy clothes, you eat bad food – but not much of it – you smoke, you drink, you bite your nails, but all that is just another extreme form of vanity. You're saying, 'You know what? I don't need all that shit. I'm too cool for that – and I still look good, so fuck you.' You're arrogant, and yesterday you paid the price. You found out that you are not immortal. Bad things can happen to you. You will die one day – it may even happen sooner than you think. No matter how cute you look in pictures, you can't pout your way out of that one. In fact, it was your pouting that got you in trouble. It serves you right – a scare like that – it serves you fucking right for thinking you were above Life. Hubris, baby. You got what you deserved back there.

I'd made myself cry. I looked crazier than ever because my tears were dissolving the dried blood and flowing pink. I winced as salt stung my cut. I passed a newsagent and caught sight of Justin's face staring out from the cover of a teen magazine. There was fire in her eyes and white-blonde hair over her face. I didn't recognise her. She still thought she was immortal, and in a way she was. But I knew what she was thinking when the picture was taken, and she and I could no longer be friends.

I found myself in the tube station on Sloane Square. Without boarding, I let three trains hiss to a halt, disgorge their passengers, swallow others and slither off into the black tunnels.

I went to a payphone and dialled my mother reverse charge.

The line was clear – clearer, in fact, than when I made local calls. She was in the garden, and I could hear the burbling of currawongs in the background. I had woken to those bird calls on so many mornings, but hadn't paid them any attention. I resolved to listen more closely when I finally got home again.

My mother was bright and cheery, and I felt the sunshine of an Australian summer shimmer through the phone before an icy wind blew and reminded me where I was. Hearing my mother's voice made me want to tell her so many things, explain how crazy I felt, how close I had come to dying – but she was gardening and she didn't hear the oddness in my voice and I didn't know how to begin to tell her. We were separated by a vast, cold ocean, and I did not know how to bring us closer. Another train pulled in.

'Oh, Mum, that's my train. I'm sorry. Better run. If I miss it I'll be waiting for ages.' I hated lying to her.

'We'll see you for Christmas, darling. I've got so much to tell you – well, it can wait I suppose! Just phone before your plane leaves.' This time the sunshine in her voice didn't warm me, just made me feel the cold on the platform more acutely.

I got on the train. I owed her at least that much truth.

The carriage was warm and the bleached faces lolled like balls of dough, their pallor piqued here and there by the red irritation of disease. It was winter in London and everyone had the flu.

No one was home at Swiss Cottage. I sat on the front steps, my bottom cold on the cement.

It occurred to me that no one had noticed I was missing and come to look for me. I remembered my angry words to Mandy: 'I'd like some *rules* – a *curfew* perhaps?' I lived in a world where disappearances and reappearances went unremarked. Mandy had once complained to me: 'So many changing faces, how can I possibly remember every girl I look after?'

'How can you let me do whatever I want? I'm a young girl!' I responded to the imaginary Mandy standing before me. But no sooner were the words out of my mouth than loneliness engulfed me. My head was buzzing softly and my face was hurting. I took off down the street, aimless as a leaf in the wind.

23
You're Still Not Listening!

Hey you walking there, what's going on, why are you so blue? You're not the only lonely person. Every face you see is crying out for love. Everyone wants someone else to understand their special talents and qualities, and love them for them. Your lot is everyone's.

You only ever experience happiness as a contrast to a previously miserable state. You sit back, glowing, and say to yourself, 'Now I am happy.' But this is only the absence of suffering.

You've tried living in a make-believe world of beautiful places, people and things but that hasn't made you happy.

There is only one avenue left: love. Love someone who loves you back and you might find happiness. To be in love makes you vulnerable – look at Caprice – but it also protects you. Love doesn't come easily to people like you. You are almost eighteen and you have become unlovable. It takes a long time to grow up –

But it only takes one night to grow old. I found myself standing ringing Jeb's door-bell, back where I had come from. He appeared in jeans and no shirt. He had a beautiful stomach – flat and muscular – but I was in no condition to care. 'I've got nowhere else to go.'

Jeb stepped aside and let me in. I thanked him in my head for not asking questions.

The flat was cosy, but my head was swimming. I didn't know if I wanted to cry or break something.

'I found you trying to get into Sesame.' Jeb broke the silence. He was making tea. 'I was just leaving – crap crowd in there last night.' I stared blankly at the teaspoon spinning around in the mug. Jeb stopped what he was doing. 'You look like death, Justin.'

'So?'

'Nothing.'

'Who cares if I look like death?'

'You don't look well. You might be sick.'

'You care about the way I look.'

'Yes, I do. You are beautiful.'

'You are . . . an . . .' I said this softly, bitterly.

Jeb came over. 'Justin baby . . .'

I felt an acid wave of hatred rising as I trembled. My nails dug into my bandaged palms, making them bleed again. The pain focused my rage into a ball of steel.

I punched Jeb hard in the face. He reeled back. The floodgates opened and the fetid lake poured out. I leapt on him and began slapping, supernaturally strong, protected by a force-field of fury.

'I hate you, Jeb. I hate you so much I could kill you right now. All of you!' The words spat themselves free.

'You make me sick with your smiles and your compliments and your fucking up-and-down gaze and your groping fingers – always groping for my panties. Fuck the lot of you. Do you think I like being grabbed and stared at and kissed and prodded? Lied to and patronized and treated like an idiot?! 'Tongue-kiss her and she'll shut up, Mandy!'

'Humour the dumb darling, Serena – she's just stupid!' Do you think I enjoy it when someone holds me down and tells me they want to butt-fuck me? That I find that flattering? Or when they stick their fingers inside me while I'm trying to get dressed?' I clawed Jeb's face and felt his flesh gathering under my nails like tissue paper.

Jeb didn't fight back. He didn't run or hide, just let me beat him up. I threw blind punches at his perfect stomach, hating him all the more.

'Or when they call me 'dumb girl'? Just because they can. Or when they chase me in the street? Or lick me while I'm sleeping in some hotel room – and the guy's married! How can I scream? And what about Maggie?! How can I scream? Who's going to listen to the dumb model?'

I screamed now and kicked at Jeb, tears pouring down my face, until he caught my foot and threw me to the carpet. I curled there in a ball, my body one hard, hurting sob.

My crying grew so big I was afraid it might tear me in two. I gasped for air and choked on my snot. It felt like I was trapped underwater. If I didn't expel this pain it would explode inside me like a grenade. It would kill me. I had never been more sure of anything in my life.

Jeb lay himself next to me on the carpet and whispered words I couldn't quite hear or understand. He didn't touch me, but his voice was soothing. Gradually my sobs calmed to trickles of teary mucus. And still Jeb continued to croon, as if I were a small furry wild animal. I hadn't the strength to stop him.

I was a void. Nothing in nothing.

I became slowly slowly aware of the itchy carpet on my cheek, aware of Jeb's soft voice and the throbbing in my right hand, and that my eyelids were too swollen to see properly. All I knew was that bright light poured in from what looked like a window and I couldn't move, nor did I want to.

I felt Jeb's hands heft me from the floor and carry me across the room. We passed through a sun-patch and its two-second warmth felt good.

Jeb laid me gently on a bed. I don't know if I slept, or passed out, or slipped into a fevered state where memory has no power. Eventually I realised there was no daylight any more, just the soft glow of a lamp by the bed, and I was curled around a shirtless Jeb. I raised my head with a start.

'Before you open your mouth, my little wild cat,' Jeb said, '*you* snuggled up to *me*. I haven't touched you.'

I sank back down. The afternoon's events were slowly coming back. I looked into Jeb's face and he smiled back at me.

He leant to kiss my forehead, then my cheeks.

'Being bashed suits you, Jeb.'

He smiled. 'You suit me.'

'Don't flirt, Jeb', I croaked, 'I don't have the energy. It gets tiring. And you know what, I'm almost eighteen anyway – over the hill, right? We've missed my window. In case you hadn't heard, I will no longer be young and beautiful after the twenty-ninth. Bail out now.'

Jeb knelt on the bed and took my wrists, pulling me to a sitting position. He made me turn to look at the reflection in the mirror on the wall above the bed. 'Look at us, Justin. We don't exactly look like the kind of couple that *Hello!* is killing to photograph.'

He was right.

Jeb's mouth had a scab of dark, dried blood in the centre, and my claw marks on his cheek were deep and inflamed. His chest was speckled with blood, so was his gold chain, and wedding ring. My nose was red, my face pale and blotchy. The cut on my cheek stuck out like a sword slash. My eyelids were puffed and purple like the hood of an angry cobra, my lips chapped. Even my bandages were looking ragged. We could have passed for survivors of an air crash in the Alaskan wilderness.

Actually I liked the way I looked. I had the face of a girl in a movie, the face of a heroine.

'I'm not kissing you for your looks right now.' Jeb was still staring at me through the looking-glass.

'I guess I'm going to have to believe that,' I said, with a nod to the mirror.

I felt strong kneeling on the bed with Jeb as we examined our battle scars. I had earnt the right to feel good. No one was going to take it away now. I even felt sexy in my puffiness – sleepy and damaged and voluptuous.

I turned to Jeb, who was still looking in the mirror. The lamp-light made him glow like a golden boy.

'What's up, sweet pea?' he said with a smile.

And I knew.

'Jeb?' My voice came out quietly, almost a whisper, but I did not falter. 'Let's make love.'

He put his hands on my shoulders and looked at me for a moment. 'You have no idea how wild you make me, baby.' And he began to kiss me softly. I felt the same electric shiver I had felt in the hot tub. My mouth melted into his. I felt powerless against his lips, like they were capable of killing me softly, softly.

You didn't think he would refuse, did you? Perhaps on account of my emotional turmoil hours before? He was still Jebbery Hoochey, after all. I won't go into details. Some matters have to be kept private, even in a story. But I will tell you that Jeb was gentle. His kisses distracted me and he crooned to me as he had done on the carpet. When it was over he gathered me in his warm arms and we slept. I heard him whisper to himself, almost too softly for me to hear, 'Beat up on me all you want, until that anger is gone – and then run off with a man far better than me.'

I smiled to myself. Did he think I wouldn't hear?

We made love again next morning. When I got out of bed I saw Jeb's gold chain and wedding ring on the bedside table. I hadn't noticed him remove them.

But I knew what would happen now. The fashion magazines had taught me that Jeb would want me out of there as fast as possible. I prepared my mind and heart for the fact that he would not call that week – perhaps ever – and that maybe I had irreparably damaged our friendship.

But it had been worth it. I told myself to look upon it as a wonderful night and morning. A turning point, a wonderful initiation.

'What are you smiling at, wild thing?'

My smile vanished.

'Nothing. I have to go.'

He watched me dress and said nothing to detain me. I congratulated myself for having preempted his desires. I wouldn't be providing material for his tales of obsessed females.

Jeb watched as I slipped on my bedraggled hibiscus dress. 'I'm going to have to borrow a coat, Jeb, unless you want me dead of hypothermia a second time, or arrested for indecency.'

Jeb smiled slowly. He fetched me his coat and scrambled into his jeans. 'I'm taking you out. You need coffee. You're in no state to go about without at least one.'

He took my hand, refusing to let go even as he struggled to slip on a heavy jumper. 'I'm not letting you run off again,' he said from under a pile of wool.

The sun was out for a second day in a row. This does not happen often in London at Christmas. Nature was blessing what I had done the night before. There was a spring in my step that morning and, I have to admit, an arrogant tilt to my head. I felt party to a secret. I had a bad man holding my hand and a scar on my face. Jeb looked as though he had been mauled by a lion.

'How's your cheek?' he asked me.

'Fine,' I replied.

'You would look pretty cool with a scar right there.' He touched my wound gently and I didn't flinch.

'Will yours scar?' I felt a little guilty.

'I certainly hope so. I want to remember my night with the wild cat.'

Pleased as I was by his reply, it confirmed what I had thought. 'My *night*?' Didn't sound like he was planning on more.

I began to feel less wild cat, more human girl. For the first time I wasn't hiding behind a pretty face – I was showing the world the disaster that was Justin. I didn't care how anyone would react and my indifference was completely liberating. I floated down the road. I had decided to go home to Sydney the next day and felt as if I could take on anything. Even my agency. I resolved to tell them I was quitting. They wouldn't be able to reach me across the ocean.

I said very little to the girls at Swiss Cottage about Jeb, just as I had said nothing to Jeb about leaving London. I told TK what had happened with Ali, but in a light-hearted, 'oh what larks' kind of way.

'It was hilarious TK – all these guys in fur guarding the door! And me swimming half-naked to shore. I'm having your dress dry-cleaned by the way. Oh, and then I tried to get into Sesame, totally muddy with no shoes on. Jeb caught me just as he was leaving the club!'

Luckily TK was wrapped in the cuddly blanket of her own affairs and didn't notice the high-wire strain in my voice. She'd had a whirl-wind two days with Nellee.

'He wants to put me in one of Jeb's movies – some horror thing. Could be funny. A change from modeling, anyhow.' Nellee wanted TK to move in with him in Hampstead. 'He has wonderful central heating. I know you shouldn't live with a guy before you get married, but it'll just be temporary and he's just . . .'

'Just go for it.' I was nonchalant, but pleased for her. 'Sometimes it's the things you are most scared of that bring the best rewards.'

'True, little Justin. True.'

I went into my icy room and began throwing the odds and ends of my life in my suitcase. I only needed one bag for everything I owned and, as I had never unpacked properly, it was an easy job.

Next I dropped forty pence in the pay phone and dialled Mandy. Checking in was a habit I couldn't break. Her voice was surprisingly subdued, almost normal. She was giggling intermittently, her voice muffled and I suddenly just knew she was with Leather Benny. She reminded me that the Agency Christmas party was on that night.

'Everyone' would be there. What a perfect stage for my send off, fuck off. As if I was going to go. Of course I was going to go. What was one more party in a list of hundreds? And how else was I going to finally find my full stop?

In a distracted moment Serena had handed the party organisation over to Mandy, who took the idea of an 'office party' literally and arranged the gathering in the Agency office itself. Serena's budget had been designed with a big bash in a trendy club in mind, and Mandy found the cash went a long way when it came to ordering booze and cute waiters with cartoon noses and bubble butts.

It didn't bother me that I had come alone. In fact I wouldn't have wanted anyone with me. I had to face this on my own.

I stood outside the office for a minute, watching the party through the big glass windows that gave onto the street. It was like some horrid fish-tank – fiendishly bright and full of smoke. People were pressed against the glass like specimens, gasping at each other, silent as fish. I smiled and slipped in through the glass door unnoticed.

The chatter whacked me like a wall of water. Cries of 'Justin!' hit and I was swept along by the crowd.

The caterers had corralled enormous bottles of champagne in

wooden cradles and the bottles dipped and bobbed like fat ponies before each empty flute glass. Eric the French, head of one of the smaller Parisian fashion houses, was guest of honour. He bobbed and dipped beside the bottles, unaware that every time he bent to kiss a hand or reached out with a kissy smile, his movements were shadowed by a large green bottle. His pleasure at the turn-out, however, was genuine. He had none of the Englishman's taste for class, and all of the European's appreciation of beauty for its own sake. For Eric, the Agency was heaven. The place was full of models and clients, minor film stars and photographers, hungry men and ravaged women. Sinews stretched towards the glasses like tightropes, rhinestones or diamonds glittered in the ditches between the bones. The pink glossy lips that laughed and kissed were just that bit too plump, as if they had sucked the flesh from the bodies they belonged to and deposited it next to their teeth.

The large offices were bursting with guests and their guests. Serena was livid at Mandy's incompetence but determined to smile through her rage. The fluorescent strip lighting did little for anyone's complexion and every woman over twenty-five (and several men) had their sunglasses on. People bustled and bumped, confused by the filing cabinets and austere office furniture which Mandy had not bothered to move for the party. Most assumed it was the new 'new' in entertaining and affected the mild boredom of the insecure.

I meeted and greeted, Eric the French poured me champagne. So many faces I knew in that room, all packed together. I smiled at them, at their reflections in the glass and my reflection too, but I had grown my own glass window inside. I was watching them from a silent place and they couldn't touch me. Nothing mattered, least of all these glossy people with taut faces, these crispy blow-dried blondes, these shiny dark men. They were amusing diversions, nothing more.

I recognised Victor Victor, turning towards me. 'Justin, my darling. Merry Christmas. I haven't seen you since –'

'Oh, I really must get some snow shoes,' I giggled. He beamed at me.

'I know! It's been too long!' he called after me as I let myself drift on.

Then Rhett, the rock 'n' roll photographer, appeared on the horizon. He smiled lazily and reached out a hand. 'Justin – long time no –'

I put my glass in his hand. 'But it's not vodka Brett!' I shouted excitedly, my smile on high-beam.

'I know!' he shouted back, grinning. 'It's been so long! We have to get together –'

I floated off, smiling inanely.

Where was Mandy?

I found her by the filing cabinet, the one that held the vital statistics of every girl in the Agency. I had watched Mandy file me away on my first day in London. TK was in there, Debbie/Caprice, Croatian Cristina, Druggie Tia. Their measurements, photos, state of their hips and lips and busts and hands and teeth all filed alphabetically (according to their first names) for easy access.

Mandy leapt on me. 'Justin-baby! Fabulous! Did you have a fun time on the boat?! Wasn't it fabulous?! Best party ever except this one, only I think it's a bit cramped in here!' She suddenly looked concerned and stretched out a hand. 'Justin-baby! Honey! Where's your drink?!'

'I don't know. I think I lost it on the way . . .'

'Let Aunty Mandy fix it all!' Her G-string rode over her waistband as she bent over to open the bottom drawer of the filing cabinet. 'Look Justin – I've restocked the office stash from the caterer's bar! We're at full-time capacity! Brilliant!' The drawer was so full of booze bottles it could hardly open. Mandy poured me a slug of vodka as deep as a glass of water. She was high, of course, but coherent.

I took a sip of the vodka. 'Mandy I'm quitting modelling.' I know she heard me.

'Did you see Benny on the way in?! Isn't he gorgeous?!' she whispered. 'I might even be *in love*!' I stared at her face. Suddenly it lost its unity and became a collection of recognisable but unrelated features. Smudged eyeliner, taupe eyeshadow smeared upwards; large red mouth mashing ice and words and tongue; eyebrow hairy as a wiggling caterpillar; large pores shining with oil.

Which bit should I address? I focused on the mouth, which pulled more than its own weight in the face.

'Mandy, I'm quitting everything. I'm going home. You'll never see me again.'

Mandy's elbow knocked her glass to the floor as she fumbled in her enormous handbag. She found half a cigarette. 'Silly Justin. No, you don't mean it. No you won't.' But the absence of exclamation marks told me she knew I did mean it, that I would indeed. I felt triumphant. Then I had a thought.

'I want my file back Mandy – my vital statistics.'

'What file, Justin-baby? We don't have files.' She was looking around nervously for a light.

'The ones right here.' I drummed the cabinet with my bitten fingers.

Her eyes began roving further afield, looking for help. 'You can't have those Justin-baby! No, no, no. They're for us to keep. What if a client wants to see you, or we need to call you about a job or –'

'Exactly. I want my file. It belongs to me. I don't want you to contact me about anything ever. Don't you see?'

'But what about campaigns?!' The exclamation marks were back. Mandy had found a way out. 'You have options! So many, Justin-baby! You are such a star! Isn't she Serena?!' She appealed to Serena who had crept up unnoticed. 'Isn't she, Victor Victor?!' He had too.

I didn't care. Even if Mandy were right, I didn't care. I was free. I didn't want the fame anymore. I didn't want the money, the attention, of anyone in that room.

Serena cut through, ice cubes clinking in her voice. 'We'll talk tomorrow, Justin. The files belong to the Agency. You do, too. It's in your contract. It's all in the files. All the girls belong to the Agency. Have another drink and Calm Down.'

Victor Victor patted me on the head and offered me a foreign cigarette.

I smiled at Victor Victor, at Serena, at Mandy, and took the cigarette. Still smiling, I said, 'Well, can I at least have a light then?' I felt their collective sigh of relief. Rogue Model Tamed. Smiles All Round. Victor Victor handed over his matches and I lit my cigarette. Eyes on Serena I then dropped my match carefully into my glass of vodka. It flared like a torch.

I stood a moment like some demented Statue of Liberty, glass aloft. Slowly I opened the top drawer of the filing cabinet and dropped the burning glass. Then I closed the drawer and walked away.

I know the thing went up in flames. I heard the screams, smelt the smoke of all that paper burning. When I reached the glass door I turned around. Mandy was throwing glasses of water at the cabinet. Serena was shouting at her. Victor Victor was hurrying backwards, his expensive shirt cuff singed. The crowd had started to surge for the door. I stepped into the street just as the flames hit Mandy's office booze stash. The explosion destroyed the entire cabinet. The last sight I saw was the Round Table catching fire.

I headed down the road. It was a hard, cold night, but I imagined I could feel the heat of the flames at my back. I did a twirl, feeling light and naughty and happy. What a terrible accident it had been! How clumsy of me! All the files gone! All the girls up in flames! And Serena's angry red face ...

24
Don't Be a Bad Girl!

7.54 a.m., 32,000 feet, somewhere over
the Takliman Desert

I was on the plane, flying home, trying to stay awake until the end of
the movie. My fingers played with a gold ring, watching the band – too
big and thick to suit my stringy fingers – slide up and then fall, spin, roll.
It was Jeb's wedding ring. He must have slipped it in my coat pocket
as we left the café. I hadn't noticed it until I fumbled for my passport
at Heathrow.

If I had been in a hot air balloon or a boat I could have thrown the
ring dramatically into the ocean. As it was, I was hurtling through dark
skies thirty-two thousand feet in the air with no hope of an open window.

Two interpretations were possible. Perhaps Jeb had slipped me his
wedding ring to remind me that, although we had had fun, although we
were friends, he was a man with a memory who did not make the same
mistake twice. Or his gift could be seen as an act of faith, a declaration
that he was prepared now to forget his fears and believe that love might
not be a mistake. He had, I knew, a plan for me – he had told me so.

What Jeb didn't know was that I had already left London. It was
almost Christmas and this time I knew I really wanted to be back
home even if it meant feeling odd around the edges of life in Sydney
as I compared myself now with the Justine I had been as a school girl.

Take speed slowly, Jeb had said, and that was exactly what I was trying to do, sitting here in the frozen moment. A woman looked up from her magazine as I passed on my way to the bathroom. Had she seen the ad on the back page – 'Where are my jeans?' – and did she recognise me? She had another magazine on her lap, and I knew it contained an animal-print story we had shot on a freezing day in front of the Duomo in Milan, one I didn't like at all.

The bathroom mirror showed me to be green, and I felt sick. Wherever I went, I seemed to encounter myself. Magazines in the hands of strangers, in waiting rooms and rubbish bins; posters above overpasses and on the sides of buses. Fractured and photographed, I was spread around cities like confetti, defying unity. And the only image of myself I even remotely recognised was that of the sick green girl in the toilet mirror.

The woman stared as I moved back to my seat. I put my finger in my nose and picked it, carefully and deliberately, wanting to confuse her with the two pictures I offered: white fur over diamond denim perfection, caught on her fabulous way to La Scala; and green, grotty nose-picker. I wanted my picking finger to be the leak of reality into her fantasy.

I watched a *Tom & Jerry* cartoon for a while. Tom was chasing Jerry through a restaurant kitchen filled with wonderful potential for extreme pain.

The chase only ended when Tom ran over the edge of a cliff. There was no going back now. He was able to walk on air, hanging suspended above it all, but only so long as his illusion supported him. The second he realised there was nothing there he dropped, ending up concertina-shaped, head down, at the foot of the Grand Canyon.

The captain's voice came through my headset and I fastened my seatbelt. Fingers tightly crossed, I hoped for a gentle landing.

Epilogue

When the Australian summer was over I went back to London. My home town didn't fit me anymore, too small in some places, too large in others, and I felt that if I didn't go back to London, knowing all I thought I knew then, I would regret my cowardice. I wanted to see if the new Justin could survive without the crutches of adoration.

My King campaign had come out, and it shocked many people. Mandy even called a couple of times, despite 'that dreadful accidental cabinet inferno' as she called it, wanting me to 'come home, darling, you're a star!' But it seemed too far away, something belonging to an underwater world.

I could laugh at my big face on billboards now, enjoy the absurdity. My face was no longer the centre of my life.

And Jeb's plan was underway.

He had me working on his new film *A Plague of Female Werewolves* for almost a month, and I loved every minute of it. It was a Hoochey Coochey Production, and I was helping Dave the art director with the backdrops and set furniture. I loved wearing my baggy jeans with tools slung through the belt loops, loved the paint splatters on my shoes and the blood red under my fingernails. I felt like a Lady Macbeth who wore pink and smoked too many cigarettes.

There was always a lot of blood to be painted on Jeb's movie sets, and Dave soon discovered I had a particular talent for creating a realistic-looking splatter.

'You have a talent for gore, Justin,' he told me solemnly while we contemplated an elaborate motorised-cheese-grater death scene. I glowed all over at his praise.

Jeb himself directed the movies. He would move like a maniac through the sets, instructing werewolves in hair suits, buxom lovelies in sheer nighties, fat cops, packs of dogs, knife-throwers, wizards, supermarket cashiers and grannies – all with such charm that they ran to do his bidding. He was dedicated, tireless and passionate about his horror. I watched his face light up in excitement as he saw his stories come to life.

I refused to move in with him, despite his attempts to convince me (though I think he was relieved). It would have been too easy, too comfortable, simply to join my life to his and tag along. Instead I moved into an apartment in Maida Vale with TK. It isn't huge – we share a double bed in one room – but it is bright and warm – two very important considerations in grey, wet London.

TK had given up full-time modelling as well and her character seemed to have softened. Nellee had convinced Jeb to put her in *Frankensavage*, his epic story of wild natives mutated through genetic experiments. TK played one of the more talkative virgin sacrifices. Her screams were so wonderfully realistic, her wide eyes conveying her terror so well, that she was soon starring in B-grade horror movies all over London. We both came home and exchanged gore stories, drinking tea with blood-covered faces. Thank goodness that the neighbours spoke very little English – but they stared.

TK pretty much ignores even her part-time modelling work. Mandy has made it easier for us by calming down as well. She is still with Leather Benny and they've even had a baby, a terrified little boy with enormous cheeks named Rolo. I take the fact that she doesn't try to tongue-kiss me when I run into her at a bar as a sign that she is indeed content.

Lara O'Hara is often in the tabloids. She married a wealthy Englishman of the media 'aristocracy' who owns tabloid magazines. *Hello*, *OK*, *Tatler* and *Harpers & Queen* ran glossy stories on the golden couple and their wedding for weeks. We learnt they had gone to live in Hadrian's (that was his name) estate in Glouscestershire, where there is a rose garden and a water-garden with lilies. Inside, their home is filled with black-and-white photos of Africa (they plan to see it for themselves one day) and expensive pot pourri. They own a green Jaguar and a green Range Rover and are trying to have a baby (who they will call Cordelia if it's a girl, Mauldwin if a boy). Mrs O'Hara is said to be very satisfied with her daughter's match.

Cristina became a celebrity in Croatia. She is still with Milos and they named their baby boy Rok. He's very pale, with Cristina's fiery black eyes, and what looked remarkably like Mick Jagger's big, red lips. TK and I keep up with their progress through irregular letters and blurry photographs in the tabloids. Cristina clutching Rok outside a supermarket; Milos, Cristina and Rok on a beach on the edge of the Adriatic Sea; Rok and Cristina playing with a savage-looking German Shepherd in a bombed-out country lane.

As for Ali, I read in a side bar in the *Guardian* that police were looking for him in connection to arms dealing to Burma. I don't think he's ever been found.

Maggie, too, slipped away. Lascari said she had gone home with her mother. I wrote her two letters but I think she wanted to let it all go. I never got a reply. Lascari told me she was still beautiful, but she wasn't ever going to be 'picture-perfect'. His attempts to woo her back to New York and DNA with offers of reconstructive surgery had been firmly refused.

'She's growing organic potatoes for McDonald's, for god's sake, living with her mother! She's nuts!'

I had hung up the phone thinking it sounded like a good idea.

Debbie/Caprice moved to Dubai. Imran had wooed and won her that night on the yacht. She calls us now and then, her accent more exotic every time, and says she has found her prince in Imran and couldn't be happier.

He drives an all-white Range Rover – white hub-caps, white steering wheel, white tyres – and the tinted windows are bullet-proof.

She's especially proud of the windows. We ask her many questions, and she answers with the indolence befitting someone who spends a lot of time lying down eating rosewater sweetmeats.

Her beautiful body is now hidden by a heavy black chador every time she leaves the house, which she can't do without a male relative as an escort. But Caprice has always enjoyed the company of men and to her this is no hardship.

She wears Chanel underneath the robes and she has made friends with some of the other women and they all hold clothes-viewing parties – women-only gatherings where they remove their chadors to display their acquisitions from the latest Paris collections. Most of the women are beautiful – certainly very well maintained – but Caprice's blonde hair and model figure have made her an instant hit as she sashays before admiring eyes. She has all the money in the world and none of the freedom – she has never been happier.

I am happy too. I still travel a lot. Jeb and I often make trips to Transylvania, or Ireland, or the Black Forest – any scary place we can think of – for research. We collect ghost stories and come back with dark ideas for sets and films. I keep trying to convince him to use my idea for a horror flick – *I Was a Teenage Fashion Model* – but he doesn't think the script would be gory enough.

Ash Rain

Corrie Hosking

A bushfire in Dell's childhood still haunts her. She dreams up new starts, but her spilling stories cannot over-write the past.

Evvie dances into Dell's life. She has run as far as she can from her family, but her country keeps calling her back.

Evvie's daughter, Luce, is most at home in the company of creatures. All she wants is her collection of bugs and a guinea pig for Christmas.

Dell meets Patrick in the pub, but he's going back to Scotland. Her life finally rupturing, Dell follows. She leaves a hole that Evvie and Luce struggle to fill. They must find each other again, without Dell. And Dell must discover how love works half a world away.

Ash Rain explores the corners and crevices where love can grow in unexpected ways.

Winner of the Adelaide Festival Award
for an Unpublished Manuscript

ISBN 1 86254 634 7

For more information visit www.wakefieldpress.com.au

Street Furniture

Matt Howard

Street Furniture is a hilarious, feel-good book about a guy who's languished forever (more or less happily) unemployed with his mates in the suburbs of Sydney. At 29 he somehow scores a publicist's job in a slick publishing firm in the city. He moves house, and hopes he won't lose his friends. And does true love await him?

'Matt Howard's spliff-happy, artful slacker of a hero Declan does to over-achieving what the Titanic did for boating. A funny, subtle and astute novel.' – Shelley Gare

**** *Australian Bookseller and Publisher*

'Very much enjoyed it.' – Magnus Fuxner

'Just gotta say: very impressed. Awesome!' – Simon Proud

ISBN 1 86254 646 0

For more information visit www.wakefieldpress.com.au

Reflections from an Indian Diary

John B. Murray

Reflections from an Indian Diary is an exploration through the hills and across the plains, into the mentality and the psyche of India. John B. Murray writes with yogic detachment to interpret India through the lens of his own spiritual experience, probing its culture and the essence of Hindu, Buddhist and Christian thought in a manner that bridges the divide between East and West.

The narrative is punctuated with anecdotes that delight the reader – an encounter with Aung San Suu Kyi and her husband in Ladakh in the 1970s, and an interview with Bhagwan Sri Rajneesh before he became an international phenomenon come to mind. And one cannot forget the author's discussions with Tibetan Buddhist Rinpoches in mountain-top gompas, or the simple village woman in Rajasthan who sang her lyrical devotional poems under the desert's night sky.

Reflections from an Indian Diary takes the reader on a physical and metaphysical pilgrimage, in the spirit of Peter Matthiessen's The Snow Leopard.

ISBN 1 86254 598 7

For more information visit www.wakefieldpress.com.au

Temples & Tuk Tuks
Lydia Laube

The dinner menu had the usual interesting items such as 'Soap' and 'A Fried Monk' not to mention 'Chicken Amok'. The waiter couldn't tell me what amok meant, but I tried it and it turned out to be, not a crazy chicken running around with a cleaver, but chicken pieces in a soup coloured a kind of caterpillar-innards green that was very tasty.

Lydia Laube discovers that Cambodia, a nation with a violent and horrific recent past, is also an ancient, beautiful country populated by friendly, generous people who like to ride motorbikes very fast around corners.

Preferring the more sedate pace of tuk tuks, Lydia chooses this mode of transport wherever she can while visiting Cambodia's magnificent temples, markets, beaches and mountains – and, of course, the killing fields.

Deciphering the menu is only part of the intrigue of this mysterious land only just now opening to tourists and travellers. Join Lydia, squashed into a taxi with nine or so others, for an unforgettable ride.

ISBN 1 86254 631 2

For more information visit www.wakefieldpress.com.au

Wakefield Press is an independent publishing and
distribution company based in Adelaide, South Australia.
We love good stories and publish beautiful books.
To see our full range of titles, please visit our website at
www.wakefieldpress.com.au.

Wakefield Press thanks Fox Creek Wines
and Arts South Australia for their support.